# Love at First Sight

## The Stories and Science Behind Instant Attraction

Earl Naumann, Ph.D.

CASABLANCA PRESS®
A DIVISION OF SOURCEBOOKS, INC.®
NAPERVILLE, ILLINOIS

This publication is designed to provide accurate and authoritative information
in regard to the subject matter covered. It is sold with the understanding that
the publisher is not engaged in rendering legal, accounting, or other professional service. If legal advice or other expert assistance is required, the services
of a competent professional person should be sought.—*From a Declaration of
Principles Jointly Adopted by a Committee of the American Bar Association
and a Committee of Publishers and Associations*

Published by Sourcebooks, Inc.
P.O. Box 4410, Naperville, Illinois 60567-4410
(630) 961-3900
FAX: (630) 961-2168

Library of Congress Cataloging-in-Publication Data
Naumann, Earl, 1946–
     Love at first sight: the stories and science behind instant attraction / Earl
Naumann.
          p. cm.
     Includes index.
     ISBN 1-57071-623-4 (alk. paper)
     1. Love. 2. Love—Case studies. I. Title.

BF575.L8 N38 2001
306.7—dc21

                                                                00-051851

Printed and bound in the United States of America
LB   10 9 8 7 6 5 4 3 2 1

# Dedication

This book is dedicated to those who have the courage to open their hearts to another, the emotional depth to love completely, the intelligence to understand what is happening, and the maturity to seize the moment.

# Acknowledgments

All research projects require a team effort. I would especially like to thank the team at Naumann & Associates that made this book a possibility. Sharmaine Anlbach was responsible for all of the interviewing and data gathering. Dan Matoske was responsible for the data analysis. Kathy Walker was responsible for putting the manuscript together. And all three made many valuable suggestions along the way. Without their assistance, this book would still be an idea, not a reality.

I would also like to thank the nearly 1,500 people who shared their time and experiences to complete the survey. Their experiences form the core of this book.

The people of Sourcebooks have been a pleasure to work with. Thanks especially to Todd Stocke for his faith in the project, and to Jennifer Fusco for her insight and recommendations. Thanks to Judy Kelly and Sarah Donaldson for their ideas and advice. They made the project flow smoothly.

# Table of Contents

Preface    vi

Part I: Understanding Love    1
Chapter 1: Understanding Love    3
Chapter 2: The Chemistry of Love    23
Chapter 3: Learning to Love from Our Family    57
Chapter 4: Learning to Love from Society    83

Part II: What the Research Says    103
Chapter 5: The Role of Our Experiences in
        Falling in Love    105
Chapter 6: The Traits That Attract Men and Women    137
Chapter 7: The Physical Traits That Attract
        Men and Women    155
Chapter 8: The Personality Traits That Attract
        Men and Women    185
Chapter 9: The Career/Achievement Traits That
        Attract Men and Women    213
Chapter 10: The Emotions Men and Women Feel
        When Experiencing Love at First Sight    233
Chapter 11: The Outcomes of Love at First Sight    261
Chapter 12: A Few Concluding Comments    285

Appendix A: Aided Survey    289
Appendix B: Unaided Survey    299
Endnotes    309
Bibliography    313
Index    315
About the Author    319

# Preface

$\mathcal{T}$he topic of love is expansive, and grappling with the entirety of the concept would be overwhelming from a research perspective. Therefore, the concept was pared down a bit. Being "in love" is an on-going event, evolving and changing over time. "Falling in love," on the other hand, is a more discreet event. Because of the monumental impact on a person's emotional life, most people can identify when they "fell in love" with someone. Therefore, the initial decision was made to focus this book and the research involved on the experience of falling in love.

Essentially, there are two ways to fall in love. One way is to do so gradually over time. For example, author John Gray outlines five stages that couples must pass through: attraction, uncertainty, exclusivity, intimacy, and engagement.[1] Cathy Troupp in her book *Why Do We Fall In Love* identifies four phases of hope, projection, disillusionment, and attachment.[2] Most writers contend that there are some phases that couples progress through somehow. Hence, most of the literature weighs in favor of "falling in love" as being a gradual occurrence.

A few years ago, there was an article in *USA Today* that discussed a different way to fall in love. The article discussed the concept of love at first sight, or immediately falling in love with someone when you first meet them. There were opinions about love at first sight provided by fifteen or so "relationship experts." All but two of the experts said love at first sight doesn't happen.

Similarly, Leil Lowndes, in her book *How To Make Anyone Fall In Love With You*, dismisses love at first sight as "Monday morning quarterbacking."[3] Anthony Walsh, in his book *The Science of Love*, states, "I do not mean to imply that love at first sight is a common phenomenon, although I suppose it does happen."[4] The general consensus among the experts is that *lust* at first sight is very possible, but love at first sight is very unlikely. But there was not empirical data to support whether love at first sight does or does not occur. Therefore, determining if love at first sight does occur was an objective of this book.

The second objective was to determine why love at first sight occurred. I wanted to find out what it was that so overwhelmed the two people who experienced love at first sight. Therefore, many questions were developed that addressed issues such as those discussed earlier in this chapter.

The third objective of the research was to determine the outcomes of love at first sight. What emotions did they feel at the time of falling in love? Was lust a dominant factor as the experts suggest? Was the experience of falling in love at first sight a fleeting emotion that quickly evaporated? Or did love at first sight lead to a lifetime of happiness?

To answer these and other questions, I applied a rigorous research design. First, I conducted a comprehensive literature review to identify the basis of interpersonal attraction. Based on the literature review, I designed a questionnaire to be used in a large-scale telephone survey. Then I had the interviewers in my research firm administer the survey to almost fifteen hundred people scattered across the United States. We randomly phoned households nationwide and asked respondents to participate in a study about love at first sight.

We had a single screening question that asked if the respondent was at least twenty-one years old. If the respondent was twenty-one or older, we proceeded with the interview. Respondents were first asked if they believed in love at first sight. If the respondent said "no," the interviewer skipped to the demographic questions. We did this to determine if "believers" are somehow different than "nonbelievers." If the respondent did believe in love at first sight, we asked if he/she had experienced it. If the respondent had not experienced love at first sight, the interviewer skipped to the demographic questions. If the respondent had experienced love at first sight, the interviewer proceeded with the survey.

At the end of the interview, respondents were asked if they would share their love at first sight experience. Their stories were tape recorded, and a verbatim transcript was developed.

There were 1,495 respondents who agreed to complete the survey. The sample consisted of 948 women (63.4 percent) and 547 men (36.6 percent). The data presented in this book is based on these responses.

## The Results

The results to the study will be used throughout this book. This section will present only some of the higher level findings. After the initial screening question to ensure respondents were at least twenty-one years of age, love at first sight was defined to provide a common base of reference. The respondent was told, "For this study, love at first sight is defined as falling in love with someone within sixty minutes of first seeing or meeting the person." Although the one-hour time frame was an arbitrary selection, I felt that the concept of an hour would be a relatively easy time frame for people to conceptualize. For many respondents, it took less than ten minutes to realize that a person was "the one."

Of all 1,495 respondents, 64.1 percent believe in love at first sight. The difference between men (65.2 percent) and women (63.6 percent) is statistically insignificant. Considering the skepticism of the relationship experts, the magnitude of this response was quite a surprise. If so many people believe love at first sight can happen, some of the theories of interpersonal attraction are in need of severe reevaluation. This is particularly true when the results of the next question are considered.

Of those 958 people who believe in love at first sight, 58.2 percent have experienced it! A clear majority of people who believe in love at first sight have had it happen to them. Now, perhaps there is a willingness among "believers" to have it happen. But as we shall see subsequently, in the vast majority of cases, it was not a casual occurrence. And some people flatly did not believe in love at first sight until it happened to them.

For example, one lady from New England was forty years old, divorced, and the mother of four kids. She had previously discussed love at first sight with her friends, and stated flatly that it couldn't happen, at least not to her. She had firmly made up her mind. But on the day of her grandmother's funeral, she met a man and, within thirty minutes, she knew he was "the one." They only dated a few times before they were married. And they have had a great life together.

To continue our "he said, she said" approach, men are more likely to experience love at first sight than women. Of the male "believers," 62.3 percent have experienced love at first sight. Of the female believers, 55.7 percent have experienced it. This difference is statistically significant. The finding is very consistent with the idea that women are more selective when selecting a mate.

## Times Experienced

There are not many repeat performances for love at first sight. Of those who have experienced love at first sight, 75.0 percent experienced it only one time. There were 17.2 percent of respondents who experienced love at first sight twice, and 4.7 percent who experienced it three times.

Here, again, the differences between men and women were statistically significant. For women, 78.5 percent experienced love at first sight only once compared to 69.6 percent for men. The most striking finding is that love at first sight is most often a once-in-a-lifetime experience. This is at least partly due to the fact that the majority of people who experience love at first sight marry the person. And the vast majority of those getting married stay married. The result is that the person who experiences love at first sight is "out of circulation" for the most part.

## Age and Love at First Sight

Love at first sight is predominantly the province of the young. Of all respondents who experienced love at first sight, 53.6 percent had it happen by age twenty (Table P.1). The most common age bracket was sixteen to twenty years old, with 41.1 percent of respondents. Somewhat surprising is the lack of any significant differences between men and women. It was expected that the men, on average, would be somewhat older. This should have shown up as a slightly older distribution. Some of the cause may have been the bracketing that masked more subtle differences. For example, a female, age sixteen, would view an eighteen-year-old male as older, but both would fall in the same age bracket. The second age question is a bit more revealing.

Respondents also were asked the age of the other person when they first experienced love at first sight. Most respondents (95.3 percent) fell in love with a person of the opposite sex. Therefore, in Table P.2, females were predominantly giving the age of males, and males were predominantly giving the age of females. Females had a higher propensity to be attracted to older males, males had a higher propensity to be attracted to younger women.

For males, 51.5 percent fell in love with a woman who was twenty years old or younger. For females, 39.4 percent fell in love with a man who was twenty years old or younger. While males had a higher likelihood to be attracted to younger females, the pattern was not extreme. For both males and females, the largest age bracket to first experience love at first sight was sixteen to twenty, followed by the twenty-one to twenty-five group. For women, 18.6 percent of the men they were attracted to were more than thirty years of age. For men, only 10.1 percent of the women were more than thirty years of age.

The most striking result of the age questions was the emphasis on youth. Perhaps young people are in a more active search mode and are more attuned to possible mates. Therefore, the young may have a higher propensity to fall in love. Although less common now than twenty to thirty years ago, getting married shortly out of high school was an accepted norm, particularly for women.

There are a significant number of single or divorced adults in the U.S. society. But only 12.6 percent of the respondents experienced love at first sight over the age of thirty. Perhaps those of us over thirty are a bit more battle-scarred and cautious when it comes to entering new relationships. Hence, we may try to not allow love at first sight to happen. We may be unwilling to lose emotional control with the same reckless abandon that we did when we were young.

This age finding also may account for why most of the "relationship experts," who are surely over thirty, don't believe in love at first sight. If they slipped through youth without experiencing love at first sight, they did not have their world rocked by the experience. Since their writings and views are tempered by their own experiences, people over thirty who have not experienced love at first sight are much more likely to be skeptical of its existence.

## Education and Love at First Sight

Education is inversely related to believing in love at first sight. People who have attended graduate school believe in love at first sight less than those who have a high school diploma or less (Table P.3). Those who have attended college or graduated from college are also less apt to be believers than high school graduates. While the differences between believers and nonbelievers are not extremely large, a very clear pattern exists in the data. Perhaps a college education encourages a more rational thought process that offsets emotional motivation or urges. Hence, the better educated are somewhat more skeptical of love at first sight.

If a person believes in love at first sight, education has little influence on whether they actually experience it. For all four education groups, the percentage of those believers who have experienced love at first sight is between 56 to 60 percent. Therefore, education may influence a person not to believe in love at first sight. But once a person believes love at first sight *could* happen, it actually does to about 58 percent of believers.

## Ethnic Background and Love at First Sight

The issue of sociological and cultural influences on patterns of loving will be discussed in subsequent chapters. The data clearly suggests that an individual's ethnic background influences their attitudes toward love at first sight. Many ethnic groups in the United States possess unique subcultures that are manifested in ways different from U.S. society as a whole. Some ethnic groups are far more disposed toward believing in love at first sight than other groups.

A very large portion of Asian/Pacific Islanders (81.8 percent) believe in love at first sight (Table P.4). Hispanics (72.9 percent) also are more apt to believe in love at first sight. The "other" category consisted of people of Eastern European, Middle Eastern, and Mediterranean heritages for the most part, and this group had a very high propensity to believe in love at first sight. Caucasians and Native Americans/Eskimos had about the same portion of believers (63 to 65 percent).

African-Americans are much less likely to believe in love at first sight, with only 55.6 percent being believers. The difference between this figure and the other groups is statistically significant. And of the African-American believers, only 50.7 percent experienced love at first sight.

Among the believers, Caucasians (58.4 percent), Hispanic (57.4 percent), and people in the "Other" category (57.2 percent) all had about the same likelihood to experience love at first sight. Among the believers, Native Americans/Eskimos (65.7 percent) and Asian/Pacific Islanders (63.9 percent) were much more likely to experience love at first sight than the other groups. The relationship between ethnic groups and love at first sight is probably due to sociological and cultural influences of some type.

The implication of these overall results is that love at first sight is not a rare experience. The majority (64.1 percent) of the people believe in love at first sight, and the majority of believers (58.2 percent) have experienced it. A person's age, sex, education, and ethic group also influence love at first sight in some way. And as we delve deeper into the research, we shall see that many other factors also influence love at first sight.

Table P.1

# Age When Love at First Sight Happened

| Ages | Females | Males | Total |
|------|---------|-------|-------|
| 15 and under | 12.6% | 12.2% | 12.5% |
| 16–20 | 40.4% | 42.1% | 41.1% |
| 21–25 | 21.9% | 19.6% | 21.4% |
| 26–30 | 12.3% | 12.6% | 12.5% |
| 31–40 | 7.5% | 6.5% | 7.1% |
| 41–50 | 4.1% | 5.6% | 4.6% |
| 51 and over | 1.2% | 0.5% | 0.9% |

Table P.2

# Age of Other Person

| Ages | Females | Males | Total |
|------|---------|-------|-------|
| 15 and under | 4.4% | 10.6% | 6.9% |
| 16–20 | 35.0% | 40.9% | 37.3% |
| 21–25 | 27.4% | 26.4% | 27.1% |
| 26–30 | 14.5% | 12.0% | 13.5% |
| 31–40 | 12.0% | 5.8% | 9.5% |
| 41–50 | 4.4% | 4.3% | 4.4% |
| 51 and over | 2.2% | 0.0% | 1.3% |

Table P.3

# Education and Belief in Love at First Sight

| Education | Believe | Don't Believe |
|-----------|---------|---------------|
| High School Diploma | 68.0% | 32.0% |
| Some College | 62.6% | 37.4% |
| College Graduate | 62.1% | 37.9% |
| Graduate School | 59.1% | 40.9% |

Table P.4

## Ethnicity and Belief in Love at First Sight

| Ethnic Group | Believe | Don't Believe |
|---|---|---|
| Native American/ Eskimo | 64.7% | 35.3% |
| Asian/Pacific Islander | 81.8% | 18.2% |
| Caucasian | 63.1% | 36.9% |
| African American | 55.6% | 44.4% |
| Hispanic | 72.9% | 27.1% |
| Other | 70.2% | 29.8% |

## ∞ PART ONE ∞

*Understanding Love*

## Chapter One

# Understanding Love

*L*ove.... Love is at once the purist and simplest, most intense and most powerful of emotions. Love is dynamic, evolving, ebbing, flowing like some irresistible tide that we humans are powerless to control. Love can lift our souls to incredible highs of ecstasy. And love can push us into the deepest, darkest despair, depression, and anguish. Love can fulfill us, make us complete, and give us strength and inner peace. Or, love can distract us, make us unable to work, unable to focus, unable to draw pleasure from life. And most of us know precious little about love, why we express love the way we do, or how to love.

There are many forms of love. There is family love, including parent-child, and particularly, mother-child love. There is compassionate love, where we care deeply for our ideals or humanity, in general. There is religious love, love of God or a higher being. And then there is romantic love, the passionate love shared by two people as significant others. These types of love are not discreet, separate subjects. They are all intertwined, influencing one another somehow. While we shall examine the different types of love, the primary focus of this book is on romantic love. It is romantic love that shapes our soul. It is romantic love that shakes the foundation of our very existence.

## The Concept of Love

Some authors and philosophers have contended that love is too profound and expansive to be defined. Others contend that love is the glue of human existence. Others simply say that to love is to live. Love is like the U.S. Supreme Court Justice's definition of pornography: "I can't define it, but I know it when I see it." Most of us cannot define love precisely, but we know when we feel it, and we know even more clearly when we lose it.

For more than three thousand years, philosophers have attempted to understand, describe, and define romantic love. One of the first philosophers to grapple with the concept of love was Plato in about 400 B.C. Plato stated that the feeling of completeness was central to the emotion of love. Plato's mythology states that pairs of humans were once physically joined together as complete beings. But because of their pride and vanity, the gods cleaved humans in two. Each half had to search through life trying to find the other half. When the two halves were reunited, each felt wholeness, completeness, and true happiness.

The concept of "soulmates" had its origins with Plato. Each human is thought to have a perfect complement somewhere. We all subconsciously search for that other soul, that other being, that complements us and makes us whole once again.

For Plato, the deepest and purist unity was devoid of sexual passion, hence the term "platonic love." In fact, Plato viewed actual sex as a debasement of the purist form of love. He contended that engaging in sex lowered humans to mere animal behavior. This detracted from the almost spiritual and ethereal experience of pure love for fellow humans.

Since Plato, the concept of love has been the continual focus of writers and philosophers for more than two thousand years. Yet, the central message of Plato remains. The emotion of love is about oneness, wholeness, completeness with another person. If we, as humans, do not love, we are not complete in life. To be loved and to give love is the very essence of life.

In spite of love's centrality to life itself, romantic love is dynamic and can be expressed in many ways. The linkage of love and marriage is a very recent human invention, for example. The linkage of love and monogamy also is very recent. For most of the history of mankind, marriage and monogamy simply did not exist. Having multiple sexual partners ensured diverse genetic shuffling, which enhanced the likelihood of survival. The current data that suggests that 40 to 50 percent of married men and women have extramarital sexual activity does not prove to be a new phenomenon. This activity has been taking place for many thousands of years.

Not only has the concept of love evolved over the millenniums, love evolves through our lifetimes and our relationships. The way we love when we are young is different than the way we love after ten years with a person. And the way we love can ebb and flow over the course of a single day. Simply put, love is a dynamic, fluid emotion that will take on many forms and manifestations.

## What Influences the Way We Love?

Just as each human has a unique fingerprint and DNA, each human has a unique pattern of loving. Fortunately, we are each malleable and flexible enough that we can learn to adapt and adjust somewhat in the way we love. But there are many influences on the way we love that are beyond our control. Perhaps most powerful, and the least understood, are the genetic tendencies and imprinting that have evolved over a million years of human history. Quite simply, we each are imprinted in certain ways to ensure the survival of the species. While we are imprinted to love, the way we love also is shaped by the sociology and structure of our family, by our culture, and by our own experiences in life. All four of these factors work together to create a pattern of love that is unique to each individual.

## Genetic Imprinting

Genetic imprinting is present in almost all of the animal kingdom. Salmon are imprinted to return to the site of their early development. Depending on the species, a young salmon knows when to go downstream to the ocean. It knows how many years to stay in the ocean. It knows when to begin the upstream migration. It knows how to make a nest (or redd, as a fisheries biologist would call it) and how to mate. It knows how to protect the fertilized eggs. All of these behaviors have been genetically imprinted in salmon.

Each bird knows when to migrate south (if you are in the Northern Hemisphere). It knows what to eat. It knows when to fly north. It knows how to build a nest unique to its species. It knows how to mate and how to care for its young. Although some behaviors are learned, most of these behaviors are the result of genetic imprinting.

Virtually all birds, fish, reptiles, and mammals have a genetic code that guides their behaviors, and especially their reproductive behavior. The genetic code of animals has evolved over thousands of years of continuous natural selection. Humans also have a genetic imprint that guides our behaviors.

The history of mankind also is one of constant evolution. Our current anatomy and physiology are the result of a million years of natural selection. The emotions that we now have are also there because they increased the likelihood of survival, both of individual offspring and the human species as a whole.

There are a whole array of chemical reactions that take place in our brain and body when we are attracted to another person. These chemical reactions ensure that we have pleasurable experiences and natural highs. This euphoria leads to sexual reproduction. When someone falling in love says they feel "chemistry" or "electricity," they are exactly correct. While this topic will be discussed in more detail in chapter two, for the most part, the chemical reactions are far beyond our control. The chemical reactions are a result of genetic imprinting and evolution.

Women are much more selective than men when choosing mates. This is also a result of genetic imprinting. Regardless of the country of origin or race, women pick mates who are good providers—thus ensuring that any resulting children will have a better chance of survival. For example, the physical strength of a male was a trait that indicated he would be a good provider. In modern society, education, income potential, and resources are also indicators of being a good provider.

The reason that women are more selective than men is that women have relatively few eggs to use and a relatively short period of time to use them. A man has millions of sperm that he can use throughout his lifetime. And once a woman becomes pregnant, she has a very long commitment to nurture and care for the child. So, biologically, the selection of a good mate is far more important to a woman than to a man.

Even if a woman does not plan to have children, she tends to use the same selection criteria as women who want children. The implication is that there are some very clear genetic tendencies at work when women select mates. The pattern is not quite as evident for men. But there are tendencies there as well.

Women use a larger and more complex set of selection criteria than men. In general, men around the world prefer younger, more physically fit women. Younger women are preferred because they are more likely to reproduce than older women. Since this tendency occurs in virtually all societies around the world, it is also thought to be genetically imprinted. Beyond the preference for younger women, men are less selective. As one female author noted, "women pick good providers, men pick anything."[5]

We all have built-in genetic tendencies to do things that ensure survival. However, we are not free to individually express those tendencies in any way that we wish. We learn how to express our tendencies through family and cultural guidelines.

## Family Structure and Sociology

Virtually all humans are genetically programmed to love. While we are programmed to love, we humans must learn how to love. Unlike most other creatures, we don't have the exact "how to" genetically imprinted in us to the detail that other creatures are imprinted. Therefore, we must initially learn how to love through our interactions with our parents and siblings. Some psychologists suggest that this learning begins before birth while a baby is in the mother's womb. Although the human brain is only half of its ultimate size at birth, there is plenty of mental capability. It is entirely possible that an unborn infant can react to emotional and chemical changes in the mother. At the very least, learning how to love begins within minutes of birth.

After hatching, birds imprint on the first living object they see. We have all heard the stories of the geese and cranes that imprinted on a human after being hatched artificially. Some may be aware that a horse foal will imprint to a human if it is dried, handled, and the person breathes into its nose. Such an imprinted foal is much easier to train as an adult. It becomes what is referred to as a "people horse." There have been cases where sheep and goats have been imprinted on one another. In one unlucky case, a male goat thought it was a sheep, and, as an adult, tried to mate with other sheep. The female sheep weren't entirely impressed by the goat's amorous advances.

The point is simply this. Just as other animals imprint shortly after birth, so do humans. The initial imprinting is in the beginning of the mother-infant relationship. As will be discussed later, most mothers can identify their own baby just by smell. And babies are even better at identifying their mother's breast by smell. Because of the power of the mother-infant imprinting and relationship, some psychologists feel the nature of this relationship is the single, most significant influence on an adult's ability to love.

Learning to love certainly begins during the early mother-infant interactions. Well before an infant learns to talk, it is learning to love from the mother. Babies will stare into the mothers' eyes for long periods. As adults, direct eye contact lasts seconds. But for infants, eye contact and facial expressions are the first forms of nonverbal communication. It is very possible that the power of direct eye contact to convey attraction for another person among adults is learned in the first few months of life.

As a child grows, the interaction patterns between family members teach a child how to love. A child will watch how his father and mother express love for one another. If a father shows little emotion, a child may form beliefs that emotional distance is appropriate for men. A son might replicate this pattern as an adult in his relationships with women. A daughter might prefer to be around men who are less expressive because she knows how to deal with them better.

If the household is headed by a single parent, say a woman for example, a child may learn that leaving is common behavior for men. The structure of the family unit and the interrelationships among family members provides a laboratory in which a child will learn subtly how to love and to interact with others.

In addition to the pattern of relationships between parents, the pattern of relationships among siblings will influence the way a child learns to love. The birth order, sex, and age gaps all exert powerful influences on childhood development. For example, a family might have four children with the youngest child a girl, the next youngest a boy four years older, and two older children, also boys. The girl may learn that men are supposed to take care of her. The youngest boy may learn to be a caregiver and nurturer of women.

Although we are clearly imprinted to love others, we must be taught how to love. And that initial learning occurs in the family unit during childhood development. But, as a child grows, other sources of learning become more influential.

## Cultural Influences

Prior to age six, the family unit is clearly the dominant learning laboratory. But once a child enters school, factors outside the family start exerting influence. This influence can come from friends, classmates, peers, teachers, friend's parents, and coaches. For example, preschool-aged boys and girls play together as equals. But in school, playmates tend to be of the same sex and boy-girl rivalries often develop. This is a learned, cultural behavior. The power of the peer influences reaches its zenith during adolescence. Cultural influences certainly are not restricted to personal interactions, however.

Entertainment, particularly television and movies, influences a child's beliefs. The endless hours that children spend in front of a television educates children about social values, love, and relationships. For example, one of the most significant impacts on the indigenous cultures in remote areas of North America was the satellite dish. Suddenly, native peoples were exposed to a society radically different from their village. Young people, particularly, realized that there were many experiences and opportunities beyond village life. And in many situations, the clash of cultures was traumatic.

Many cultural values about love are learned in the family unit. Others are learned from the broader society. Still others are learned through our own experiences.

## Life Experiences

We continue to learn, change, and evolve throughout our lives. Each experience teaches us something. Collectively, our love experiences shape and mold our pattern of loving and relating to other people. Our experiences can cause us to have hope that we can find a better place in life, to find emotional growth and fulfillment. Most of us hope to find that true love that will complete our existence.

Our experiences can teach us forgiveness when others disappoint us. We learn how to let the sorrow and disappointment of yesterday go so that the present and the future can happen.

Our experiences will teach us how to communicate, both verbally and nonverbally, in a loving relationship. Our experiences can teach us to be more emotionally open. Or our experiences might teach us to withdraw and avoid conflict in a loving relationship.

The way we learn to love is highly complex. Our pattern of loving begins with genetic imprinting that is molded by our family, by society, and by our personal experiences. However, there are some writers who dismiss much of the genetic and sociological aspects of loving. Instead, these writers view mate selection as a more rational, economic type of process.

## Love as a Rational Choice

The writers who view loving as a more rational decision process suggest that loving relationships are based on the equity theory. Each person has a series of traits, benefits, and assets that can be contributed to a relationship. In the mate selection process, an individual attempts to obtain equal or better value in the form of a partner. This is sort of a human, cost/benefit analysis.

The traits and assets most often evaluated are physical appearance, attractiveness, current resources, income potential, personality, knowledge/education, personal values, and social status. There may be other traits that could be important to some people. But these, in total, are balanced out in a crude ledger. A good match occurs when the sum of a male's traits are approximately equal to the sum of a female's traits.

This may all sound very cold and clinical in our modern society. But, remember, the "love leads to marriage" concept is a fairly recent human invention. Arranged marriages are still commonplace in many cultures. There may be some of the "good provider" type of genetic imprinting at work somehow when evaluating a potential mates' traits. One study asked males and females if they would marry a person if that person possessed every desired trait *except* for love. Males were pretty emphatic with 60 percent saying "no." Only 25 percent of women indicated that they would not marry the person. Fully 75 percent of the women were undecided or indicated that they would marry the person.

As one author noted, if a woman can find the perfect man, she should marry him. If she can't find the perfect man, she should invent him.[6] Apparently, women are somewhat more ready to adapt and learn to love a mate than men. This suggests that women are more inclined to settle for compassionate love. Men, conversely, are more interested in the passion of romantic love.

## Summary

There are many factors that influence how we express love such as genetic imprinting, family structure and sociology, cultural factors, and our personal experiences. We start with a sort of genetic roadmap. But we overlay the genetic tendencies with learned behavior from our family development, from our society, from our personal experiences. And to some degree, we learn to evaluate the traits of our prospective mates. From the complex maze of interactions, we develop patterns of loving.

These factors and patterns also probably have something to do with how we fall in love, as well. And to understand love at first sight, we must address factors in each category.

A person's sex, age, education, and ethnic group all are related to believing in love at first sight and/or experiencing it. As we shall see, there are also many other fascinating relationships. Without a doubt, love at first sight is a far more common experience than the many experts believe.

# A Montana Cowboy

$\mathcal{M}$y parents owned a neighborhood grocery store in Billings, Montana. Everyone in the family worked in the store. My mother and father worked there in the day, and us kids would help out in the evening. After my mother died, things became more difficult. My father hired a lady, Phyllis, to help out during the day. She was about twenty and lived in the neighborhood, so it was convenient for her. The man of my life was her brother.

It was a cold winter evening in 1957 when I met him. I was sixteen. I can still remember every detail of that evening. I was wearing a black jumper and a pink blouse. My hair was long and brown, not the gray it is now.

Phyllis' brother wanted to meet me. He had seen me at the bus stop and in the store. Phyllis was playing the matchmaker, so she brought him over to the house that evening to introduce us. They came to the back door, because it was closest to the store, and knocked.

When he came in, he took off his cowboy hat. He was a handsome man, with black hair, dark brown eyes, and sharp features. He was twenty-five. He was tall and slender, with wide shoulders. He stood straight and strong. He was wearing a brown jacket, jeans, of course, cowboy boots, and a white Stetson hat. He looked like he could have been the model for those lanky cowboys in a Charlie Russell painting.

*He was a real gentleman, very soft-spoken. He was a good listener, and a good speaker too, but initially was shy and reserved. He had wonderful mannerisms in the way he moved and looked at me with those hawk-like eyes. It was like he saw every detail.*

*He had been in the Navy and knew a lot of different things, but he wasn't a know-it-all type of person. He was very modest and reserved, but he had this quiet confidence, very self-assured. I knew within a few minutes that this was a man I could spend the rest of my life with. I suppose a twenty-five-year-old man might be a little old for a sixteen-year-old high school girl, but I honestly never even thought about his age.*

*We visited all that evening. It was so easy talking to him. He was working in Livingston, Montana, about 150 miles away, and had to leave the next day. He immediately wrote me a letter and invited me to go to the Grand Old Opera in Billings.*

*The next weekend we went to the Opera and saw Meryl Haggard and Faron Young. It was another cold evening so we went for coffee. Since I was sixteen, we couldn't go to the bars. I never drank coffee much before, but I drank coffee all that night. We talked and talked and just hit it off.*

*He courted me for almost a year. He would drive the 150 miles every two weeks to see me. In between, we wrote to each other all the time. Then, on Christmas, he asked me to marry him. We got married the next June as soon as I graduated from high school.*

*He taught me how to love and sheltered me for almost thirty years. His love surrounded me and immersed me in his warmth. He had such kindness and gentleness about him, and those eyes of his never missed a thing. If I was feeling a little blue, he always noticed and cheered me up. His laugh was like music that lingered in my heart. Most men know little about the laws governing life, about the art of living. But he knew, he really knew.*

*We were married for twenty-seven years. We had two sons and a daughter. The boys are almost exact replicas of their father. He taught them well. My daughter-in-laws are lucky to have husbands like that, and they share that with me all the time.*

*We lived a happy, happy life. Right to the end we could still sit and talk like that first evening. The fire was still there through all those years, except it got deeper and deeper. It seemed that we fell more and more in love every year. When you are young and in love, you don't believe you could love someone more. But when you are with that special person, love grows and grows, almost like it is alive.*

*The worst experience in my life was when he died. He started having chest pains one evening, so we went to the hospital. The doctors said that he would need open heart surgery to correct a valve problem. Some complications arose after the surgery, and he died rather suddenly. He was only fifty-four when he died. We had such plans for life, but it shows that you never know.*

*When I close my eyes, I can still feel my fingers running through his black hair, feel his breath on my neck, feel his strong arms around me. For a long time I would wear his shirts so I could smell him. While his smell faded from his clothes, it never faded from my memories. I miss his touch so much. At night sometimes, I reach for him, wishing I could feel his heartbeat against me once more.*

*I can still hear the music of his words in my heart. There is a picture in my memory of each special time in our life, of when we first became one, of when our children were born, and of when our grandchildren were born. It's like there is a scrapbook of memories of good times overflowing in my mind. The real photographs have faded with age over the years, but the memories never will.*

*Love At First Sight*

*For a while, I felt such emptiness. I was mired in the darkness of my own pain. I felt sorry for all of the things that we would never do, never feel, never see. I thought that we would have at least another twenty years together.*

*My children are what got me through. They brought the life back to me, helped me see light again. For a while, I didn't know who I was. But there is so much of him in our children that I constantly felt his presence. Seeing the children, who are now adults, do things brings flashbacks of those happy memories: a warm spring day, a fall morning in the mountains, the softness of twilight, or a mountain sunrise. They convinced me that I shouldn't extinguish the spark and joy of life with my sorrow and tears. They wanted to see me smile and laugh again.*

*Not a day goes by without thinking of him. Sometimes I get a glimpse of him walking toward me, arms outstretched. He is always in my heart. He was my soulmate who left too soon. Someday our souls will be united again. I will love him even better then.*

# Fall Magic In Vermont

*F*all in New England can be almost magical. The countryside is ablaze in natural beauty. The trees are a kaleidoscope of reds, yellows, oranges, and greens of every hue. Many communities have fall foliage festivals, and Bradford, Vermont, was no exception. Adding to the festivals was the fact that the year was 1976, the U. S. bicentennial. It was a fall that I'll never forget.

I was twenty-five and employed in a small woodworking shop making cider presses. As part of the festival in Bradford, businesses were encouraged to have an open house so the public could see how things were done. In our business, people could see how cider presses were designed and made. Because the town is so small, a few people would drift in throughout the day, with probably no more than twenty-five all day long. As with most small towns, I already knew most of those people.

She came in with a girlfriend. She was slender with shoulder length brown hair and beautiful brown eyes. She was wearing jeans that fit her well and a denim jacket. I felt an immediate attraction to her and enjoyed showing her around. I honestly couldn't tell you a thing about her friend. They weren't really in the shop long, perhaps twenty minutes.

After they left, I was talking with a friend that I worked with. I remember telling him that I was sure that she was the person that I was going to marry. I don't know what possessed me to say that, it was totally out of character for me. I didn't know her name, age, or anything about her. I just had a premonition that she was going to be my wife. Finding out about someone in Bradford isn't too hard, we were bound to have eventually met.

I was renting a room at the time from a family in Bradford that had a large house. I told them about her, and it turned out that she and her sister had been babysitters for the family's children a few years ago. Her name was Donna, and she was a few years younger than me. The family told me a little about her.

When I finally mustered up enough courage to go over to her house, I had quite a surprise. She was living with her parents for a while as she was going through a divorce. When I got to her house, I found out her father was a friend of mine. Her father and I had worked on several construction projects, and we were on the same carpentry crew once. It seemed strange initially, courting a friend's daughter. That was when she asked me out on our first date.

It wasn't your typical first date. We decided to go explore an old, abandoned cemetery. The fall colors were absolutely beautiful that day. It was clear and sunny, but a typically cool New England day. After hiking through the hills for hours, we finally found the cemetery. It was overgrown and unkempt, many of the headstones had fallen over. We wondered about the forgotten lives of those buried there. It seemed people used to die so young, living hard, short lives. There seemed to be many children buried there. And now nature was gradually reclaiming their resting-place. Old cemeteries seem to make people more thoughtful and philosophical.

While we were at the cemetery, we sat down and used a headstone for a backrest. The surrounding hillside was spectacularly beautiful. We held each other's hand, and I felt a little awkward for a minute. I was hypersensitive to her touch. She was sitting on my right so that our legs and hips were touching.

We leaned toward each other and kissed. Her lips were moist and soft, really sexy. There seemed to be so much warmth and passion. When we first kissed, it seemed that my heart was adrift in a moment so sacred and pure. We ended up laying down in each other's arms in a rather passionate embrace. I caressed her soft skin and held her close. We got leaves all over us. I had to pick the leaves out of her hair. A cemetery may not seem like a very romantic spot, but it was that day. There was this serenity about it. Or maybe it was her, or the fall colors. Or maybe there was something in the air. Whatever it was, it was special.

On our third or fourth date, I decided to impress her with my cooking ability. I remember cooking several traditional New England dishes and topped it off with Indian puddings. It must have worked.

We quickly became best friends, she was someone that I could share anything with. It was as if she filled my heart with music and a joy of living. When I was feeling down, just her touch, her smile would lift my spirits. As each moment unfurled, our hearts grew closer and closer.

We spent almost all of our free time together. About six months after we first met, she moved in with me. It was a little strange having my friend's daughter move in, especially since she moved directly from her parent's house to mine. But since her parents and I got along real well, things worked out nicely.

The following year, we planned a short trip to San Diego, California, to visit my family. Our short trip ended up being a year and a half long. We spent a lot of time at the beach and I taught her to surf. We would go up to La Jolla and snorkel in the rocky coves.

*We lived in Mission Beach, between San Diego and La Jolla. In the evening we'd walk along the beach and watch the beautiful sunsets. Sea World was only a few minutes away and watching the killer whales was fun. The lifestyle in San Diego focuses on the sun, beach, and ocean, so it was quite a contrast from Vermont. While it was fun out there, we weren't true Californians, we missed Vermont.*

*It was fall again when we moved back to Vermont from California, almost exactly three years after we first met. There was something very comforting about seeing all of the fall colors again. It was like an artist painted the hills as a welcome home.*

*The reason that we came back from California was to get married. Most of our friends and family, except my parents, lived around here. Coming back here was truly home for us.*

*Fall is always a special time of the year, since that is when we met and when we married. Every fall the splendor of the countryside is a celebration of our anniversary.*

*We have been married for over twenty years now, and time has flown by. I can still see every detail of that time when she walked through the door of the shop, wearing her jeans. It is hard for me to believe that I told my friend that I was going to marry her before I even knew her name. Life twists and turns in ways we never expect or anticipate. I'm just thankful for the roads we each took that brought her to me in Bradford.*

## Chapter Two

# The Chemistry of Love

Have you ever cried at an emotional movie when you really didn't want to? You may have been consciously trying to keep from crying, but the tears ran down your face anyway? Have you ever seen someone sob uncontrollably at a time of sorrow? Have you ever seen someone get instantly very angry over nothing at all? Have you ever seen "road rage"? All of these situations are a type of emotional hijacking that takes place in our brain. Certain parts of our brain stimulate hormones that cause emotions to overwhelm rational thought. We are seemingly carried along on an emotional roller coaster ride. Experiencing love at first sight very possibly could be one of these emotional hijackings.

When a person suddenly experiences love at first sight, something about the other person stimulates a flood of emotions. As we shall see in later chapters, many people felt "excitement," "chemistry," "electricity," or a "powerful aura." They felt pulled along, almost out of control, truly swept off of their feet. Most felt a euphoria or high. Some said that their heart just went "pitter-patter." All of these people were feeling a natural high that happens in our brain when we are around someone we love. The chemicals that are released in several parts of our brain and body act very much like many illegal, euphoric drugs. And the chemicals are addictive, we learn to need them. We go through withdrawal symptoms when we are deprived of them.

For example, an infant may cry when separated from its mother. When held by its mother, the infant may become calm and content. There are chemical changes that take place in the infant's brain that stimulate these emotional swings.

The functioning of every brain is unique. There are significant differences between men and women in terms of brain structure and neurochemistry. Just as there are differences in intelligence between people, there may be differences that cause some people to be more predisposed to love at first sight than others. But to understand how this could be, we must lay a foundation of how a human brain develops.

## The Human Brain

Of all creatures, humans, at birth, have the least developed brains relative to adults of the species. By the end of the first year of life, the human brain will be two to three times its birth weight. Most mammals give birth to young that can walk and run within minutes of birth. For example, a calf can walk after a few minutes and is directly dependent on the mother for three or four months. An infant can't even begin to care for itself for four or five years.

This extended development period has led some to refer to the human gestation period as a two-part process. Utero-gestation occurs from conception and lasts until birth. Extero-gestation lasts from birth until the first year of life. The external gestation period requires just as comprehensive care and nurturing as dur-

*Love at First Sight*

ing pregnancy. During the first year, the infant, and its brain, grow rapidly and increase in physical and mental capability.

At birth, the portions of the human brain that control the basic bodily functions necessary for life are genetically programmed to be well developed. Other brain functions are almost nonexistent, and will develop in the first year or two of life. Throughout embryonic development, the brain generally grows from the bottom up. Thus, the lower brain functions tend to be more fully developed at birth.

The human brain is extremely complex, and any simplifications are inherently crude. But we have to start somewhere. The human brain has three major parts. One part is the brain stem and other nearby lobes found at the bottom of the brain. One part is the limbic structure that sits atop and surrounds the brain stem. The third part is the neocortex, which is at the top and has all of the convolutions and wrinkles. Each part of the brain has control over different aspects of human physiology and behavior. But each part of the brain also interacts with other parts through a highly complex neural network. The neural network in a single brain is many times more complex than the entire world phone system and can carry far more messages in a day.

## The Lower Brain

The brain stem, olfactory lobe, medulla oblongata, midbrain, and pons are collectively referred to as the Reptilian brain. In reptiles, this is all the brain structure that is present. And it is completely adequate for lower species to have a functioning life. Most of what a reptile needs to know is genetically programmed into the brain. It knows how and what to eat, how to mate and nest, where to live, and so forth. But there is no capacity for emotion and rational thought processes.

In a human infant, the lower brain is well developed at birth, as it must be. This portion of the brain controls the basic bodily functions and activities. The heart beat, breathing, sucking, swallowing, and body metabolism are predominantly controlled here. Later, control over motor activities such as walking, running, and swimming are controlled here, as well.

Also controlled here is an infant's reflexive ability to smile. All humans are genetically imprinted initially to smile when pleasurable events occur. This is an infant's first type of nonverbal communication with another human. And a smile is the only reward an infant can give until it grows and develops more.

Babies learn to mimic the facial expressions of adults. When an adult smiles, the infant smiles. When an adult frowns at a baby, the infant often will begin to cry. These are primarily lower brain responses. It has been found that female infants usually smile more than male infants. This does not imply that they have a happier infancy, however.

The lower brain is pretty much in control for the first few months of an infant's life. During this time, the other portions of the brain are growing rapidly and the infant is learning about the environment into which it has been cast. Gradually, the other portions of the brain exert more and more influence.

## The Limbic Structure

The limbic structure is perched above and around the lower brain. The limbic structure is the seat of most emotions, such as love and anger. Many emotional patterns are genetically programmed into the limbic structure and are much the same for all people. For example, emotions such as anger, sadness, happiness, disgust, and surprise result in the same facial expressions among people in every country in the world. The need to love is part of this genetic emotional programming because there must be a caregiving, nurturing bond between a mother and her infant. The mother needs to love the infant in order to care for it during the long period of development and maturation. The mechanism that ensures this nurturing is the mother-infant bond. And the need to love is housed predominantly in the limbic system.

The limbic structure wraps around the outer portion of the brain. On each side of the brain, there is a portion of the limbic structure known as the amygdala. The amygdala acts as the center of emotional memory, and, along with the neocortex, emotional learning. When a person jumps when they hear a loud, unexpected noise, it is because the amygdala sent a message to other parts of the brain, which instructed the body to respond.

Whitewater rafting is one of my recreational passions. A few years ago, a group of us were floating the Middle Fork of the Salmon River in Idaho's backcountry. One evening, I went for a hike along a trail that parallels the river. The trail was well maintained, but knee-high grass had fallen over, partially obscuring the trail. While walking along, I heard a rattlesnake rattle within a few inches of my feet. I instantly jumped about three feet in the air and landed about six feet away. My jumping was a reflex action because the amygdala processed the sound of the rattle as extreme danger and seized control of my body.

On a different Middle Fork trip, one of my sons brought four or five of his college-age friends along. There are pack bridges across the river for hikers and horses at several places. One of the pack bridges is about fifty to sixty feet above the river, and we usually stop and jump off for an adrenaline rush. One of the guys was a big body builder, strong, and macho. When he climbed up to the bridge and looked down, he was paralyzed with fear. Even though his friends jumped off with no ill effects, Phil was basically paralyzed. His amygdala had processed the situation as fear and danger, and locked up his rational thought processes.

If a person has a damaged or dysfunctional amygdala, they exhibit no emotions. They don't get high, low, angry, or happy. And often, they don't love. When a person lacks emotions or the ability to express emotions, the condition is referred to as "alexithymia." A person with alexithymia has difficulty understanding, describing, or expressing emotions. They can't tell someone that they love them, and they don't know how to respond when someone else expresses love for them. People with alexithymia often complain of vague medical problems because they have a feeling of illness inside when the real problem is emotional distress. Since these people don't know what emotions that they, themselves, are feeling, they are fundamentally incapable of expressing deep emotions to others. Being in love with an alexithymia person can be a very cold, emotionless, frustrating experience. They simply have no emotional depth to give. The condition of alexithymia is caused by a dysfunctional amygdala or a dysfunctional linkage between the amygdala and the neocortex.

The amygdala quickly receives and processes information from our eyes, ears, and nose. Since there is a direct link from our senses to the amygdala, the amygdala can store memories unconsciously. Sights, sounds, and particularly smells can be stored for long periods of time and then compared to current experiences. This can elicit very clear emotional responses. When we discuss pheromones later in this chapter, we will discuss genetic imprinting and how learning about smells can elicit an emotional response.

When there is a high level of emotional arousal, the amygdala imprints the memories more strongly. That is why people remember the events surrounding love at first sight so clearly.

Even though love at first sight may have occurred decades before, the images of that moment are etched into our memories with minute detail. If you are old enough to remember, the events such as J.F.K.'s assassination or the explosion of the space shuttle *Challenger* stimulate extremely detailed memories of exactly where you were at the time. We would be very hard-pressed to remember what happened four days before or five days later, however.

I can recall several early childhood events clearly, and all of these involved some degree of emotional stress. Before I was two, I wandered away from my house, fell in a creek, and nearly drowned. Luckily, my brother pulled me out. When I was three, my family went to the California coast and I slept in a cave on the beach. While still three, my stepfather was driving a grey, Willy's 4x4-wagon sidehill around the hills near Santa Rosa, California. My mother got very upset because she thought that the Willy's was going to roll over. I can recall many events prior to the age of four, but the more interesting experiences occurred as I got older.

When I was about nine, I went fishing with two young friends. It was summer and the stream was low and we didn't catch any fish. But I caught something much more interesting. While walking up the streambed, we came across a rattlesnake about eighteen inches long. We pinned it down with our fishing poles while I took a shoelace out of my tennis shoe. I made a loop in the end of my shoelace and slipped it around the snake's head. My chums and I proceeded to proudly walk home with a live rattlesnake on the end of my shoelace (which I was holding in my hand). As we walked by a neighbor's house, I showed him my prize. For some reason, he decided to call my mother. I can still recall the look on her face when I got home. It wasn't a look of joy. I have no idea what happened to that snake, but my mother's reaction is etched in my brain. Such is the power of emotional arousal on the imprinting of memories.

Advertisers have known the impact of emotional arousal for years. If an advertisement can get you psychologically or emotionally aroused, you will remember the ad, and, hopefully, the product. Therefore, a television ad will have a scene that will stimulate you in some way. Perhaps, a beer ad shown in California would show people playing beach volleyball. In Colorado, the beer ad might use skiing or whitewater rafting. In Minnesota, the ad might feature a hockey game. All ads would be attempting to increase brand recognition through psychological arousal.

If we lose a loved one in some way, we may find it very difficult to be productive and to focus at work. We may lose weight or gain weight. We may have trouble sleeping at night. This is because the amygdala is creating neural static that is difficult for the neocortex to process. Hence, we have something akin to a neural thunderstorm taking place in our brains. It often takes several years for the emotional memories to fade enough to gain normalcy.

It is very possible that those people who experience love at first sight have a more active amygdala. These people would experience a wider range and greater depth of emotions. Because of potentially greater emotional sensitivity at the subconscious level, these people might be more prone to the emotional hijacking of love at first sight than skeptics.

The amygdala is particularly important to human development and the ability to love. While the lower brain is more fully developed at birth, the limbic system, including the amygdala, grows proportionally more after birth. This implies that emotional learning through early childhood experiences is more important than genetic imprinting. The impact of childhood experiences will be discussed in the following chapter.

The limbic system is the primary seat of emotions and emotional memory. While lower brain functions are more independent from other parts of the brain, the limbic system actively interacts with the third major portion of the brain, the neocortex. Thus, while the emotions generally originate in the limbic areas, the neocortex guides how we express those emotions.

## The Neocortex

The neocortex is at the top of the brain, a mass of convolutions and wrinkles. The neocortex is where our rational, and sometimes irrational, thought processes and reasoning take place. This is where our working memory resides.

Like the limbic structure, the neocortex is less well developed than the lower brain functions at birth. The neocortex grows rapidly in mass and processing capability during early childhood development. Thus, the neocortex is like a framework or architecture upon which life's experiences will be imprinted.

The neocortex is where most of our lifetime memories and learning takes place. So as the neocortex grows, it is storing memories. Some of the early memories are stored before an infant has words to describe them. In fact, a good deal of learning about family relationships occurs before age six, a time when a child can not fully understand *why* things happen. The child observes things happening and the memories are stored in the neocortex. Understanding these early memories is the focus of a good deal of adult psychoanalysis.

The neocortex consists of two hemispheres or lobes that are separated by a thick band of nerve fibers. This has led to the "left brain, right brain" discussions and distinctions. The left side of the brain appears to focus on rational, logical thought such as mathematics, computer programming, languages, and some scientific applications. The right side of the brain focuses more on visual and emotional processing. There are significant differences between male left-brain and right-brain functioning.

The distinction between the left and right functions is more pronounced in males than females. The male brain compartmentalizes functions more than females. A female brain operates more holistically, with less distinction between the left and right lobes. This gives rise to less emphasis on analytical thought processes and more emphasis on social and emotional integration and sensitivity.

Apparently, the evolution of the female brain has enhanced the caregiving, nurturing capability necessary for child rearing. And this more holistic approach may give women, in general, a greater capacity for love. This might show up as a need for family and mate acceptance and reenforcement. The greater left brain emphasis in males may lead to more of an emphasis on self, such as personal skills or physical development. This could be a result of the need for males to be good providers.

The distinction in brain structures between males and females begins when the human embryo is at about six weeks of development. A male embryo at this stage will receive an "androgen bath." This androgen bath will cause male characteristics to develop in the embryo such as male hormones, physical differences, and differences in the brain. The stimulus for this androgen bath is the presence of the Y, or male, chromosome. If the androgen bath does not occur for some reason, a "female" brain will develop in a male body. This produces tendencies toward male homosexuality due to the presence of more female hormones in the body.[7]

*Love at First Sight*

The neocortex is where most learning takes place. While many aspects of individual preferences and tendencies are genetically imprinted, much more is learned. Keeping the focus on love, the family, social, and cultural values are learned during childhood development. These shape the way that we express love later in life. This comprehensive storing, cataloging, and interpreting of memories occurs first at the subconscious level, and later at both the subconscious and conscious level. It is over this foundation of learning that we map our individual love experiences, and develop even more learning.

To illustrate the powerful memory capacity of the neocortex, it is thought that all life experiences are stored there somewhere. While we may periodically go through our personal computers and delete old files and "defrag" temporary files, the brain doesn't operate so cleanly. During the latter stages of my mother's life, she suffered from Parkinson's disease. Once when I visited her, she carried on a conversation with me from over fifty years ago, before I was even born. She was complaining about some farmhands stealing tools from a ranch that she had owned. I personally have had flashbacks where I see an image from twenty, thirty, or forty years ago. For some reason, it suddenly appears, like a still picture or just a few seconds of activity. But I could describe everything in that image in minute detail. All of these images or conversations are flowing from deep in the recesses of the neocortex, very much like the archives of a large library. The stimulus for such flashbacks is probably a wayward electrochemical signal in the neocortex.

## The Neural Network

There are billions of cells in the human brain. These cells communicate with nearby cells and across neural pathways to other parts of the brain. For example, there are neural pathways between the amygdala and the left, prefrontal lobe of the neocortex. The amygdala identifies an emotion by comparing memories to the current situation. A message is sent to the neocortex to determine the appropriate emotional response. An emotion identified as anger, fear, or sorrow will elicit a different response than an emotion of love.

This type of neural communication occurs through a whole series of electrochemical signals that are passed on from cell to cell. The junction between nerve cells is a tiny gap referred to as a synapse. Chemicals, referred to as neurotransmitters, carry information across these tiny synapses. There are many types of neurotransmitters that can be used for different messages. One of the neurotransmitters is peptides, large strings of amino acids. Peptides are very large and have the ability to carry large amounts of information between neural cells.

Of the peptides, endorphins are directly related to love. When a mother holds and caresses an infant, the infant's brain releases endorphins that create a feeling of comfort, contentment, and euphoria. When the mother and infant are separated, the infant's endorphin level drops dramatically, and the infant becomes distressed and anxious, and begins crying.

As with all neurotransmitters, the brain must know exactly *where* the endorphins must be released to create the desired effect. Released in one place, the infant may feel contentment; released somewhere else, the infant may feel sleepy. Peptides, in general, and endorphins are more heavily concentrated in the limbic region of the brain. Since this is the center of emotions, peptides appear to be linked most directly to emotional behaviors.

Other neurotransmitters are epinephrine, norepinephrine, and seratonin. These have widespread use throughout the brain and have been linked to emotions. For example, abnormally low levels of seratonin are linked to feelings of melancholy and depression.

We perceive our environment through our senses of sight, smell, touch, and hearing. Most sensory information goes to the thalamus, and then messages are sent simultaneously by the thalamus to the neocortex and the amygdala. The amygdala then sends messages to the hypothalamus. The hypothalamus then directs the pituitary gland to release the appropriate hormones. This direct linkage from sensory input to the thalamus to the amygdala to the hypothalamus can bypass the rational thinking of the neocortex.

This bypass is probably how the emotional hijacking of love at first sight occurs. The message from the thalamus is translated by the amygdala as "love." The amygdala releases a flood of endorphins in the limbic system, creating a feeling of euphoria. Simultaneously, the pituitary stimulates a release of adrenaline, which increases our heart rate, increases the metabolism of blood sugar, and stimulates appocrine glands which causes us to sweat. Making matters worse is the release of phenylethylamine (PEA) and dopamine, both of which induce a natural high just as the endorphins do.

The implication is that there is not just a single chemical reaction taking place in our bodies. There are a whole series of reactions that result in the emotion of love. All of the chemical changes have a similar end result however, a euphoric, natural high.

Like any chemical reaction, the body will build up tolerances. Gradually, the chemical reactions caused by love abate. The euphoria of passionate, romantic love fades for most people, to be replaced by compassionate, caring love. Some men and women rue the evolution from romantic love to compassionate love as a pretty lousy trade.

The fading of the strong chemical reaction associated with love after a few years may be the cause of many extramarital affairs. A spouse may yearn strongly for the love-induced high and search elsewhere. We've all heard the expressions of "the fire went out" or "I didn't feel anything anymore." Most married people who stray find an extramarital affair "exciting," but accompanied by a good deal of guilt. Keep in mind, the institution of monogamous marriages is a very recent social innovation. The power of a million years of evolution is hard to overcome in a few thousand years. It may be that plural sexual relationships generated a more effective genetic shuffling. Knowing *why* the love-induced euphoria fades would be quite interesting.

## Pheromones

The senses of sight, hearing, and touch can input information to the thalamus both consciously and subconsciously. In the first year of life, the majority of sensory input is subconscious. But as the neocortex grows, more conscious sensory input is captured. A child watches his parents and siblings, and through trial and error learns about appropriate and inappropriate behaviors. Just as a newborn infant will mimic facial expressions, a child will pattern behavior from those around him or her. There is another sense, smell, that operates primarily on a more subconscious level.

I was once at a business meeting and one of the ladies in attendance was cold due to the air conditioning. So I let her wear my jacket. I could smell her scent for about a week after that. It was not just perfume, although she was probably wearing some. The scent was *her*. I have been out with women and could smell some of them for a day or so. This was after I had changed clothes and showered. Yet, I could smell the essence of the woman. Something about particular women created a lingering scent.

Some people will pick up their spouse's clothing and bury their face in the shirt. They are smelling the essence of their mate. All of these examples illustrate the power of pheromones.

At its simplest, pheromones are chemical signals. Most, but not all, pheromones are excreted externally and influence the behavior or physiology of others of the same species. Male pheromones generally act as an aphrodisiac on females. Female pheromones generally act as an attractant for males. Before discussing human pheromones, demonstrating their presence in other species is illustrative.

## Pheromones in Mammals

Many female mammals give off strong pheromones when they are in estrus (or heat). A male dog can smell a female dog in heat from miles away. The female is excreting minute, airborne pheromones that drift along on air currents. This occurs with many, if not most, mammalian species. Female cows, horses, cats, rabbits, squirrels, deer, elk, and bears all come in heat.

Male lions and bears kill any young they can. When a new male lion gains control of a pride of lions, he immediately kills all of the sexually immature lions in the pride. The absence of the young causes the adult females to come in heat. In this way, the male ensures the passing on of his genes at the expense of his predecessor. When a female bear's cubs are killed, the sow will come into heat. But pheromones are not restricted to females.

I have a friend who has a small herd of longhorn cattle. All are cows, or females. None of the cows showed any signs of being in heat since there was no bull around. However, when he brought a bull onto his property, all of the cows came into heat within a few weeks. Although the bull was separated from the cows, the bull excreted pheromones that caused the cows' sexual cycle to become active.

## Human Pheromones

Among insects, reptiles, and mammals, there are many examples of pheromones at work. So the question naturally arises, do humans excrete pheromones? The answer is certainly yes. It is less clear exactly how human pheromones work. For the most part, pheromones work subconsciously with genetic imprinting to change human physiology.

It is fairly well known that women in close proximity to one another demonstrate menstrual synchrony. For example, all women in a women's dormitory do not exhibit menstrual synchrony. Only women who spend a good deal of time together demonstrate synchrony. The greater the amount of time together, the greater the menstrual synchrony. Human menstrual blood contains a pheromone, trimethylamine, that women can subconsciously smell. Somehow, this pheromone causes a woman's menstrual physiology to change.

Women who spend a considerable time apart from men have longer and more varied menstrual cycles. Women around men more frequently have shorter and more regular menstrual cycles. Men excrete pheromones that influence a woman's menstrual physiology without their physical presence. For example, some studies have used only a pad containing male sweat to achieve the same results. Women exposed to such pads three times per week had shorter, more regular menstrual cycles.

Girls who are around men enter puberty earlier than girls who have little contact with men. The presence of male pheromones apparently stimulates the sexual development of women in some way, in addition to influencing menstruation.

Studies have shown that women who are ovulating are more sensitive to smell than at other times of the month. And a woman's vaginal odor will also vary throughout the month. These are probably due to some type of sexual signal that is being emitted.

Human sperm contains many olfactory receptors. These would not be needed unless they played a role in reproduction. Some scientists believe that the human egg emits a chemical that sperm follow upstream until the egg is found. Male semen also contains prostagladins, which stimulates uterine contractions. Perhaps these contractions are an aid to sperm making their way to the fallopian tube where the eggs are located.

Human pheromones are excreted primarily through apocrine and eccrine glands. Apocrine glands excrete a modified sebaceous substance that is fatty and oily. The facial areas have many apocrine glands. When your face and hair become oily, it is due to apocrine excretions. A primary reason for kissing a person's face and neck is to smell them.

Eccrine glands are sweat glands and are more widely dispersed across the body. Most eccrine excretions act to cool the body during periods of exertion. But eccrine glands on the hands and feet sweat during times of emotional arousal. Perhaps these glands are giving off some type of chemical signal of sexual interest.

There are significant differences in the presence of apocrine and eccrine glands across different racial groups. Africans have the most and Asians have the least.[8] Scientists also have found that different ethnic groups have different odors. One smell is not better or worse, but there are subtle differences. Just as there are ethnic differences in odor, there may be unique family odors.

Other mammals have a unique family odor. For example, a dog that has just given birth to a litter of six or seven pups can easily identify a strange pup slipped into the litter. Usually, the strange pup will be pushed away. Elephants are thought to be able to smell the family odor on the bones of a long dead family member. The elephants will fondle and carry the bones of a dead family member and ignore the bones of a nonrelated elephant. Family odors may occur in humans, as well.

In one study, mothers who had just given birth were blindfolded and presented with three newborn infants.[9] The mothers were asked to identify their own baby by smell alone. The mothers were able to correctly identify their own baby 61 percent of the time. Only 37 percent of the fathers were able to correctly identify their own baby, very close to the 33 percent expected by random chance. This suggests that families do have a distinct odor signature.

Within about a month of birth, a breastfed infant can accurately detect its own mother's breast. When presented with an unfamiliar breast, most infants will turn their head away. This suggests that the mother's odor is quickly imprinted into the amygdala, neocortex, and olfactory lobes of the brain. It is entirely possible that the infant subsequently learns the scent of other family members such as the father or siblings.

If humans do have unique family odor signatures, as it appears, odor may have a role in love at first sight. There have been women that I have dated that have smelled extremely good. There have been women who had no unique odor. And there have been a few that I did not like the smell of. I am not talking about perfumes, and I am not talking about overwhelming body odors. I am referring to that unique subtle odor that is the essence of a particular person.

It may be that I find odors that are similar to my family's odor are pleasing. Odors that are disparate may be much less pleasing. I can't tell you why a particular woman smells good, I just know it happens.

Some (137) of the people in our research mentioned a person's smell or odor as attracting them to some degree. Since most pheromones work at the subconscious level, this was probably a very subtle type of attraction. The people probably knew someone smelled good, but would find it difficult to explain why.

Some humans have far more sensitive olfactory senses than others. For example, some people are one thousand times more sensitive to certain scents than others. Scientists believe that the sense of smell is ten thousand times more sensitive than our sense of taste. And our scent preferences evolve throughout life.

Male and female children under age eight like similar scents. But after age eight, significant scent preferences begin to emerge. Boys and girls prefer different smells. And the scent preferences gradually evolve as children grow and mature. Again, it is apparent that something happens to our sense of smell throughout our lifetimes. It is unknown why our preferences for smells changes, but it may have something to do with sexual maturation, as in other mammals.

## Summary

The structure and functioning of the human brain play a primary role in our patterns of loving. There is no question that we are genetically programmed to love. But the way we express love is a learned behavior, just as the language we use is learned. And the learning takes place both consciously and unconsciously. Understanding the emotional functioning of the brain helps us to understand the physiological impact of love at first sight.

Just as people are taller or shorter than others, each person has a different pattern of loving. And the pattern of loving is influenced by a combination of genetics, socio-cultural factors, family behavior, and individual experiences. It is very likely that differences in brain structure and neurochemistry may predispose one person to experience love at first sight when a unique combination of stimuli are presented in the form of a mate.

# The Heart of the Darkness

❧

*N***ikki.** *Even several years after seeing her last, writing her name still stirs powerful emotions. Heartache. Longing. Thoughts that I try to suppress and shove back into the dark, hidden recesses of my soul. Thoughts that are too distracting and emotionally draining. For the first year after "goodbye," a day never passed without thinking of her a dozen times. She was like a ghost, haunting my life. Especially in the emptiness of late at night, laying in bed in the dark, listening to some CD. It seemed every song was about her.*

*Gradually, slowly her constant presence inside ebbed away like a receding tide, leaving for now but certain to return. Nikki. As with all old loves, there is still curiosity, wondering what she is doing, where she is. There is also the inescapable "what if?"— thoughts that should not even be considered.*

*Nikki hated to be called Nicole. Too formal, too constrained. Nikki seemed to fit her free spirit, her inner fire, the constant sparkle in her eye. Her age was forty, but her heart was fourteen. To understand her, if that is possible for anyone, you need to know a little more of her life.*

*Nikki came from small town USA. Probably one of those Midwestern towns John Mellencamp sings about. Raised on a small farm a few miles from a town of five thousand, she fancied herself to be a country kid, a real cowgirl. But she wasn't. She had sold out on that heritage years ago, when she began trying to transform herself into something different. A task never completed.*

*In grade school, she did have a horse and loved to ride across the flat, Midwestern prairie. In high school, she experimented, like most teenagers do, with smoking, sex, drinking, and drugs. Most of these vices she never completely gave up. She was a little more daring than most, a little wilder. She was the cheerleader that all the guys wanted. There was also an emptiness inside her that was never fulfilled, a thirst that was never quenched. That was probably something that she and I had in common.*

*She went off to college at the small state university. She met the football star. Walking down the aisle on her wedding day, she knew she was making a mistake. She wasn't even sure what love was. And she still doesn't know. Her father told her to take his car keys and run, he sensed what his daughter was feeling. But she didn't want to disappoint all the friends and relatives. Getting married to a football star was supposed to be part of her escape and transformation.*

*It wasn't long before the physical and emotional abuse started, or so she said. Perhaps she caused some of it with her flirting and wandering eye. She thought that having a baby would help, but it didn't. After several years of marriage, she needed out. I was never sure if the stories of physical and emotional abuse were really true or were an excuse to justify her affair. She found a rich white knight to rescue her and her young son from her gloom, and her husband. Rich as in many, many millions. As she once said, money has powerful advantages. It enabled her to get away from her husband and live a life of luxury. She wasn't in love with the white knight, but she liked the lifestyle. Her attempted transformation continued.*

*For fifteen years she was the trophy bride, adorning the arm of her white knight, CEO husband. Million dollar houses. Flights on the Concorde. All the best country clubs and tennis clubs. CEO's wives clubs. Part of the social upper crust. But she felt she needed to do something, to accomplish something. She had seen the hollowness of many executive wives and wanted more for herself. A few strings were pulled, and dollars invested, and she had an executive position. Money still had its advantages.*

*Her white knight was now sixty, over twenty years her senior, and had forgotten what sex was, if he ever really knew. He had never been emotionally warm or sharing. As Nikki described it, they had a business relationship. He provided her with an opulent lifestyle. She provided him with companionship. She still didn't know what love was, and didn't really care if she ever found out. And this is about when we met.*

*She was new in her executive position and ill equipped for success. Being a trophy bride builds good social skills but poor job skills. So she looked for consultants to help her. By chance, she found me. We talked frequently on the phone. Truthfully, I sensed something different about her from the start. We both found reasons to call each other, often several times a day, more than we really needed to. She decided I should give a presentation to her company. That is when it all began.*

*Nikki met me at the airport. Her image will never be forgotten. Her long, camel cashmere coat shielded her from the cold February wind. Her designer silk scarf was wrapped around her neck, billowing in the breeze. Her designer purse was over her right shoulder. She wore black leather gloves. Her eyes were ablaze with life.*

*Nikki is attractive, but not like the models in a magazine. She has the high cheekbones of the Plains Indians or Cherokee. Her* long black hair is coarse and thick. Her brown eyes were large and round. But she flatly denied having Indian blood in her veins. Her lips were red and moist. Like most of us over forty, she carries a few extra pounds but still has a nice figure. There was something special about her, although it took me a while to figure it out. As I extended my hand to greet her, she threw her arms around me and gave me a warm embrace.

In an instant, I knew I was in trouble. She acted as if we were long lost friends; she was still the perfect hostess. I felt fear and uncertainty. This is a business relationship, I kept telling myself. Stay in control. And for the first six months of working with her, I did maintain control. But then it happened.

Nikki was always friendly, sometimes too much so. She stood a little too close, she would brush against my body, invade my space. She would put her hand on my arm. Sometimes our eyes would meet and neither would look away, or say anything. The connection had been made. But I maintained control. I tried to ignore her hints and invitations, that social dance that men and women learn. Until she grabbed my tie and whispered, "We need to have an affair." Those words came very easy for her. My initial impulse was to pull back, get some breathing room, to run. I caught the next plane out of town that day. On the three-hour flight back home I was churning with mixed emotions. Part of me wanted her passion. The rational part of me said stay away, keep in control. She was a beautiful, exciting, but very married woman.

Running from Nikki was a stalling tactic. From a business standpoint, an intimate relationship could be a disaster. Her company was a good account. From a personal standpoint, an intimate relationship could be even worse. Having an affair with a married woman, particularly one married to a white knight and money, is not a recipe for happiness.

*Our business relationship required that I have frequent contact with Nikki and her company. My supposed self-control quickly melted under the warmth of her smile and her wet, eager kiss. She possessed the magic key that unlocked the chains around my heart. I was powerless to resist her easy invasion and conquest. As lovers often do, we met wherever and whenever we could. I knew from the start that I was toast. I was gone, hook, line, and sinker. I knew in my heart that I loved her in the instant that I first saw her. The affair was something I was unable to resist, it was almost inevitable.*

*I constantly questioned myself, wondering why I let myself become involved with a married woman. I think that it was like a characteristic that you ignore. If you really love someone, you don't care if they are a few pounds overweight, you ignore mannerisms you don't like. For the most part, I accepted and ignored the fact that she was married. And since her husband lived in another state, it wasn't much of a constraint.*

*From the start, I felt that Nikki was missing something. I never expected her to leave her white knight and money. But I did need her to share her heart, her warmth, and her love. But that was simply beyond her. She would gladly share her smile, laughter, and her body. That was enough for her. But she could not share her heart or her love. She was something of a chameleon, changing her colors and moods to fit any situation. That was a skill learned as a trophy bride. I sensed that she was emotionally shallow, always playing a game.*

*For a while, I just didn't understand. I told her that I needed more warmth, more sharing. Consistent with my personality, I only know how to love a woman completely. While I rarely share my heart, when I do, I want it to be on a very deep emotional level. She said that she cared for me more than any man she had* ever known, that we were building a significant relationship. She talked of children, of the future. Foolishly, I believed her.

Perhaps she said those things because she thought I wanted to hear them. She said I was a very deep person, very evolved in the meaning of life. She said "I love you." But her words were hollow, insincere, coming from her head and not her heart. I told her not to ever say that unless she was absolutely certain of it. After that, my I love yous were always met with the same stone, cold silence.

When I realized that she would never share emotionally with me, my sexual passion for her faded. She had always been sexually dysfunctional, which is a nice way of saying that she had never in her life experienced an orgasm through anything resembling normal intercourse. I started to see that her sexual dysfunction and her emotional dysfunction, the inability to love a man, must be related somehow. Since she didn't feel love for me, while this may be strange for a man to say, I felt she was trifling with me, toying with me, to satisfy her own desires.

I felt that I was simply convenient for her. I was around often enough and met her minimum qualifications. That wasn't good enough for me so I began to emotionally withdraw and to create some distance between us. She would knock on my hotel room door, but I would ignore her. She would phone, but her calls went unanswered. She probably did the same to me. The end of our relationship was not unexpected.

We were sitting in her dining room sharing a bottle of expensive Chardonnay from her well-stocked wine cellar. We were having the same old conversation. I was saddened and frustrated by the lack of emotional sharing. She couldn't understand why I wasn't satisfied with our sexual relationship. Most of her previous lovers had apparently been completely satisfied with "just sex." Perhaps in my twenties, sex alone would have been sufficient. But sex without emotion was unfulfilling at my age. I needed both. The discussion seemed to be going nowhere. All the words had been spoken, but the feeling wasn't right, the issue remained unresolved. Finally, Nikki said, "I want to maintain our sexual relationship, but loving you is a road that I'll never go down."

As I sat there in silence, reality crashed over me. Gradually, I realized that I was in love with the illusion that Nikki had tried to create, that she was a smart, warm, caring person who could share her heart and soul. At that moment, I saw through love's illusion and reality stepped into view. The completeness of her emotional and sexual dysfunction was devastating. She had finally revealed her true self. And it was the heart of the darkness.

Minutes passed in silence as we sat there. I kept hearing her words pound in my head, "Loving you is a road that I'll never go down." This forty-year-old lady had been married twice and had many lovers, but she had never really loved any man. Somehow, she was emotionally stunted, emotionally inaccessible, incapable of love. Perhaps living with her cold white knight for fifteen years had taken a greater toll than her abusive first husband. What a sad life, I thought, to be forty years old and have never experienced the joy and exhilaration of complete love. The only things that she really valued were her son, designer things, and money. Even the white knight was unimportant; he was just the means to what she wanted. I turned and looked at the frozen look on her emotionless face. As I turned away, I realized that she was nobody I had really known, she was a perfect stranger.

Slowly, I stood without looking at her. As I walked across the dining room, I said, "I guess there is nothing more to say." I didn't want to leave, to give her up, but I couldn't accept her terms. The whole scene was surreal, like things were moving in slow motion, it seemed everything was in a haze. She sat at the dining room *table, motionless. My footsteps in flight made a hollow sound as I walked across the hardwood floor and out of the front door. Without looking back, I drove away. That was the last time I saw Nikki.*

# The Easter Egg Hunt

*I*t seems like another world, long ago and far away. It was 1926, and things were much different then. I was twelve years old and lived in Rocky Ford, Colorado, a pretty small town. Rocky Ford is about fifty miles east of Pueblo in the rolling grassland country of southeastern Colorado. It was a good place to grow up.

By today's standards, life was hard. There was no television, thank goodness, and even radio reception was poor. So everyone learned to entertain themselves, mostly by reading. My family was very close knit, and my parents were very strict Christians. As a result, we studied the bible a lot, something my father was very good at. Like most men, my father worked six days a week, but Sunday was for church and family.

One of the high points of the week was when my father would buy a Sunday newspaper. All of the kids would read the funny papers, or comics, as they are now called. That one paper was how we kept up with what was going on in the world. While life was harder, there was a simplicity and purity in life that young people today don't understand.

Because our family was close, all of the holidays were spent with relatives. My father's brother and his wife were our only relatives in the area, and they lived about twenty miles away, out in the country. We went out there to be with them one Easter, and that is where it happened.

My aunt and uncle had several children, and one of the girls was about my age. We had become good friends over the years. My cousin attended a little one room country school. This little country school also doubled as the church on Sundays. We all went to the Easter service there that day. After church, there was to be a big Easter egg hunt at the school for kids of all sizes. My cousin had invited me to go with her on that egg hunt.

The men had started at the schoolhouse and had gone across the prairie hiding Easter eggs. They used real, hard-boiled eggs that had been colored, not the plastic ones they use today. It seemed like there were eggs for a mile, but it probably wasn't that far. A bunch of us girls were together hustling around and gathering up those eggs. On the way back to the schoolhouse for the picnic, some boys ambushed us as we crossed a small bridge. They were throwing the hard-boiled eggs at us, and we were screaming and yelling. They were just a bunch of feisty, adolescent boys.

One of the boys started to throw an egg at me. I looked at him and said, "If you hit me, I'll hit you back." Something about the softness in his face, something about it just captured my eye. His name was Charles, and he was fifteen.

Later that day we were getting ready to play baseball, and Charles and another boy, Mike, were fighting over which team I was going to be on. I ended up on Charles' team. As I was running the base paths, one of the other boys accidentally hit me in the head with a baseball. It almost knocked me out. I was lying on the ground, and Charles rushed over, gently picked my head up, placed it on his leg, and started rubbing it. He adamantly yelled for someone to get me some cold water. Luckily, I wasn't hurt too badly. Charles was very protective and gentle with me.

That evening we went home to Rocky Ford. After I got home from school on Monday, there were two cards in the mailbox waiting for me. They were from the two boys who were fighting over me, Charles and Mike. Mike was nice, but Charles had my heart from the minute I saw him on that bridge.

Charles was about five feet, four inches tall and was real nice looking. He was always well dressed. His mother was a little tiny French woman, and his father was Dutch. His father was a blacksmith who had brought his wife into this area in a covered wagon. In those days, the railroad used to stop in Kansas.

Charles wanted to come to town to see me. He was old enough to drive a car so he would always come to my house. My mother would not let us go out alone, even to the picture show, because she thought I was too young. I actually was pretty young, I was almost thirteen. Mama didn't think girls should start dating before they were fifteen. So my older sister would go to the show with us, but she would always sneak off with some guy. Both my sister and I would be alone with our boyfriends. Finally, after about a year, mama let me go out without a chaperone. I was only thirteen when Charles and I started dating by ourselves.

Charles was kind and full of fun. He always had a smile on his face that gave me a warm feeling inside. I went with Charles for four years, and he was the only boyfriend I ever had or wanted. I was seventeen when we got married on September 5, 1931. It took us three years to get our first child. She was born at my mother's house, as all four of our children were. All of the relatives knew how to take care of everything. She was a tiny little thing, being very premature.

Back then they didn't have incubators for babies, so my mother made a bed for her in one of my dad's shoeboxes. That tells you how tiny she was. I guess it was a miracle that she lived. My dad was so proud as it was his first grandchild. We ended up with two boys and two girls.

*Sometimes, when we were first married, Charles and I would get on our hands and knees, looking for a four-leaf clover. When we found one, we'd hold each other close and make a wish and seal the wish with a kiss. On a summer night, we used to lay out on a blanket and watch for falling stars. We would make a wish on the falling star and seal it with a kiss, too. It seemed that all we ever wished for was love and happiness. I wonder if young people do those things anymore.*

*My hands used to be soft and tender, now they are old, wrinkled, and stiff. My hair was auburn, now it's gray and thin. I've learned that there is great beauty in life, but I fear few people find it. Most people are too blind, searching for something, but not sure what they are looking for. The days become weeks, weeks become months, months become years, and the years rob us of our youth. What really matters in life is love; it is life's great lesson. The more you love, the more beauty there is in life and all the things you do.*

*When a baby comes into this world, the only thing certain is the mother's love. Hopefully, the father is there to share that love also, but in this crazy world, that isn't always so. If the baby is lucky, there are a few grandparents to give love as well. The best we can hope for when we die is to be loved by the same number of people as when we are born. A really successful life is marked by being loved by more people. That means a person has been a conduit of love and happiness to others. They have made the world a better place.*

*Charles and I were married for over fifty-two years when he passed away in 1984. When you finally leave this world, you don't take much with you, but you leave behind memories. The most cherished memories of Charles and I aren't when we bought something. The best times were when we shared laughter and love and sometimes even tears. Those memories of Charles will always* be in my heart. The only really sad time in my life was when Charles left this world to be with the Lord. He left me alone, but his memories and the knowledge that he is in a better place gives me comfort until we are together again.

## Chapter Three

# Learning to Love from Our Family

*W*e learn how to love. It is that simple. Well, almost that simple. As we saw in chapter two, we are genetically programmed to love, so we begin life with some preprogrammed tendencies that are unique to each person. This genetic template forms the framework around which more specific behaviors will be wrapped. These behaviors are learned in the unique environment into which each human is born.

There are three types of environmental influences that shape human behavior, and particularly the ability to express love effectively. First, there are the family structures and behaviors, which probably are most important. This includes parents; grandparents; the number, age, and sex of siblings; and the patterns of interaction. The family unit is the incubator where we learn from our first role models. Then there are socio-cultural values and modes of acceptable behavior that we run into, especially during adolescence. We learn what is good and bad and much more from society. And, finally, there are our own unique experiences that we have in love and relationships. The human cortex has the ability to learn both consciously and unconsciously from our personal experiences. All of these influences work together to make each of us truly unique in the way we love. Fortunately, the uniqueness may be an attractant for a potential mate.

## The Family Unit

We begin learning about love and how to express it in the first few minutes of life. The learning continues through early childhood in the crucible of the family. We continue to learn through the joys and pains of adolescence. And we continue to learn how to express love throughout adulthood, although at a slower rate. From the very moment of birth to the moment of death, we weave relationships together continuously to create the fabric of who we are.

## Mother-Infant Relationship

Some psychologists believe that we spend our entire life trying to replicate the initial mother-infant relationship. Most psychologists believe that the mother-infant relationship is the single most powerful influence on our ability to love as adults. If an infant is deprived of mother love, the infant will most certainly have problems in relationships as an adult.[10] In order to love as an adult, we must have been loved as a child. And the pattern begins minutes after birth.

Mothers who have immediate nude contact with their baby have much stronger feelings of maternal attachment toward the child than mothers with no nude contact. For example, a mother gave birth to an infant that had health problems. The infant was immediately placed in an incubator in intensive care. The mother nursed the infant, but, otherwise, had little physical contact with the baby. The mother, years later, said that she felt more distant from that child from the start than her other three children. She did not form the same maternal attachment as she had with her other children.[11]

Until very recently, the skin contact between a mother and infant was greatly reduced in most hospitals. A mother would give birth to an infant. The doctors would deliver the infant, cut the umbilical cord, and perform other tasks on the newborn. Then, nurses would take the infant, dry the baby, wrap the baby in a soft blanket, and give the baby to the mother. In the interest of cleanliness and sanitation, nude skin contact was virtually eliminated.

If skin contact has an impact on maternal attachment, it is also likely that it would have an impact on the infant as well. Perhaps infants with immediate skin contact develop stronger attachments to their mother. This may show up in subsequent relationship behavior. In the history of human evolution, clean, sterile hospitals are a recent development, existing for only one hundred years or so. It may be that the current clinical treatment of newborns does influence subsequent behaviors.

While the impact of skin contact is somewhat speculative since conducting experiments is difficult, the impact of a mother breastfeeding an infant is much clearer. Breastfed babies outperform non-breastfed infants on almost every physical, mental, and emotional trait. A breastfed baby will have better motor skills and coordination than a non-breastfed baby, for example. A breastfed baby is less likely to experience social problems later in life. Breastfeeding clearly conveys benefits to the infant.[12]

A mother's milk is not only extremely nutritious, but helps the infant develop immunities to various diseases. There is some evidence that breastfeeding benefits go well beyond just nutrition and immunology for the infant, however. When a mother nurses an infant, large quantities of the hormone oxytocin are released into her bloodstream. Oxytocin induces maternal attachment and caring toward the infant. Mothers who nurse infants have much higher levels of oxytocin than mothers who bottle-feed their infants. The implication is that breastfeeding stimulates hormonal changes in the mother that enhance the mother-infant relationship.

A mother's milk also contains cystine, a complex amino acid. In chapter two, we saw the important role that amino acids play in the functioning of our neural networks. We also saw how rapidly the brain grows in the first year of life. It may be that the cystine in the mother's milk aids in the mental development of the infant's rapidly growing brain.

In addition to skin contact and breastfeeding, the whole pattern of mother-infant interaction provides a foundation for subsequent relationships. Infants who are held, touched, and stimulated more tend to have better motor skills. Infants who are talked to frequently begin talking at a younger age. Infants who are smiled at, tend to smile more. And infants who are warmly loved begin developing a better ability to love.[13]

Infants align their feelings unconsciously with their mother. This mirroring is sometimes referred to as emotional synchrony between mother and infant. When the mother is happy, the infant tends to be happy. When the mother is upset, the infant becomes upset. Initially, this emotional exchange is conducted primarily through the mother's facial expressions and tone of voice. This is where the infant first learns how to display emotions. And it is through this first intimate relationship that an infant initially learns how to love. The mother is the first, and, usually, the most influential role model for the first several years of life. It is from this secure base of a mother's love and acceptance that subsequent patterns of relationship will be built. A poor mother-infant relationship will plague an infant for life.

As a child grows, other patterns of interaction emerge that influence patterns of loving. Certainly, the father-infant relationship also grows and evolves, and the father also becomes a role model. The child will observe the mother-father relationship and learn about adult male-female interactions. But for the first few years of life, most of the patterns of loving are set by the mother, and most are unconsciously learned by the child. This initial mother-infant relationship is subsequently shaped by the family structure and behavior.

Love at first sight may be influenced by the parent's relationship. One woman noted that the man who she was attracted to had parents who had a similar love at first sight experience. The parents were very young when they met in high school and fell in love. His parents have been married for fifty-five years. Knowing that his parents fell in love at first sight may have predisposed the man toward love at first sight. He also married the woman.

## The Family Structure

Just as an infant mirrors the emotions of its mother, a child gradually learns patterns of interacting with other family members. Most notably the father, mother, and siblings are the dominant influences. But the maternal and paternal grandparents also exert an influence since they raised the mother and father, respectively. The family structure is the framework for behavioral interactions among family members.

Probably the easiest way to understand a family structure is to develop a relationship tree that includes all of the parents and siblings for three generations. The analysis of family structure should go beyond just a biological roadmap. To understand the complexities of the family in adequate detail, the tree should also include all of the significant relationships that each person has experienced. Each relationship leaves its mark on the personality of a person somehow. And each of these individual, complex personalities of parents become the role model that children use to develop patterns of loving.

Within each of the family units, the number of siblings, their ages, and their sex all influence a family member's personality. For example, if your father was an only child, he would probably have a different personality than if he were a youngest child. Therefore, the father who is an only child would present his children with a different role model. Since children learn about relationships from their parents, it is important to understand the family units in which both parents were raised. While many issues should be considered, birth order, age, and sex are very critical.

## Birth Order

An individual's birth order has a major impact on personality and patterns of interactions with other people and it also influences patterns of loving. There are four places in the birth order that have very clear tendencies associated with them. These are the only child, the eldest child, the middle child, and the lastborn.

## The Only Child

The only child has undivided parental attention for all of their life, there are no siblings to compete or interact with. Through the only child's early years, the primary interaction is with the parents. Since the only child is modeling adult behaviors, they are perceived to be mature for their age. He or she is often conservative, reenforcing the parent's views and values.

The only child tends to be reliable, conscientious, and responsible. This is at least in part due to the fact the only child experiences higher parental expectations. The only child also typically is subject to stricter discipline. Because of parental expectations and discipline, the only child tends to be well-organized, studious, and more goal-oriented.

The only child may experience greater difficulty in activities, like a job or marriage, that require good social skills. The only child has never had to share possessions with siblings, has never had to take care of others, has never had to compromise desires that conflicted with another. In essence, the only child has never had the opportunity to develop peer level social skills in the family unit. He has learned how to be independent and self-confident, take care of himself, and be content being alone. As a loner, the only child has less need for peer acceptance and praise.

Because the only child interacts only with adults in the household, he may prefer the company of adults as he grows older. It is common for an only child to be attracted to a much older mate. For example, a female only child who was in her early twenties and in college preferred to date men in their late thirties and forties. Her father found it frustrating when his daughter dated his friends and business associates. The daughter simply felt more comfortable with older men instead of the "immature" college-aged males who were her own age. When the daughter ultimately did marry a man near her own age, the marriage was in trouble from the start, as she had difficulty with her husband's "irresponsible" behavior and lack of "goals."

Since the only child closely patterns the behavior of the parents, there is a potential problem. If the parents, and especially the mother, are overprotective, the only child may take on the characteristics of a last born. For example, a woman had an only child, a son. The woman never worked outside the home until her son was seventeen years old. As a result, the son was the focus of the mother's attention every day, all day. She catered to his every desire. She cleaned his room for him, bought his clothes, and told him what to wear. She met with his teachers continually to find out why her son didn't excel in class. She made her already attractive son have cosmetic plastic surgery so he would look "perfect." She was the overbearing soccer mom, pushing the coaches to play her son more. The child never wanted for anything. And the child never learned to make a decision for himself, his mother did that for him. As the son grew older, he was a loner, insecure, and unable to make career and life choices.

This example illustrates another strong tendency for an only child. The mother-infant bond is never diminished by a subsequent infant. Therefore, the mother-child bond continues through adulthood. The only child is very likely to maintain close emotional ties to the mother, even as a married adult. Thus, the spouse of an only child is likely to feel that the mother-in-law plays an undue role in the marriage.

### The Eldest Child

The eldest child, or firstborn, shares many of the traits of an only child. The eldest child tends to be serious, conscientious, and reliable. She is likely to be achievement-oriented, trying to excel at all pursuits whether academic, athletic, or professional. She likes to be in control of her own destiny and doesn't like to rely on others.

Because of their innate drive to excel, firstborns or only children are more likely to be astronauts, doctors, engineers, attorneys, or politicians. All of these professions have a higher proportion of firstborns than would be expected based on the general population.

Like only children, firstborns are the center of attention. Their first steps, words, and actions make them the center of attention. Because they are older than their siblings, the parents have higher expectations of them. Firstborns are expected to be more responsible.

The major distinction between an eldest and an only child occurs because of the presence of siblings. The only child is the center of parental attention for life. The eldest child is the center of attention for a period of time. The length of the period of time is quite important.

If an eldest child receives full parental attention for roughly five or six years or more, the eldest will behave more like an only child. Large age gaps between children, in effect, create a separate sibling structure. For example, if the age gap between the first and second child is eight years, the second child also will acquire the characteristics of an eldest child. By the age of five or six, a child is beginning to shift focus from the exclusive attention on parents to others. The six-year-old begins school and will focus on teachers, peers, and classmates. In essence, attending school forces a child to develop a social network beyond just the parents.

If an eldest child is followed by another child within five years or so, there are major changes in the firstborn's life. The firstborn is the center of parental attention until the second child is born. Of necessity, the mother must shift her attention to the new infant. Even the attention of grandparents and adult friends of the parents shifts to the new baby. This diversion of parental attention typically has a long-lasting effect on the firstborn. Since the mother focuses more on the new infant, the firstborn feels jealousy and often competes for the mother's attention in some way. After realizing that the infant is a permanent fixture, the eldest child will shift their focus toward the father. Because of this, eldest children often have the strongest paternal bond of any children. The father becomes more of the role model, regardless of whether the child is a male or female.

If the eldest is a male, he often becomes "just like his father," mimicking all of the father's subtle mannerisms. If the eldest is a female, she also uses the father as a role model. The eldest daughter tends to be more career-oriented and is less fulfilled as a homemaker. If the father enjoys sports, the daughter is more apt to become athletically involved. If the father enjoys fishing, the daughter is likely to become an active fisherwoman. The eldest daughter is likely to be a bit of a "tomboy."

While both male and female eldest children experience feelings of loss and betrayal at the arrival of the new infant, females are more likely to carry this resentment forward into adulthood. This may lead to frustration when the eldest daughter must assume the role of homemaker herself, a role she disdained because of her mother.

Eldest children, because of the diminished mother-child bond, are much more likely to be prone to jealousy in relationships and marriages. They may have a subtle insecurity and compensate by overachieving, even to the extent of being a workaholic. This insecurity causes firstborns to have lower self-esteem and a greater need for approval from others.

## The Middle Child

Middle children are cast into a difficult role. They never have the total focus of the parent's attention. As a result, the birth of a younger sibling has much less impact on a middle child than an oldest. And instead of just two role models, the father and mother, the middle child also has at least one older sibling to use as a role model.

Since the elder sibling is older, larger, and more physically dominant, middle children cannot compete physically. Therefore, they must learn to compete in other ways for parental attention and for their role in the family unit. The most obvious tendencies of a middle child are a desire to avoid confrontation and to develop good negotiation skills. When an argument occurs in a relationship, the middle child, as an adult, will try to stay calm and discuss the issue in a rational, logical way. If discussion fails, the middle child will likely withdraw psychologically from the argument with the attitude "nothing that I say will make a difference."

The middle child usually avoids direct competition with their older sibling by choosing activities or areas of excellence neglected by the eldest. If the eldest was a great athlete, the middle child may focus on academics. If the eldest was a great student, the middle child may focus on athletics. If the eldest was a skier, the middle child may be a snow boarder. By differentiating in their areas of excellence, middle children avoid direct competition with older, more experienced siblings.

Because middle children must use their wits to establish their place in the family order, they usually develop the best social skills. They are perceptive because they had to be, watching what happened to other siblings, learning from other's mistakes. The middle child typically makes friends easily and has a larger number of friends than a firstborn.

Because of their superior social skills, the middle child is most likely to have stable relationships and marriages. They are also more likely to be monogamous. For example, a firstborn is more likely to need approval of others, and this could lead to extra-marital affairs.

The typical behavior of the middle child is illustrated by the story of Larry and Carolyn from Vermont. "I am a middle child and Carolyn is a middle child, and we both think that is important. One of the things that I think is an advantage, especially in a marriage, is that it seems to me that middle children are healers. I think that as a middle child, you tend to be someone who tries to reach a compromise. We are not fighters. We have never had major, serious arguments because we are both willing to work out the details. We both found that is what we did within our own families."

## The Lastborn

Lastborns are, by definition, the babies of the family. Someone, both parents and older siblings, is there to take care of them. Lastborns learn to be taken care of, and they learn that someone is watching out for them. This leads to lastborns being the least responsible of birth order positions. They don't have to be responsible since they learn to expect that someone else will do that for them.

Lastborns are the subject of the parents' attention, and, often, the ridicule of older siblings. Parents give approval for the last-born's activities. But older siblings are critical of little brother or sister getting into their things. Older siblings sometimes resent having to take care of junior. When sibling rivalries break out, the parents are most likely to scold the older sibling.

All of this causes lastborns to be more impulsive and rebel-lious. Their moods will swing quickly from happy to angry. As adolescents, they are more likely to rebel openly against parental authority. This could lead to more experimentation with alcohol or drugs. While this may sound rather negative, the lastborn has some very positive traits.

They are very personable and easygoing. They are much more tolerant of other people having different viewpoints and values. Lastborns are usually spontaneous, fun-loving people, the life of the party. And lastborns show their emotions more easily, they are caring and affectionate.

## Sibling Relationships
### Gender

The birth order of children has a direct impact on personality. But birth order works together with the sex of siblings. As with birth order, there are some tendencies because of the sex of siblings. When all children are of the same sex, whether boys or girls, the children learn to interact with other siblings of the same sex. And there is only one opposite sex role model, the father or mother. Therefore, the behaviors of the opposite sex parent provides the only source of learning about how that gender behaves. As a result, the characteristics of the opposite sex parent are relatively important when all children are of the same sex.

### Older Sister-Younger Brother

When an older sister-younger brother situation exists, both children are affected, particularly if there is less than three or four years difference in their ages. The oldest sister typically harbors some resentment toward the mother and younger sibling for damaging her mother-infant relationship. The oldest sister may develop a disdain for household duties, including babysitting her younger brother. She may choose to emphasize her professional career and not have children. Some oldest sisters will harbor some resent toward males because of the younger brother's inept behavior. The other common pattern for the oldest sister is quite different than this situation.

The older sister may assume the role of a caregiver. In effect, this creates two mother figures in the younger brother's life—his own mother and his watchful older sister. This can cause the younger brother to want to be taken care of by women later in life. A younger brother may be attracted to a woman who is an only child or an eldest daughter. The only-child woman would likely have difficulty knowing how to "take care" of a man. Conversely, the eldest daughter may find the role of taking care of a man very comfortable.

## Older Brother-Younger Sister

As with the older sister-younger brother relationship, there are also two somewhat different patterns that often emerge for an older brother-younger sister. If the older brother is an eldest child, he is more likely to harbor some resentment toward the younger sister because of the damage to his mother-infant bond. This may result in jealousy toward and competition with the younger female. This could lead to some level of lack of respect for women in the adult years. For example, an eldest brother of a younger sister is more apt to have many casual sexual relationships with women and to not feel bad about dropping a woman and moving on to another.

If the older brother is a middle son, the male is more apt to assume a caregiver role. The middle son would be more apt to take care of the younger sister and interact with her more closely. He would also likely be protective of his younger sister in social relationships. When the middle son has a younger sister, the male will learn how to relate to women and how to care for them. These characteristics, along with the other middle son traits, make the middle son more likely to have smoother, more enduring relationships with women as an adult.

## Summary

While the need for love is genetically imprinted in humans and emotions are created through complex activities in our brain, the way we express love is predominantly a learned behavior. We initially learn to love from our parents, for better or for worse. The lessons that we learn depend largely upon our primary role models, our parents. If our parents learned undesirable behaviors from their parents, we are likely to carry on with some similar behaviors ourselves. And we will likely pass them on to our children.

The behaviors that we learn from our parents are honed, refined, and modified based on interactions with our siblings. The birth order, sex, and age of siblings all influence our patterns of behavior and interacting with others in some way. And these factors certainly influence our preferences for loving.

Most humans are comfortable with what they know and understand, at both the conscious and unconscious level. If we sense that another person has a similar background and value system, we often feel "comfortable" with that person without knowing exactly why. This was one of the most common emotional reactions to love at first sight.

Somehow, we sense who is "the right one" for us very quickly. We have the uncanny ability to select mates who were raised in a situation similar to our own. We often select a mate whose birth order provides the best match for our own birth order. We select a mate with personality traits that we find desirable. And all of this occurs in less than an hour for those who experience love at first sight.

# Regrets

*I grew up in Northern Michigan, isolated and insulated from the rest of the world. I graduated from high school in 1959, when few people were familiar with anything outside a one hundred-mile radius of their home town. I knew nothing about Martin Luther King and the racial problems the rest of the country was dealing with. I knew nothing of the promise of the Korean War. I knew nothing of anything outside of my family and community. It was a time of ignorance, whether by choice or by chance. Our families made our choices for us, and for me that meant that my college and my profession were chosen. There was no inkling to even think about disobeying. I now view those years before college as Chapter One of my life, sort of an overview introduction to life, but not detailed or well developed, or even well written.*

*The socially appropriate careers for women were nursing and teaching. My parents chose teaching with little input from me. Going to college at one of the big universities like Michigan State or University of Michigan was out of the question. There were too many chances for a girl to get in trouble there, according to my parents. Even Northern Michigan University in Marquette, which was fairly close to where I lived, was too big.*

*My parents thought that I would fit in better at a small school. A church school would be even better because the students, especially the boys, would have higher moral values. Since we were*

*Catholic, my parents selected a small Catholic college in northern Wisconsin. In many respects, that is where Chapter Two of my own life began.*

*Into my sophomore year in college, I finally realized that my mother and father were not beside me every moment. Somehow, I thought they knew my every move before. It finally dawned on me that I had some freedom, and with that the skies opened a little. I began to experiment with new things. My friends and I would go out on Friday and Saturday nights and have some libation and good talk. Sometimes we had more libation than talk, and sometimes the reverse was true. We felt safe in our little group. My parents would have been horrified if they knew I was drinking, although only a few drinks would last all night.*

*One Saturday night we all went to a local lounge that had a band playing. Some of the members of this band were college students, and, since the college had only 400 students, we knew these people well. I was sitting at the bar, not really knowing what to do with myself, trying to smoke my first cigarette just to have something to do with my hands. I truly looked pretty awful. All the practicing I had done in front of the mirror didn't seem to have done me any good. Smoking a cigarette was another one of those rites of passage that signified that I was my own person. Little did I know at that moment that Chapter Two was about to end.*

*Anyway, I looked up and across the bar from me sat one of the band members. He had on a white shirt and dark pants, and had black hair in a crew cut, and black horn-rimmed glasses. That was the Buddy Holly look that was popular then. The band even played a lot of Buddy Holly and Elvis songs.*

*Our eyes met. But more than our eyes, our souls met too. We had this instant connection between us. It was like we could look into each other's souls and see all of the hidden thoughts and fears and desires. In an instant, neither of us had any secrets from one another. The deepest part of my soul suddenly lay naked before his eyes with no fear or embarrassment.*

*He got up and walked around the bar to where I was. I swear my hands were trembling and a nervous exhilaration went through my body. I had never felt excitement like that with any man before. I instantly knew that something special was happening. He was Chapter Three.*

*He said, "Hi, I'm David." His voice was so warm and smooth, almost soothing. His dark brown eyes seemed to sparkle and glow and look right through me. It seemed that we were destined to be together.*

*The band was only on a short break, so he didn't have much time. He offered to buy me a drink, which is probably the standard opening line for every man. We talked for a few minutes then he got back on stage. He was so friendly and easy to talk to. Before he left he asked me not to leave until we could talk some more.*

*While he played the guitar, I couldn't take my eyes off of him. He was always looking in my direction and our eyes, unblinking, would meet and convey longing and gentleness. I don't think that I even saw the rest of the band, just him.*

*At the next break, he came and sat next to me. He asked if he could take me home later. As we drove home, I felt so comfortable with him, like he was a long-lost friend. When we got back to my dorm, he kissed me goodnight, and this electricity shot through me. It was an incredible feeling. Later I found that he had cancelled a planned tryst with another girl so he could be with me.*

*It wasn't long before David and I began spending all of our spare time together. I loved his laugh, his attitude, everything about him. He was the first man who ever made me feel pretty, witty, and wise. I wasn't too wise in the ways of the world, but he took me under his wing and helped me more than I could ever imagine. He was the first man that I ever made love with, and he was so tender and patient with me. He helped me grow as a human and realize that I was my own person, a good person, capable of making my own decisions. We loved each other with all our hearts. He was sitting beside me the day that Kennedy was killed. He supported me when I made a fool of myself. He promised me nothing but gave all that he had. But, he was Native American.*

*I really didn't think the difference in the color of our skin mattered, it surely didn't to me. I was so excited to tell my mother that I was so happy and so in love. I went home one weekend full of the excitement of our plans and hopes. I expected my mother to be happy for me, her daughter was in love. As I told her about my love, her face tightened, and then she said to me, "Kathleen, please don't marry this man. Please don't do this to me. How can we explain having an Indian in the family?" I felt total shock and disbelief.*

*My mother made me feel that I had betrayed and embarrassed her. She made me feel that I had made this huge mistake. I was being emotionally torn in two. I felt this tremendous love for David. But I also felt this love and respect for my parents. Ultimately, my parents won the battle. They were spared the supposed public humiliation at the cost of my broken heart. That is when Chapter Three ended. If I knew then what I know now, the decision would have been different.*

*David and I never married, although our relationship in one form or another continued for over twenty years. For quite a while after I was told that David was socially unacceptable, my life had no meaning or direction. I kept losing him over and over again in my mind every day.*

*I eventually chose a man with a similar background to my family and me and began Chapter Four. He was a teacher like myself and a good Catholic. My mother was happy. The week before we were married, David came to me and begged me not to go through with it. I did, though. And, within a month of the marriage vows, the beatings began. It took David a while to find out about this, and when he wanted to come to get me, I had to say no. I think David cared for me and respected me more than anyone ever has, including my parents and my husband.*

*When I finally left my husband, my mother was again mortified that she had to answer questions about a divorce. It seemed strange, because I thought that I was the one with the bruises. She was still more concerned about what other people would think of her, rather than what was best for me. She was still living in a different world.*

*When I got divorced, David was married. He was the man that I longed to be with, but I didn't want to be a home-wrecker. I married a second time and stayed married for twenty-two years and then finally left. My second marriage was Chapter Five, and it was worthy of only the one sentence. A few years after I remarried, David's marriage also ended in divorce.*

*David is always in my heart, my thoughts, and my prayers. While in my second marriage, I chose not to stay in contact with him for self-preservation. It is hard to make a marriage work when the love of your life is someone else. I found that, ultimately, it was impossible.*

*My parents were a product of their parents and their environment. They truly wanted the best for me. But they were misguided. At some point, children make the transition to adults, to unique individuals. The best that a parent can hope for is that their children have a happy life. If only my parents had seen and valued my happiness and respected my ability to make decisions. Had they done that, David and I would have had a wonderful life together. Marrying David would probably also have helped my parents to overcome their outdated stereotypes. I was simply too young and naive to stand up to them when I should have.*

*You see parents that are controlling, making all the decisions for their children. They tell the children what to wear, what classes to take, what college to attend, which major to chose. Little by little those parents are destroying their children's self-confidence and maturity, weakening their ability to make decisions. Transition to adulthood is more difficult when this occurs. It certainly was for me. Sharing love and happiness is the foundation of a good life. I wish I had learned that lesson sooner.*

*There is a Robert Frost poem about choices in life,* The Road Not Taken. *That poem is at the crux of my life, and it brings tears every time that I read it. Little did I know that the choice between David and my parents was the focal point of my life, the single most important decision that I ever made. How sad to be over thirty years removed and still know that I took the wrong road, what terrible regret.*

*When I close my eyes and think of David, and I do more often than I should, it is 1960, a time of endless possibilities in my life, and we are looking across this bar in Northern Wisconsin. Our souls, once again, unite. Someday, David. Someday.*

# Stuck in Lodi

❧

*A*fter many years of therapy, I know exactly when I first fell in love. It was the summer of 1965 in Lodi, California. Lodi is about thirty miles south of Sacramento in the San Joaquin valley, a very fertile farming area.

I've known the man that I met that summer, Don, for almost thirty-five years now. He is the love of my life. I still feel that first glow of love for him sometimes. But at the same time, he is very unhealthy for me emotionally. I can't tell you how many tears I've shed over him.

In 1965, I was an eighteen-year-old single parent, just out of high school. My daughter was so special to me, even though her father and I were never married. I was one of those teenage pregnancy statistics. In truth, I wasn't very smart or mature about sex and didn't take the right precautions. I didn't think getting pregnant would happen to me. I wonder how many high school girls have said that.

I was raised in what is now called a dysfunctional family. My mother and father split up when I was pretty small, and he didn't ever come around much. He never paid any child support either, so there wasn't a lot of money in our house. My mother had a lot of boyfriends who lived with us. She even married a couple of them, but nothing ever lasted. Some of the men were pretty nice, but some wanted to have sex with me, too.

*It didn't help matters that my mother was an alcoholic. She was an attractive woman, but there was always a lot of drinking and fighting. It didn't help build my self-esteem. As a result, I was pretty shy and not particularly trusting of men in general.*

*A friend of mine invited me to go to a party with her. She was friends with one of Don's sisters, and the party was at her house. Don's sister and I became very good friends that summer.*

*As soon as I walked into the house, Don walked up to me and asked me what I wanted to drink. Don was about six feet, two inches tall and had these wonderful dimples. To look at him, you would think of kindness, laughter, and mischief all at once. He was absolutely the life of the party, everybody admired him. He was the center of the whole thing.*

*At the time he was twenty-three, so he was an "older" man to me. To visualize him, the character of "the Fonz" from the TV show* Happy Days *could have been patterned after him. He was a magnetic personality that men and women were drawn to.*

*As we walked into the kitchen, I was flattered that he even noticed me. I wasn't used to having attention from a very "cool" guy. Just being around him my pulse quickened and I felt flush. I was sensitive to his presence and the sound of his voice. It mesmerized me. In my heart, I knew right then that he was the one. I was completely in love. And it only took a few minutes.*

*He was attracted to me because I completely adored him. I was an attractive girl, about five feet six inches, with auburn hair and a slender build. But he could have any girl. It was very much a hero worship situation from my perspective.*

*Nothing happened between us that night. He was just very attentive to me and would put his arm around me. It felt like electricity ran through my body when he touched me. When I went home and went to bed, he was all I could think about.*

After that night, I was always included in their parties. If Don didn't invite me, his sister would. A lot of the parties were tailgate parties out in the country. The guys would ride their dirt bikes and have races and hill climbs. Just to be included in that group was really something to me.

Naturally, Don was the expert on the motorcycles. The other guys always wanted Don's help or advice on something. He seemed to know about cars, motorcycles, and everything. Everybody looked up to him.

I was also over at his house a lot. He lived with his parents and they were really nice, much different than my own family. He was the only boy in the family, and he had three sisters. It was like they took me in and adopted me.

One day, after I had gone to several parties, I stopped by his house to see his sister. Actually, seeing his sister was just an excuse, I really wanted to see him. When I got there, Don was the only one home. After only a few minutes there, he took me in his arms and kissed me. For me, electricity ran through my whole body. I was tingling. That was the first time we made love. I'd had sex before, but with him it was making love. It was totally different that anything I had experienced. I felt so special and lucky that he wanted me, this shy wallflower.

I never felt that Don was exclusively mine. I'm sure that he went out with other women. But I knew that from the start, so it didn't bother me. I just knew that the times we had together were incredibly good. Maybe he was just using me, but I enjoyed being with him so much that I didn't mind. It was like we both enjoyed each other with no real strings attached or long-term expectations. That summer was a whirlwind of parties, fun, and intimacy.

At the time, my mother was married to a guy who was in the Air Force. He got transferred to an air base in Japan. It was part *of the Vietnam war build up. So in the fall, we went to Japan for a year and a half. Don and I exchanged a few letters during that time, but then it faded out. When the letters quit coming, I assumed that he found someone else to occupy his attention. Honestly, being an attractive eighteen-year-old girl living on an airbase had its advantages for me, too. My social schedule was always full after the first month over there.*

*The day before I returned from Japan, he called my best friend in Stockton to find out about me. She got his phone number from him and said that she would pass it along to me. When I got back the next day, she was the first person that I called, and she gave me his number. I phoned him a few days later.*

*When we got back together, it was like we had never been apart. There has always been this sort of instant karma between us. That really typified our relationship over the next thirty years.*

*We would be separated for years with virtually no contact. Then one of us would show up, and we'd have an affair for a while. Then we'd go our separate ways. Then we would run into each other, and that damn instant karma thing would happen. Neither of us could ever say no to the other, no matter what the situation was. We were always there to fulfill the other's needs, whatever they were.*

*We talked about having some type of paranormal connection. I would be thinking that I'd like to see him and the phone would ring. It would be him. Or he'd be thinking of me and I would call him. Just the other day, we talked.*

*We were reminiscing about thirty-five years of knowing each other. My daughter was just a baby then, and now she is thirty-six. We have always had special feelings for each other, we always feel a very strong connection. But we could never make a relationship last permanently.*

*Don was raised in a family of women, and I think he has some deep resentment of women. Being raised with just sisters, he learned to manipulate women in a way. At first, when we get together, he is very supportive, very loving, and very attentive. But after a while he starts using things against me, holding a grudge. It is like he gradually transfers his resentment of women in general to me, or anybody else he's with. He has never been able to maintain any long-term relationship with a woman. This underlying problem emerges every time we get together and give it a try again.*

*For a long time, I hoped he would change and get more mature. But it just hasn't happened. He is absolutely the love of my life. I have always felt that, right from the first night at the party. My love for him has made it hard for me to have a solid relationship with someone else. I have never met another man that stirs the feelings that he does.*

## Chapter Four

# Learning to Love from Society

There is no question that early childhood experiences before the age of five or six play a predominant role in shaping an individual's pattern of loving. But these early experiences only provide the foundation and framework for loving. A person's own experiences and society, more broadly, will add additional dimensions of intimate relationships. Learning about these factors begins as soon as a child begins encountering the world outside of the family unit.

## Childhood Experiences

Until the age of about five, the social behaviors of boys and girls are about the same. Something happens at that point that causes a shift in previous behavior. The event that causes changes is probably the increased influence of peer level behavior. By age five, a child is encountering daycare, kindergarten, and other preschool activities. These social interactions with peers have a profound influence on the rapidly developing child.

Before age five, children have about the same number of male and female friends. They often engage in similar activities, although differences in preferences are already there (girls can play with dolls, boys shouldn't, for example). After age five, there is a shift toward friends of the same sex. By age seven, boys play almost exclusively with boys, and girls play almost exclusively with girls. This pattern generally continues through puberty when the opposite sex again becomes appealing.

During the period from about age five until they reach puberty, boys learn how to act like boys from other boys. Boy's social groups are large, louder, and more active. They are often focused around sports activities. The boys are taught to be independent and to minimize emotions.[14] For example, if a boy gets hurt slightly and begins to cry, other boys are likely to ridicule him as a "crybaby." The boy is taught a lesson about showing emotions. The lessons learned about being male during this period extend to adulthood.

While the boys are focusing on independence and self-development, girls typically pursue a different path. The social groups for girls are smaller and more intimate with an emphasis on being good friends. The desired values are friendship, communication, and sharing emotions. Girls learn how to read nonverbal cues better, to express emotions more openly, and to communicate better.[15] These patterns are also carried over into adulthood by women.

These two patterns are central to intimate adult relationships. In a marriage, men have a greater aversion to arguments, are much more likely to stonewall, and take much longer to recover. Conversely, women are more likely to be critical and want to talk about issues in more detail. Women are more willing to engage in an argument and are likely to recover quickly from an argument.[16]

These patterns, learned in childhood, can be the source of endless frustration and bewilderment later in life. A man might say, "I just don't understand women." A woman might say, "How can men be so stupid?"

## Social Roles

The roles for boys and girls gradually evolve into adult roles and patterns of interacting. But the evolution to social roles that conform to the values of society may not be a good fit for everyone, particularly females. In one study of teenagers, only 29 percent of girls were "happy with who I am" compared to 46 percent of teenage boys.[17] The implication is that society expects girls to look and behave in certain ways. For example, for girls, "looks" is the most important characteristic, and only 10 to 25 percent of teenage girls "like the way they look." Most girls thought that they were overweight or that portions of their anatomy weren't developed enough. Because boys have been taught to be independent and develop a good self-image, they are apparently more secure in who they are.

If anyone doubts the divergent acceptable roles, think back to your teenage days. How would you describe a teenager who is a "bad girl"? How would you describe a "good girl"? A "bad girl" probably conjures up images of a girl who is sexually promiscuous, who smokes, drinks, and is rebellious. A "good girl" probably does well in school, respects her parents, has no behavior problems, and is also viewed as a virgin.

Now do the same for a "bad boy" and a "good boy." The "bad boy" may be associated with alcohol or drugs and probably some behavior problems requiring the legal system. A "good boy" is probably viewed as a good student or good athlete with no behavior problems.

Sexual activity, or lack thereof, is more often used as a descriptor for girls. It is much less frequently used to describe boys, either positively or negatively. The assumption is that all boys will be sexually active to some degree, a role more acceptable to society.

In a very general sense, good girls in most societies around the world are expected to subserviate their sexual desires to conform to social values. In most societies, boys are granted much more sexual latitude. This double standard is probably the cause of a good deal of marital infidelity.

Occasionally, even a good wife may want to throw off the shackles of being "good" and be "bad." Some women find being the perfect wife is much less fulfilling than they would like it to be. And since boys are granted more sexual latitude, an extramarital affair is often just an extension of previous behavior patterns.

There is no question that society teaches acceptable roles to boys, girls, men, women, husbands, wives, mothers, and fathers. The roles may not conform to the individual desires, leading to a lack of fulfillment or frustration. But there are other aspects of interpersonal relationships that are also taught by society. These are verbal and nonverbal cues that let another person know that you are interested in them.

## Signaling

Just as society teaches us about acceptable roles, society teaches us how to send nonverbal cues and how to interpret them. As you might expect, women are generally more adept at sending and interpreting nonverbal cues than men. Naturally, sending a signal indicating interest and not having the man understand the message is frustrating for the woman—but it is a fairly common occurrence.

It is a commonly held belief that men are the pursuers of women. Men are thought to initiate contact and then romance the woman until she goes to bed with him. In reality, this is the exception, not the rule. Research shows that 65 to 70 percent of the initial contact is made by women.[18] It is simply done in such a way that the man thinks that he initiated the contact.

For example, a woman at a party might see a man she is interested in. She might make eye contact with the man, smile shyly, and look away, looking back at him briefly about ten seconds later, and then quickly look away again. This sequence has "invitation" written all over it from the woman's perspective. She would clearly view this as initiating contact. A few minutes later, the man might walk over and introduce himself. He would probably think that he initiated contact with the woman because he spoke first. But in the dance of relationships, he was simply responding to her nonverbal invitation.

When women initiate relationships with men, they use a wider array of signals than men and they use them more subtly. Monica Moore studied the use of nonverbal solicitation signals used by women in party situations.[19] Nearly all of the signals involve eye contact. The top fifteen signals are presented in Figure 4.1. Of the top six signals, only dancing alone did not include direct eye contact. Direct eye contact accompanied by a warm smile is clearly the dominant signal. If we recall the discussion of mother-infant mirroring, you will notice that this behavior was first used within weeks of birth. Some behaviors are pretty enduring.

## Relationship Synchrony

Once the initial contact is made between a man and a woman, society has taught us a sequence of actions that must take place for a relationship to emerge. If steps in the sequence are missed, a relationship seldom develops. Timothy Perper studied the sequence in singles bars and identified five distinct steps.[20] In a situation other than a singles bar, the first three steps probably are necessary. The other two would follow on the first date.

1. The first step is a nonverbal signal of some type. The signal must be sent, received, interpreted, and responded to in someway. If a signal is sent, but elicits no response, the sender usually will interpret the nonresponse as a turn down or refusal. However, it may be that the signal has not been received by the target. Given the differences between men's and women's social sensitivity, it is more likely that the male would simply not see the signal sent by the woman. Regardless of the reason, failure to respond appropriately to the nonverbal invitation will end the potential for a relationship.

One of the male respondents in our own study gave an excellent example of the power of a smile as a signal. "We made eye contact and she smiled when she walked by. She saw me and I smiled, and then she went and sat down. Her smiling at me was pretty important. It gave me encouragement. I wasn't the boldest of people when it came to the girls, so that gave me encouragement to seek her out the next day."

2. The second step is for someone to begin talking. The beginning could be a simple hello, an offer to buy a drink, or asking for a dance. If a person does not respond to the comment in some way, the relationship sequence ends.

3. The third step involves body language. The target must turn toward the speaker in some way. Initially, it may be only a

turning of the head. But if the relationship is to develop, both people gradually will turn to face one another directly. It may take hours, minutes, or seconds, but, at some point, the two people must face each other openly with no defensive posture. This may be a primitive form of display so two people could evaluate each other.

4. The fourth step is to touch. The touch can be subtle, where the two people involved brush against one another very slightly. Perhaps one person holds the other's hand to look at a ring. Perhaps the man takes her hand while helping the lady up. When touching occurs, the individual has allowed their "personal space" to be penetrated. For example, a woman could take a man's hand and give him a gentle squeeze. The message might be "I want you to hug me."

One of the ladies in our research can attest to the power of a subtle touch. "We were sitting around the table playing dice games. We had a nice conversation, and, as we were playing dice, he kept, I thought it was just accidentally at first, but he kept touching my hand. At first I didn't really pay much attention to it, but as the night wore on, I started paying close attention. I definitely liked feeling him touch me. We haven't stopped seeing each other since. It has been nine years."

5. The fifth step is synchronization. The couples begin doing the same things at the same time. Most obvious is each taking a drink at the same time. But they may also look away and then back at each other. They may change body positions or shift in their chairs. They may both order a drink at the same time. The message that they are sending to one another is that they

are in tune with the other person. They each have the same interests, feelings, and desires. They are also signaling that they might be physically in tune in other ways.

During this five-step sequence, there is another consistent phenomenon. The amount of eye contact increases. The two people gradually look intently at one another without looking away. This sends a message to the other person that he or she is fascinating and important. Gradually, the eye contact moves away from the face to the hair and neck, and then downward. This is done subtly, but conveys a message that, "All of you looks good," or, "You've got a great body." The slow downward gaze also conveys a strong sexual interest.

## Moving to the Next Level

Once an initial relationship exists between a man and a woman, it is usually the woman who initiates the advancement of the relationship. Again, research shows that about two-thirds of the time it is the woman who makes the first move. But once again, the woman often does it in such a way as to make the man think he pursued her. For example, a woman might invite a man to dinner. When he arrives, there are candles on the table, a bottle of wine, and soft, sensuous music playing. The woman may be wearing a new dress that shows off her figure. The woman has taken the initiative to create a situation where the man won't be able to resist her charms. The man may feel he made the first move by kissing her or caressing her. But he would be wrong.

Of course, most sexual invitations aren't quite as complex. It could be a passionate kiss. It could be an embrace. In the love stories in this book, you will see a wide variety of signals being used, most by women. Some are very subtle, some are not.

## Social Sensitivity

Social sensitivity is the ability to express emotions ourselves and interpret emotions in those around us. One aspect of social sensitivity is social attunement, meaning that you sense another's emotional state and adjust yours to fit. This is also sometimes referred to as emotional synchrony. For example, if you sense a person is sad, you soothe them by talking with a softer, subdued tone of voice. You may get close to them and touch them, offering comfort. You sense the other person's emotions and transfer their mood to you.

You have probably heard the saying "If you smile, the world smiles with you." This is because happiness is more expressive than sadness and is easier to transfer to another. People want to have fun and be around others who have fun. This may be why a smile is the most commonly used invitation signal.

Women typically have a higher level of social sensitivity than men and also demonstrate a higher level of social attunement. Women are more willing to adjust their moods around others. In other words, women are more flexible and adaptable emotionally. There is a danger in this from a relationship standpoint.

Setting the emotional tone of a relationship is a sign of power and dominance in the relationship. Since the woman is more apt to adapt emotionally, the male often sets the emotional tone. If the woman has to adjust too far from what she really wants, she undoubtedly will feel frustration at not being able to "be herself." She may feel that she is "walking on egg-shells all of the time." And the man may not even be aware of her frustration.

Although there is no firm research on the issue, those who are more socially sensitive may be more inclined to experience love at first sight. Socially sensitive people are more adept at reading signals in others. This means that they pick up on the other person's emotional arousal and respond in kind. In other words, two socially sensitive people are likely to immediately sense the mutual attraction, become socially and emotionally attuned quickly, and feel a very high level of comfort, like they have known each other for years.

The social sensitivity extends well beyond nonverbal signals of interest, however. Socially sensitive people can detect behavior patterns that are familiar. These behavior patterns could be common family structures and experiences or a favorable birth order, for example. Most often, these interpretations are subconscious. But some behaviors can easily be interpreted at the conscious level.

When I was a senior at the University of Oregon, I participated in a child development class. For two or three Saturday mornings, we watched a gymnasium full of young children play. There were all types of toys and games for the kids to play with, but there was no organized activity. All of the children were on their own to engage in whatever activity that they wished. Each of the children was wearing a number on a piece of paper pinned to their back.

Each of the students was randomly assigned a number. We were told to stay on the stage, watch our assigned child, note his or her behavior patterns, and then write a story about his family situation. We were not told whether the child was an only, eldest, middle, or youngest child. We were to speculate about the child's birth order personality, performance in school, whether the various siblings were male or female, whether the child had many friends, and so forth.

The parent of each child had written their own one-page description of the child. When the students compared their write-up to the parents, the accuracy was amazing. Something on the order of 70 percent of the descriptions were accurate.

The implication of this situation is that people have an uncanny ability to watch the behavior of another and interpret those behaviors with a high degree of accuracy. People who are more socially sensitive are probably much better than others. And the interpretation goes far beyond the nonverbal signals that are consciously sent and received between two people looking, or not looking, for love.

## Summary

Once a child ventures out of the home, society begins teaching many lessons. Society teaches about the acceptable roles for being male or female, husband or wife, mother or father. As in school, some learn these lessons very well, and others learn not so well. But these lessons further mold and refine the patterns of loving that genetics and our family taught. Collectively, these three influences get us ready for the journey that we make down life's highway. It is along this journey that our personal experiences further shape the way we love.

Figure 4.1

## Successful Signals Used By Women

Smile broadly at him

Throw a short glance

Dance alone to the music

Look straight at him and flip her hair

Stare at him

Look at him, toss her head, look back

Accidentally brush against him

Nod her head at him

Point to an empty chair

Tilt her head and touch her neck

Lick her lips while making eye contact

Primp while keeping eye contact

Parade close to him with exaggerated hip movement

Ask for his help

Tap something to get his attention

# Vietnam Drove Us Apart

*I met my husband when I was fourteen and he was fifteen. We felt like we were soulmates right from the start, but there was a nineteen-year period where we never saw each other.*

*I had started my first year of junior high and was feeling pretty grown up. It was 1963 in Hoboken, New Jersey. Our Lady of Grace church was just a few blocks from my house, and the youth group was having a dance. The dance consisted of playing records in the auditorium, so it wasn't anything fancy. Some of my girlfriends and I decided to go there for a while.*

*The auditorium had two levels, and all of the girls were dancing on the lower level. Most of the boys were too shy, bashful, or insecure to ask the girls to dance. After we had been there for a while, one of my girlfriends told me there was someone that wanted to meet me. He was upstairs leaning over the railing. I glanced up to see who it was, and we made eye contact.*

*He was a good-looking boy. He had curly dark hair and blue eyes. I found out later that he was Italian. Since I'm Irish and very fair skinned, he was just about the opposite of me. His name was Dan. My girlfriend motioned for him to come down and meet me.*

*He was very nice. We talked and danced and found we had a lot in common. We went to the same grammar school, he was a year ahead of me, but our paths had never crossed. We both came from big families and only lived a few blocks apart. We just seemed to get along real well. We talked about everything.*

*Right from the start I had the feeling that there was something special about him. But he also made me nervous. He was the first boy that I ever dated, I didn't have any experience at all with that. As we continued dating, I knew our relationship was going to evolve in other ways too.*

*We dated exclusively all the way through high school. Neither of us had any interest in anyone else. We seemed to have a very close, natural bond and connection between us. Being together was how life was supposed to be for us. He was kind and sweet and romantic. He was always doing the little things like sending me cards and flowers. He was a very caring person. When I was nineteen, and he was twenty, we got engaged, only a year or so after high school.*

*He got drafted about then and went first to Korea and then to Vietnam. That was a pretty tough time for a lot of people. When your fiancé, the love of your life, goes off to war, you worry all the time. I prayed every night that the Lord would bring him back safely. I wrote him letters three or four times a week. He would write, but not as often. I noticed a gradual change in the mood of his letters. At first he was lonely and emotional, and gradually his letters became more cynical and bitter and less frequent.*

*Dan had never been far from New Jersey. Until the war took him away, he had never even been on an airplane. He was a big city kid, through and through. With all of the things to do in New York and New Jersey, there wasn't much of a need to travel far. When he first got drafted, he was actually excited. He thought the whole thing was going to be a big adventure.*

*When he went to South Korea, he thought it was an interesting and exciting place. Things were so cheap, he would buy me gifts in*

*Love at First Sight*

the Itaewon shopping area in Seoul and mail them back to me. But as soon as he got to Vietnam, everything changed.

When he stepped off the military transport plane in Vietnam, the unbearable heat and humidity were suffocating. He had experienced humidity in New Jersey, but not like over there. As he walked across the tarmac, there were long rows of black body bags lined up, full of dead soldiers. There were wounded soldiers with bloody bandages boarding the plane as soon as he got off. The look in the eyes of those soldiers was a mixture of desperation, emptiness, despair, and relief. It was like they knew things that Dan didn't. A few shouted derisive comments at them. He realized within ten minutes of stepping off the plane that it was not the adventure he had expected.

When Dan left New Jersey, he was a sweet, caring person, my high school sweetheart. When he came back, he was a stranger. He was quiet and withdrawn, his eyes were hollow, lifeless. The sparkle of joy and life had been extinguished. He wouldn't talk about the war. It was as if there was this code of silence, as if you hadn't been there, you couldn't possibly understand. I believe he was going through post-traumatic stress disorder.

He was also addicted to drugs, and I wouldn't condone or participate in that. His drug addiction was like a second war that he was fighting alone. He was on a downward spiral, and he wouldn't let me get close to him. He couldn't keep a job and just hung out with friends. We weren't getting along very well then because I always had a strong work ethic and was very responsible. It seemed that his Vietnam experience changed him into a very empty, undesirable person. It hurt so bad to see him like that, especially after knowing what a nice person he used to be.

Before he left, he got along well with my family. They accepted him openly because they knew he was going to be my husband.

My family, especially my older brother, saw the changes in him even more clearly than I did after he returned. They saw the drug use and the inability to hold a job. They felt he had no future, at all. My family grew to have a pretty strong dislike for him because of his lifestyle and the way he treated me.

The final straw in our relationship wasn't his drug use, though. While we were still engaged, he got another girl pregnant. It broke my heart and was a terrible time for me. At that point, we went our separate ways. Several years later, he married that girl, and they had a daughter and a son.

The year or two after he came back from Vietnam were hard on me emotionally. He was the only boy that I had ever dated, and I loved him deeply. I kept trying, probably longer than I should have, hoping that the Dan I used to know would reemerge.

Ultimately, I met another man, Scott, and we moved to Michigan. We never married or had any children, but we had an eighteen-year relationship. That relationship ended about seven years ago—the same time that Dan got a divorce.

About three years after Dan and I broke up, he started working as a firefighter. The funny part is that he was working with my brother, who is also a firefighter. Some mutual friends told him not to discuss me with my brother. My brother had wanted to beat some sense into Dan for the way he had treated me after Vietnam. Dan and my brother worked together for over ten years before they ever discussed me.

Dan was still a sore subject with my family, especially at that time. My brother viewed work as work and family should be kept out of it. My brother didn't give Dan my address until after he was divorced.

I was pretty surprised when he phoned me after not talking to each other for nineteen years. It had been a long time coming. He decided to fly up to Michigan and see me. I was forty-four then, and he was forty-five, we weren't kids anymore.

When I met him at the airport, it was just like the previous nineteen years had not gone by. It was really like a time warp. It was wonderful. I had my best friend in life back, and I could talk to him about anything. He had recovered from the horrors of Vietnam and was the same nice person that I used to know.

He came to Michigan for a weekend and stayed for two weeks. We had a fabulous time and felt so close to each other. Our spirits had been split apart almost twenty years earlier, and, when they were reunited, the closeness and euphoria were incredible. The underlying love we had for each other transcended the twenty years as if it were a moment. Whoever said true love never totally dies was right. We both knew after just a few days that we would be married. We have now been married for six years. It was just too bad we didn't realize how wonderful our marriage would be twenty years ago.

When a person's hopes and dreams are lost somewhere on life's highway, often people don't realize the depth of the loss. It's only when they find them again that people realize how precious and cherished the dreams were. What is it about age and time and pride that causes us to undermine and destroy the glory of love? There is a lot of truth in the saying "You don't know what you've got until it's gone." Fortunately, Dan and I were able to find our way back to where we were supposed to be, together. Our lives are now moving in harmony once again.

# He Was Married

It was totally against my standards to admire a married man. To make it even worse, he had four children. And I met him in church. But the minute that I saw him I wanted a husband that was like him.

I first met him in 1974 at the College Heights Baptist Church in Casper, Wyoming. I was a college student and had just joined the church. I guess I was probably about nineteen at the time.

When I first met him, I was taken by how handsome he was. I used to go on and on to my mother about him. Talking to your mother about a married man seems strange, but he represented my ideal of what a husband should be. I always felt a strong physical attraction, but there was much more than that.

I got to know him and his family through the church. I liked the way he communicated with his wife and how sensitive he was to her needs. He always seemed so tender and loving toward his family.

At the time, he was thirty-seven. He had sandy blond hair and beautiful, piercing blue eyes. He was just so charismatic that people were drawn to him. He had a wonderful strong laugh and a quick, witty sense of humor. It was just so much fun being around him. When I talked with him, it was like we were the only people in the world, even if there was a room full of people. Just visiting with him and talking to him was so intimate.

Please don't misunderstand, we wouldn't have even considered having an affair. There was just this very strong connection between us as two people. I think he was attracted to me by how long and pretty my hair was, and probably by how pretty I was in my youth. But for both of us it was always just a very complete, comfortable connection.

Eventually, he and his family moved away due to a job transfer. He was gone for quite a few years. I was at church in 1989, and it was announced that his wife had died of cancer. I had no idea that she was even ill, so it came as quite a shock to me.

The next year, 1990, he returned to Casper and started attending church again. For some crazy reason, I was going to set him up with a friend of mine for a date. That is when he said, "What I'd really like to do is go out with you." It didn't take long for us to realize that the connection between us was still there. It had been sixteen years since we had first met, and my attraction for him hadn't faded one bit. He was my ideal of what a husband should be, right from the start. In spite of all the men I had dated, nobody made me feel the way he did.

Some of my friends have asked about our age difference. His oldest child is just a few years younger than me. Honestly, I never even thought that the age difference was an issue. My feelings for him were so strong. His children were pretty much grown when we married, and they have been very supportive. They can see the love and happiness that we share for each other.

After the Christmas Cantata at our church, about fifty members of the congregation went to the Pastor's house. He had planned the whole thing and asked me to marry him in front of everyone. It was very romantic. We were married June 1, 1991.

He is so wonderful and always sees the bright side of things. When I was single, I always thought how wonderful it would be to share my life with someone like him. The past nine years of being married to him have been even better than I could have imagined.

# PART TWO

# *What the Research Says*

## Chapter Five

# The Role of Our Experiences in Falling in Love

*G*enetics, family, and socio-cultural influences intertwine to create a pattern of loving that is unique to each of us. A successful, enduring relationship may be the result of two patterns of loving meshing harmoniously. The comfort level with the other person is high and friction levels low. On the other hand, the more disparate the patterns of loving, the more tension there is likely to be in a relationship. For example, a man and woman might find each other initially very appealing. As they get to know each other better, small annoyances emerge. Perhaps he thinks she talks too much. Perhaps she thinks he doesn't listen.

In reality, the man is simply acting out his learned behavior and the woman is acting out hers. While they may be compatible in many ways, their perceptions of acceptable behavior differ in the amount of conversation for him and the level of social sensitivity for her. If each is unwilling to change their expectations of desired behavior, the relationship may deteriorate further.

Unfortunately, it may require a good deal of time together for some people to learn all of the nuances and details of the other person. And many of the details may not emerge until a couple is living together on a full-time basis. For other people, learning about another person can happen very, very quickly. This is the experience of falling in love at first sight.

While it is not possible to examine every aspect of falling in love at first sight, this research attempted to identify some of the common patterns that individuals share. The following research findings are based on the total sample of individuals scattered across the United States. In total, 1,495 people participated in the research. As mentioned in chapter one, the sample consisted of 948 women (63.4 percent) and 547 men (36.6 percent).

Of the total sample of 1,495, 958 people (64.1 percent) believe that love at first sight can happen. Therefore, when references are made to "believers," the results are based on a sample of 958. Of the 958, 558 people (58.2 percent) have experienced love at first sight. Therefore, the results for those who have "experienced" love at first sight are based on a sample of 558. Both sample sizes of 958 and 558 are large enough to have a high degree of statistical validity.

For many questions, the sample of 558 people was further partitioned into male and female categories. There were 337 women and 221 men in each of these categories. Again, the sample sizes for men and women are sufficiently large to have good statistical validity.

The following discussions will begin with what distinguishes those who believe in love at first sight from those who don't. The discussions also will address those who have experienced it. Then the discussions will focus on the differences between men and women who have experienced love at first sight.

## Geographic Location

Many people believe that where a person is raised will influence their value systems. The physical location of where a person lives shapes the environmental influences that impact early childhood development. This influence is probably most critical in the period from about age five through age twelve.

For example, the childhood experiences of a person raised on a farm with few close neighbors would be quite different from a person raised in the suburbs of Chicago or Los Angeles. The parents of a "country kid" might be more apt to let the child wander off by himself to explore his part of the world. The parents of a "city kid" might be a little more controlling and keep closer track of where the child is and what she is doing. These differences in the environment would certainly have some impact on a child's, and subsequent adult's, personality.

This belief is illustrated by a story from Arvid in Vermont. "We thought that there were some very important values that we had learned from growing up in a small town and in a small area. We felt that we wanted to give our children the opportunity to experience the similar thing that we had. So, we came back here to give them that chance. But, we found out something. We found out that the values and experiences that we had growing up here in this small town were as much a part of the time we were growing up as they were the place that we grew up in."

For this research, the respondents were given five alternatives. These were rural, a small town with a population of less than ten thousand, a city with a population of ten thousand to one hundred thousand, a city with a population of one hundred thousand to five hundred thousand, and a city with a population of over five hundred thousand. The research examined the percentage of respondents in each area that believed in love at first sight and the percentage of respondents who experienced it. These results are presented in Table 5.1.

The first most striking finding is that people in rural areas are much more likely to believe in love at first sight. Fully 70.1 percent of rural respondents were believers, followed by those from a small town, where 64.8 percent of respondents are believers. Perhaps those who live in small towns or rural America are a bit less cynical of people in general. For example, if you were walking down a street in a small town in Montana and passed a stranger on the sidewalk, the stranger would probably say "Hello!" That probably would not happen in Chicago or New York. If it did happen, you'd think the stranger was a tourist.

While people in rural areas are most likely to believe in love at first sight, they are among the least likely to experience it. Only 54.6 percent of rural respondents have experienced love at first sight, the second lowest proportion of any group. Conversely, 68.4 percent of respondents from big cities have experienced love at first sight. The difference of nearly fourteen percentage points is quite large. Perhaps the law of averages is at work here. Because of their environment, people in rural areas come in contact with fewer potential mates. And it is more likely that people in a rural environment already know most of the potential mates in their geographic area to some degree. Hence, falling in love with someone is less likely to fit our definition of love at first sight (knowing you love someone within sixty minutes of meeting them).

Conversely, people in large cities have more contact with a much wider array of individuals. It is very probable that a person knows a very small percentage of the people that they might meet in a day. Therefore, a chance encounter with a potential mate is most apt to be with a stranger. Accordingly, the chance of falling in love within sixty minutes of the first meeting is greater.

There is no question that a person's geographic environment influences their perceptions in some way. The old saying "You can take the boy out of the country, but you can't take the country out of the boy" illustrates the belief that there are unique country values. Likewise, there are probably unique "city values." Unfortunately, we can't say exactly why the values are different, but we know they impact perceptions of love at first sight.

## Marital Status

It was thought that a respondent's marital status might influence their perceptions of love at first sight in some way. A person who is married might have more positive views since they have a seemingly successful relationship with a mate, for example. Some significant differences emerged, but not exactly what was expected. These results are presented in Table 5.2.

The majority of single respondents (68.6 percent) were likely to believe in love at first sight. Perhaps single people are the most hopeful of finding that "someone special" or "Mr. Right." It is also likely that a good portion of the single respondents were already in a relationship, since 57.2 percent had also experienced love at first sight.

As expected, respondents who were married had a relatively high propensity to believe in love at first sight (64.5 percent). Those who were divorced were less likely to do so. But the most striking finding here was for widowers.

Widowers had a very low probability of believing in love at first sight. Only 52.9 percent of these respondents were believers. These results may have less to do with marital status than with age. Widowers tended to be much older than the average respondent. The respondent who was seventy to eighty years old was born in the period of 1920-1930. People raised in this time period would have substantially different values, and probably be more conservative, than a person who was born in the 1940s and searched for a mate in the 1960s.

Widowers also had the lowest proportion of believers who actually experienced love at first sight. Only 50.7 percent of widowers had experienced love at first sight. The reason is probably the same as the previous discussion for whether they believe in love at first sight or not. The proportion of those experiencing love at first sight is about the same for the other three groups. While single respondents were the least likely to have experienced love at first sight after widowers, the percentage would probably go up over time. Presumably, most singles are searching for a mate to some degree. Since 57.2 percent of singles already have experienced love at first sight, a portion of the remaining singles will probably experience it in the future. Conversely, the percentage of married and divorced respondents who have experienced love at first sight would be more stable since the majority of married people and some divorced people are not in an active search mode.

## Times Married

If a person has been married more times, that person may be more prone to enter relationships quickly. Hence, they would be more likely to believe in love at first sight and to have experienced it. This contention was well supported by the research (Table 5.3). Of the respondents who had been married four times, 76.5 percent believed in love at first sight. Of those married five or more times, all of them believed in love at first sight. Getting married repeatedly seems to convince respondents that love at first sight is possible. Or, perhaps, they experience love at first sight and get married as a result, repeatedly. Whatever the direction of causality, people who have been married four or more times are very likely to be believers. They are also very likely to have experienced love at first sight.

The respondents who were married four times had experienced love at first sight 76.9 percent of the time. Fully 80 percent of the respondents who had been married five or more times had experienced love at first sight. Apparently, for these two groups of respondents, love at first sight is a very common occurrence. One note of caution should be added for these two groups, however. Each of these groups had only twenty to thirty respondents. With small sample sizes, we must be cautious in interpreting the results.

Those who had been married once, twice, or three times had about the same probability to believe in love at first sight (62 to 67 percent). They also had about the same probability to have experienced it (56 to 59 percent).

### Education

As noted in chapter one, a person's education level is inversely related to believing in love at first sight. Only 59.1 percent of the respondents who attended graduate school believed in love at first sight (Table 5.4). Roughly 62 percent of those who attended college believe in love at first sight. But 68.0 percent of those with a high school diploma, or less, believe in love at first sight. The reasons for this are not immediately obvious.

It may be that a college experience teaches some individuals to be more analytical in their thought processes and to not leap as quickly into emotional relationships. It may be the experience of moving away from home that often accompanies a college experience. This may lead people to be somewhat more independent. While education level is related to the probability of believing in love at first sight, it is not related to the probability of experiencing.

Once a person believes in love at first sight, most groups have a nearly equal probability of actually experiencing it. Those with high school, some college, and college graduates, all had percentages of experiencing love at first sight in the 55 to 57 percent range. Once again, those with graduate education are different.

While those who attended graduate school were the least likely to believe in love at first sight, if they did believe, they were the most likely to experience it. There were 63.8 percent of respondents with graduate education who experienced love at first sight. It may be that the extended college experience gave graduate students more exposure to potential mates who were also attending college.

## Parents' Marital Status

As discussed in a previous chapter, the nature of the parents' relationship has a direct impact on the value systems of children. Therefore, the research addressed the structure of the parent's relationship. It was thought that a parental divorce might make people more skeptical of love at first sight. However, that does not appear to be the case (Table 5.5).

There are two caveats necessary before discussing the results of this question. One category, parents never married, had only twelve respondents. With so few respondents, drawing firm conclusions is tenuous. However, this category had the highest probability of believing in love at first sight (85.7 percent) and experiencing it (66.7 percent). Perhaps there is something at work in this situation.

The second caveat deals with the "other" category. When the questionnaire was developed, I overlooked the possibility of one or both parents being deceased. There were 120 respondents in this category. Since these respondents tended to be older, they had a lower probability of believing (57.9 percent).

The differences for the remaining three categories for believing in or experiencing love at first sight are not large. Experiencing a divorce does not cause a person to be more skeptical of love at first sight. In fact, those who experienced a divorce while living at home were slightly more likely (66.5 percent) to be believers. Maybe, the divorce influenced the individual to long for a personal relationship for themselves.

These three categories also had very similar probabilities (56 to 58 percent) of experiencing love at first sight. It may well be that the structure of the parents' relationship may not be a good predictor of a child's attitudes. Perhaps the age of a child at divorce would be more revealing. It would seem to be more difficult for a younger child. Or perhaps the quality of the parent's relationship would be important. A close, loving relationship between parents would be a more nurturing environment than a cold, distant relationship or one typified by constant bickering.

## Family Structure

In addition to the question on the parent's marital status, there was also a question that addressed the family structure. This question examined the adult figures in the family or the head of household. These results are presented in Table 5.6.

It was felt that a more secure family unit, being raised by both biological parents, would make a person more secure and confident. This should lead to a higher propensity to believe in love at first sight. This was not the case.

Of the 1,495 respondents, 1,157 (77.4 percent), were raised in a household with both biological parents. This percentage was positively related to age. This probably reflects the shift in society's current view of divorce as a common, acceptable event. Therefore, younger people were more likely to have experienced a parental divorce. Older respondents were less likely to have experienced a parental divorce.

Because of their large proportion of the sample, the percentage of believers (63 percent) among respondents raised by both biological parents was very close to the total sample average of 64.1 percent. The second most common category was being raised in a household headed by a single female. Of the 126 respondents in this category, 70.6 percent believed in love at first sight. This proportion is quite high and suggests that a single female head of household situation may create a more open emotional environment. Also quite high was the percentage of believers (73.1 percent) for the respondents who were raised by relatives.

Being raised with a step parent (54.8 percent) or by a single male head of household (54.5 percent) had about the same percentage of believers. Both percentages are quite low. Perhaps the lower social sensitivity of males provides a less emotional adult role model in the household. This may result in a more skeptical view of fast-developing relationships. Likewise, some step parent situations lead to emotional conflict in the household, possibly contributing to a more constrained view of relationships by the children.

While the family structure appears to influence believing in love at first sight, it has little impact on whether a person actually experiences it. Four of the five categories have between 56 to 61 percent of respondents who have experienced love at first sight. Only those raised in a household headed by a single male were significantly different, with 75.0 percent experiencing love at first sight. However, this category had only twenty-eight respondents. With such a small sample size, we must be cautious in drawing firm conclusions.

There appear to be a number of factors that influence whether a person believes in love at first sight and whether a person experiences love at first sight. People who live in rural areas, people who are single, people who have been married four or more times, and people who have not attended college are much more likely to believe. But once a person believes in love at first sight, there are not as many factors influencing whether they actually experience it. People living in large cities and those who have been married four or more times are much more likely to actually experience love at first sight.

## The Differences Between Men and Woman

As mentioned previously, there were 558 respondents in the study who had experienced love at first sight. Of these, 337 were female, and 221 were male. The following sections of this chapter make comparisons between females and males on a variety of issues. Subsequent portions of the book delve into a wider array of differences between men and women who have experienced love at first sight.

### Times Experienced

As suggested in previous chapters, women tend to be more selective than men when selecting a mate. That contention is supported by the data. For women, experiencing love at first sight is most often—78.5 percent of the time—a one-time occurrence. For men, 69.6 percent experience love at first sight just once. While love at first sight is most often a one-time event, it is decidedly more so for women.

Only 4.9 percent of women have experienced love at first sight three or more times. This compares to 12.4 percent of men who have experienced love at first sight three or more times. The implication is that men are more willing to repeat the event. This difference could be due to the fact that men usually are expected to have more intimate relationships than women. While sexual intimacy certainly does not require any type of love, some men may be more apt to equate the intimacy with love. Therefore, the men might feel that they have experienced love at first sight more often.

## Relationship Status

The respondents were asked what type of relationship they were in at the time of love at first sight. There were no major differences between males and females. There were 80.0 percent of men and 79.8 percent of women who were unattached or not in a relationship (Table 5.8). There were 10.2 percent of men and 12.9 percent of women who were in a relationship with someone else. There were 5.1 percent of men and 3.4 percent of women who were currently married to someone else. And there were 4.7 percent of men and 4.0 percent of women who were married to someone else, but separated from their spouse when love at first sight occurred.

The most striking finding is that about 80 percent of all people who experience love at first sight are single and not involved with another person. Thus, these people are in a more active search mode for a mate. As a result, they are probably more sensitive to verbal and nonverbal cues given off by a potential mate. Thus, they are probably more ready for a love at first sight experience. But a person does not have to be unattached to fall in love with someone else.

There were 20 percent of respondents who were already married or in some type of relationship with another person when lightening struck. The implication is that people do not turn off their social sensitivity to a potential mate just because they already have one. A significant portion of people continue to notice others. And, at the least, 20 percent of people let the situation develop into love. As you will see in some of the stories, the married person was shocked that they could develop such powerful feelings for someone other than their spouse so quickly.

## Relationship Status of "Other" Person

While there were no significant differences between men and women regarding their own status, there were differences in the status of the other person (Table 5.9). For men, the "other" person was unattached 74.8 percent of the time, but for women, the "other" person was unattached 83.1 percent of the time. Thus, men are more likely to experience love at first sight with a person who already is involved with someone else. Women are more inclined to focus on a single, unattached person.

For men, 14.5 percent of the time the other person was already in a relationship, and 10.7 percent of the time the other person was married. For women, these figures were 10.5 percent and 6.4 percent, respectively. Apparently, women use the other person's relationship status as more of a filter than men, screening out more of those who are already taken.

## Shared Traits

There always has been a good deal of debate about whether people are attracted to someone who is similar to themselves or different from themselves. In reality, the truth probably falls somewhere in between. Most people want someone who is similar to them in important ways. But most people also want their mate to possess some traits that they, personally, don't possess. The different traits complement them and make them whole in some way.

The argument for being attracted to someone who is similar is based on experience and comfort. We have learned how to behave by watching others around us, predominantly in the family in which we were raised. We know how to deal with recognizable behavior patterns. People who are highly socially sensitive, pick up on the cues given off by others, interpret them, and integrate them into a broader perception of the person. While these perceptions are not always accurate, we form them anyway. Often, people project onto a potential mate the traits that they would like to see.

Most probably have heard the phrase "Looking through rose-colored glasses." The implication is that the tint gives the viewer a rosy, beautiful view of the world which may not include the true colors. So too, a person may project traits onto another which may be exaggerated or inaccurate. But, regardless of the accuracy of this interpretation and projection process, it goes on constantly when we meet other people, particularly a potential mate.

Some will argue that too much similarity is boring, that what people are really looking for is someone who makes us better than what we are alone. This is clearly an extension of Plato's concept of wholeness or completeness. This also implies that we have some "shadow traits" tucked away in our subconscious. These shadow traits are the ideal traits that we would like to possess ourselves. When we see these traits in another—real or projected—we feel that person would complement us, make us better. And we might refer to that person as "different."

If the differences in traits and behavior are too great, we would find the situation emotionally challenging. To reach a status quo, we would have only two choices. Either the other person would have to change their behavior in some way, or we would have to change our own expectations. Whether we try to change another or change ourselves, behavioral change is always difficult.

I have a longtime friend who encountered this situation. He met a girl in college and got married. The major difference between them was religion. He was Lutheran, and she was Mormon. She was absolutely convinced that she could convert him to Mormonism, and she spent years trying. The more he learned about Mormonism, the more skeptical he became of the religion. The harder she pushed him, the wider the gap between them became, and after eight to ten years, they finally divorced.

The following two stories illustrate the different views on similar and opposites. The first believes similarity attracts. "We were both looking for a relationship. We had both dated and had not found anyone that we were the least bit interested in. She had a blue Mustang, and I had a white Mustang, and that was kind of a common interest that we had. We have a lot of basic ideas in common about how we should run a home and ideas about how money should be spent. We care deeply about children and we both wanted children, but those were all secondary. There was just a warmth of spirit that touched me on that day."

The second story illustrates the power of opposites attracting one another. "He had dark hair, dark eyes. He had a magnetism about him, and I just knew that it was a connection. The magnetism that was there was like a charm. There was a definite connection. We are opposites in many things. He had a dry sense of humor and was very quiet. I was more bubbly, more outgoing. So, I think it was the opposites attract kind of thing."

The implication of this is that we probably want someone who is substantially similar to ourselves, but who also possesses additional complementary traits. However, we usually don't want the complementary traits to be too far removed or significant differences will need to be overcome. The similarity validates who we are and creates a level of comfort. The more similar two people are, the easier it will be for them to develop a shared reality of life together. The complementary traits create a synergy, leading to a feeling of wholeness and completeness. These make the whole better than the individual parts. A woman noted that when she met her future husband, "…we were on the same level, both intellectually and spiritually. We were just tuned into the same page." And this balance between similarity and differences is generally supported by the research.

Since the research was conducted over the telephone, conducting a personality test was impossible. However, the respondents were asked a series of questions about themselves and the other person. The results to these questions are presented in Table 5.10.

There are no major differences between men and women on the traits of religion, ethnic group, and race. Being of the same religion is less important than being of the same ethnic group or race, as indicated by the lower percentages. And, women have a slightly greater preference for someone of the same religion.

The question regarding homosexuality was sensitive enough that some respondents actually terminated the interview when the question was asked. Although both percentages were low, 6.5 percent of men were attracted to other men while only 3.0 percent of women were attracted to other women.

After the clearly identified traits, the respondents were asked if the other person was similar or different from them in significant ways. The results seem to suggest that both similarities and differences were appealing (Table 5.11).

Women had a slightly higher preference for someone who was different than men did (38.8 percent versus 34.6 percent). Men were slightly more likely to say that the other person was both similar and different (28.0 percent versus 23.1 percent). Very few (4 to 5 percent) of men or women said "neither."

The implication seems to be what would be expected based on the previous discussion. People like for some similarity to exist. But they also like differences to be there that will complement them in some way.

## Similar to Parents

As discussed in previous chapters, our parents are our first role models. We learn patterns of adult behavior from them. If the childhood experiences were positive, we might look for the same traits in a spouse. The theory contends that people should be attracted to someone who has traits of the opposite sex parent. A daughter would seek a mate who has traits displayed by her father. A son would seek a mate who has traits displayed by his mother. There is some support for this contention in this research (Table 5.12).

For men, 15.8 percent were attracted to women who were similar to their mothers. Based on birth order effects, this should be most prevalent for an only child who never had the mother-infant bond diminished.

For women, 26.3 percent were attracted to men who had traits similar to their fathers. Based on birth order effects, this should be most prevalent for an eldest daughter who has younger siblings. The eldest daughter would have shifted her focus to the father after the mother gave birth to a younger sibling.

Based on the discussions of parental role models and birth order effects, these results are about what would be expected. But, at the conscious level, the vast majority of respondents (63 to 72 percent) indicated that the other person was not similar to either parent. On a deeper, more subtle level, there may be greater similarity than these results suggest.

## Summary

There appear to be many external factors that influence whether a person believes in and experiences love at first sight. Where a person lives, their marital status, their education level, all influence love at first sight in some way. The individual's parents' relationship and family structure also influence love at first sight.

Most people experienced love at first sight only once, but men were somewhat more likely to experience it several times. Both men and women usually experience love at first sight with a person who is unattached. But, about 20 percent of the time, the other person is in a relationship of some type.

There is support for both "similars" and "opposites" attracting one another. Most likely, people are attracted to someone who is both similar and different.

The most striking finding presented in this chapter is that most people believe in love at first sight, and the majority of believers actually experience it. But these perceptions and behaviors vary in some predictable ways.

Table 5.1

## Where You Live

| Geographic Area | Believe | Experienced |
|---|---|---|
| Rural | 70.1% | 54.6% |
| Small Town | 64.8% | 59.5% |
| City with 10,000-100,000 | 61.1% | 53.9% |
| City with 100,000-500,000 | 57.7% | 61.4% |
| City with over 500,000 | 62.9% | 68.4% |

Table 5.2

## Marital Status

| Present Relationship | Believe | Experienced |
|---|---|---|
| Divorced | 60.6% | 61.3% |
| Married | 64.5% | 58.2% |
| Single | 68.6% | 57.2% |
| Widowed | 52.9% | 50.7% |

Table 5.3

# Times Married

| Times Married | Believe | Experienced |
|---|---|---|
| Once | 62.0% | 57.3% |
| Twice | 67.4% | 59.6% |
| Three Times | 62.5% | 56.7% |
| Four Times | 76.5% | 76.9% |
| Five or More | 100.0% | 80.0% |

Table 5.4

# Education

| Education Level | Believe | Experienced |
|---|---|---|
| Graduate School | 59.1% | 63.8% |
| College Graduate | 62.1% | 57.1% |
| Some College | 62.6% | 54.9% |
| High School Graduate/Less | 68.0% | 57.6% |

Table 5.5

# Parents' Relationship

| Parents' Relationship | Believe | Experienced |
|---|---|---|
| Parents Still Married | 62.9% | 58.3% |
| Parents Divorced After | 62.0% | 57.8% |
| Parents Divorced While | 66.5% | 56.7% |
| Parents Never Married | 85.7% | 66.7% |
| Other | 57.9% | 57.5% |

Table 5.6

# Family Structure

| Family Structure | Believe | Experienced |
|---|---|---|
| Raised by 2 Biological Parents | 63.0% | 56.1% |
| Raised by Single Female | 70.6% | 59.3% |
| Raised by Single Male | 54.5% | 75.0% |
| Raised with Step Parent | 54.8% | 60.9% |
| Raised by Relatives | 73.1% | 52.0% |
| Other | 60.0% | 61.1% |

Table 5.7

## Times Experienced

| Times Experienced | Male | Female |
|---|---|---|
| Once | 69.6% | 78.5% |
| Twice | 18.0% | 16.6% |
| Three Times | 6.9% | 3.3% |
| Four Times | 1.8% | 0.6% |
| Five or More | 3.7% | 1.0% |

Table 5.8

## Relationship Status of Respondent

| Relationship Status | Male | Female |
|---|---|---|
| Unattached | 80.0% | 79.8% |
| In a Relationship with Someone Else | 10.2% | 12.9% |
| Married to Someone Else | 5.1% | 3.4% |
| Married but Separated | 4.7% | 4.0% |

Table 5.9

## Relationship Status of "Other" Person

| Relationship Status | Male | Female |
|---|---|---|
| Unattached | 74.8% | 83.1% |
| In a Relationship with Someone Else | 14.5% | 10.5% |
| Married to Someone Else | 5.6% | 4.6% |
| Married but Separated | 5.1% | 1.8% |

Table 5.10

## Shared Traits (percent "Yes")

| Traits | Male | Female |
|---|---|---|
| Same Religion | 58.4% | 62.1% |
| Same Ethnic Group | 87.0% | 86.2% |
| Same Race | 91.6% | 89.7% |
| Same Sex | 6.5% | 3.0% |

Table 5.11

## Similar or Different

| Category | Male | Female |
|---|---|---|
| Different from You in Significant Ways | 34.6% | 38.8% |
| Similar to You in Significant Ways | 32.2% | 33.8% |
| Both | 28.0% | 23.1% |
| Neither | 5.1% | 4.3% |

Table 5.12

## Similar to Parents (percent "Yes")

| Category | Male | Female |
|---|---|---|
| Similar to Father | 3.3% | 26.3% |
| Similar to Mother | 15.8% | 3.4% |
| Both | 8.1% | 6.9% |
| Neither | 72.7% | 63.3% |

# We Were Both
## Married

◦❦◦

*I*t was a warm Saturday in June in 1972. My husband and I were doing some work on our house in Pennsylvania. There wasn't much food in the house so I went to the grocery store a few miles away to buy some things for lunch. That quick trip to the store changed my life in a totally unexpected way.

As I got to town, all of this steam started coming out from under the hood of my car. At first, I thought it was smoke and my car was on fire. Luckily, it wasn't that bad. Fortunately, my car broke down right in front of a Mobil service station.

I walked into the service station and got an attendant to look at the car. He raised the hood and found the problem quickly. It turned out to be a broken radiator hose. It only took a few minutes for him to put a new hose on and fill the radiator with fluid. We talked casually while I watched him work.

As the attendant was almost finished, he stopped and looked me directly in the eyes and said, "You are going to be my wife." I was stunned, but I couldn't look away. It was like our eyes locked in to each other and the world disappeared. I knew he was right. This guy was a perfect stranger, we didn't even know each other's names at that point. But I knew that he and I were going to be married. I have absolutely no idea what caused him to say that or why I was certain that he was right. The feeling was unlike anything that I had experienced in my life.

*At the time, I was twenty-five and had been married for six years. I guess you could say that I was happily married. I had never cheated on my husband or tried to have an affair. Yet in an instant, I knew all that was going to change. I knew that this stranger and I were going to have an affair. I knew I was going to get divorced, and I knew I was going to marry him.*

*I was scared to death. I really felt afraid of the feelings that seemed to explode in me. I got nervous and my hands started sweating. I was exhilarated, scared, excited, and confused, all at the same time. This just wasn't like me to do something like this.*

*Steve's situation wasn't much different. He was thirty-six and had been married for quite a while. He had coal black, wavy hair, and brown eyes. His voice was deep and smooth and sexy. He just seemed to exude this powerful sex appeal. I guess he felt the same way about me. And this all happened in about fifteen minutes.*

*I was selling real estate then, and my office was only two blocks from the service station. But we had never met before that day, even though we worked so close to each other.*

*After I went back home and fixed lunch for my husband, all I could think of was Steve. I was excited and fearful at the same time, feeling a real sense of danger. Two hours earlier that day, I was a contented, happily married woman. Now I was eager to see this stranger again. That night and all the next day, I thought of Steve constantly. I wondered what he was like, the music he listened to, the food he ate, the things he did. I had this overwhelming curiosity to know everything about him.*

*On Monday, Steve saw my car at the real estate office and phoned me. I still had all the confusing emotions. I badly wanted to see him but was afraid to because I knew what would happen. We had lunch and talked very rationally, but I was having these sexual fantasies about him. We reached the rational decision to not* get involved, however, and we really tried to stay away from each other. But we just couldn't, the attraction was too strong.

Initially, Steve would call me at the office or I would call him. We just talked and didn't plan anything sinister. It was always so easy to talk to him, and hearing his deep sexy voice was almost addictive. When the phone would ring, I would hope it was him. I always felt this eager anticipation with him, something I never felt with my husband. The emotions were just so powerful.

It wasn't very long before we arranged to spend an afternoon together. Our original intention was to spend a few hours together and just talk things out. We had never really spent much time together and had never been alone. As soon as we were alone, Steve took me in his arms and kissed me. That one kiss was all it took. The chemistry between us was just unbelievable. It was like we just had to have each other. We spent all afternoon making really intense love. It was just incredibly good. It was like we had known each other all our lives. The intimacy felt so comfortable and so right. But it wasn't just about sex. I think the sex was so good because I was attracted to him in so many other ways.

After that afternoon, we couldn't stay apart. For the next year, we talked or saw each other every day. The flexibility of my job made it pretty easy to arrange for time with Steve. I felt tremendous guilt about having an affair, but I just had to be with him. The sexual intensity that he had that first afternoon never faded a bit. I had never wanted a man so much.

We continued our affair for about a year. Having an affair is not just fun and games, it puts an emotional strain on everybody. I felt like I was walking a tightrope without a net, living a masquerade. My husband was a good man. But Steve and I shared a blind emotion and consuming passion, he took me so high. My time with Steve was exciting and alive.

*Initially, Steve and I probably wanted to make sure that the feelings weren't just a passing infatuation. The more we were together the stronger the feelings became. We couldn't escape what was meant to be. Once we asked our spouses for a divorce, we both moved out and began living together. That was a pretty difficult time, since both our spouses had a lot of resentment. We got married as soon as our divorces were final. That was in 1974, over twenty-five years ago.*

*Steve and I have had a good, happy marriage. That first afternoon, he said that I was the woman that he'd been looking for all of his life. If you know your destination in life, everything works out. I was his destination, and he was mine. We just didn't know it until we met. Unfortunately, most people don't know their destination or what they really want in life, so they drift along day by day, living lives of quiet desperation.*

*I'm sure that the workings of love are a pure and absolute mystery. The love that Steve and I share transformed me and revealed my true self. Drinking of his love gives my life a direction and meaning I had never known before. He has helped me experience the true beauty of life.*

# Lightning Strikes Twice

❦

*I* graduated from high school in Grafton, Vermont, in 1967, and had just completed my first year at the Hanover School of Nursing. I was still involved with my high school sweetheart, but he had just been drafted and sent to Vietnam. I spent the summer of 1968 back home at my parent's house in Grafton.

My parents would have get-togethers with their friends periodically, and that is where I met him. There were a bunch of people at the house and we didn't actually talk then. We just saw each other across the room. We made eye contact and there was some sort of instant attraction. It's like we both communicated this powerful desire to be with each other without saying a word. There was this electricity flowing back and forth between us. That night, when I went to bed, I kept thinking about him, wondering who he was.

The very next night he showed up at my parents house for no apparent reason. Actually, he said he was just stopping by to say hello, but I was the real reason he came over.

He was about five feet, eleven inches tall, had dark skin, dark hair, and brown eyes. He was a handsome, kind, gentle man. He was twenty-nine, ten years older than me. He was divorced and had one child. Being older than the boys I had gone out with, he seemed so mature and distinguished, a real man. He was very quiet and responsible.

*I guess I was a total contrast to him. I was blonde, five feet, three inches, with an athletic build. I'm very out-going, a real "take charge" kind of person. To him I probably seemed like an energetic teenager. But I fell head over heels in love with him and completely forgot about my high school sweetheart.*

*Going out with an older, divorced man had a sort of dangerous appeal to it. I don't think that my parents really approved at first, even though he was their friend. I was probably being a little rebellious, establishing my own identity as an adult. But there was a very strong, physical attraction. The high school boys that I had gone out with always wanted to have sex, but this was the first man that I really wanted sexually.*

*After our first date, he kissed me and my toes tingled. That tingling feeling happened every time he kissed me for years. That summer was the beginning of a pretty intense relationship. We got married eight months later, after I finished my second year of nursing school.*

*For the next fifteen years we had a very traditional marriage. We had three kids, and I was a stay at home mother. Gradually, I became very active in the children's school. The kids were all in school so I had a little more time to myself. The school had an opening for a school nurse and they asked me to apply. Since my work schedule would match the kid's school schedule, I decided to try it.*

*My husband was a mechanic and he had started his own business. He worked there seven days a week, with long hours every day. He put all of his energy into the business and had little time for the family, even me. It seemed we hardly ever talked and rarely made love. I guess that I compensated by focusing more on the kids and my job. We just seemed to drift apart. Lots of marriages probably evolve that way, gradually getting colder and colder with no one incident to blame. I read somewhere that in marriages, couples either get closer or they grow apart, they hardly ever stay the same. I think that's probably true. Whatever the cause, there wasn't much warmth in my marriage anymore.*

*In the fall of 1984, I was in the school office, and a new teacher walked in. It was his first year teaching at the school, and, as it turned out, he was my son's seventh grade math teacher. I was totally in awe, I couldn't see anything else but him. Within the first minute of him coming through that door, I knew that I had to have him.*

*Of course, I was still married. I had occasionally fantasized about having an affair, especially as my husband and I had grown farther apart. I had a lot of unmet needs. But I never took any steps to actually have an affair. But when I saw that man, there was absolutely no doubt that I wanted him. The only real question then was when and how it would happen.*

*He was six foot, two inches tall, very dark skin, and black hair. He was well dressed, very much the suit and tie type person. He was twenty-nine, the same age as my husband had been when we were married, but he had never been married. I was thirty-four at the time.*

*After he walked into the school office that day, I was totally obsessed with him. I would have done anything to make love with him. Since I didn't know him at all, the attraction must have been his good looks, purely physical. I clearly made all the moves and pursued him. But it didn't take much pursuing. He said he felt the same way when we first met. With those kind of mutual feelings, the fireworks happened very quickly.*

*He not only hadn't been married, he had had few relationships with women. He was quiet and serious. He liked the fact that I was bubbly and outgoing, it made him lighten up and have fun.*

*As soon as we were lovers, I left my husband and moved in with him. We were living together within a month of that day in the office. We lived together for two years before we were married. After we were married, we had a son who is now twelve. We are still married, but have been separated for a year.*

*I think the fact that I had three kids from my previous marriage complicated our relationship. My kids were in the twelve to fifteen year age range when we married, so that is a difficult time. He had his ideas about what the kids should and shouldn't do. Because my first husband was not around much, the kids weren't used to having a man controlling them. The fact that he was the reason I got a divorce didn't help much.*

*I constantly felt caught in the middle, trying to please him and trying to please my children at the same time. In some respects, communication between us was an issue because we saw things differently, but didn't talk them out. Perhaps with my first three kids out of high school and on their own we'll be able to get back together. Right now we are in a holding pattern, we love each other, but the tension in the house was just too high.*

## Chapter Six

# The Traits That Attract Men and Women

As discussed earlier, some experts argue that mate selection is based on equity theory. Each person possesses a variety of traits that could be appealing to the opposite sex or another person. We develop a perception of our own self-worth by assessing and valuing all of our own traits. Then we compare our aggregate package to that of a potential mate. If the potential mate brings a roughly equivalent bundle of traits, we may develop an interest in the other person. But if the other person has a perceived much greater self-worth, we may conclude that "they are out of my league." If the perceived self-worth of the other person is much lower than our own, we may conclude that "we can do better than him/her."

There is some research evidence that this does occur. Some researchers have found that couples usually are very close to one another in appearance. Using the infamous ten-point scale, psychologists have found that 60 percent of the couples are within one point of each other on an attractiveness rating, and 85 percent of couples are within two points of one another. It is pretty unusual for there to be a substantial gap in attractiveness among couples when they are young. [21]

In another study of the impact of attractiveness, schoolgirls were rated on their physical attractiveness. Twenty years later, they were contacted. The most attractive girls had married "better." Their husbands were more successful and wealthier than those married to the "less attractive" girls. [22]

But these two studies were tracking only one trait, physical attractiveness. While that trait is important, it certainly is not the only trait considered in the evaluation process. A variety of traits may be considered when evaluating a potential mate. Some of these traits are presented in Table 6.1. These are rather generic categories of traits that could be broken down into much more detail.

For example, physical appearance could include many dimensions such as height, weight, body shape, or physical condition. Or it could be even more detailed to include body measurements, type of hair, skin color, or complexion. Physical appearance also may include a person's attire, such as the dashing sailor in uniform. The point is simply this, each category of traits contains many more specific dimensions that could be important to a particular individual.

The traits that people use to evaluate one another are probably the result of a complex interaction of genetics, family experiences, and socio-cultural values. But, somehow, we evaluate all of these traits collectively and make a judgement of the acceptability of another person. And there does not have to be absolute equity between partners on each trait. Strengths in one area can offset shortcomings in another.

To illustrate, the lady in one of the love at first sight stories was in her early twenties, very attractive, and in a rocky marriage. She met a very wealthy man who was twenty years her senior. There was no love or passion on her part toward the man. He was not extremely handsome or a physical specimen. But he was wealthy, and, for the lady, that one trait was sufficient to offset weaknesses in other areas.

The closer that two people are on the traits individually and collectively, the more likely they are to have a happy relationship or marriage. The more disparate two people are, the more likely problems will arise. For example, the lady who married for money had a string of affairs to make up for the sexual intimacy lacking in her marriage.

In an attempt to simplify the traits in Table 6.1 for research purposes, the traits were collapsed into three categories. The three categories were physical traits, personality traits, and career/achievement traits. As we shall see in subsequent chapters, each of these categories were further broken down into eight to twelve more specific dimensions.

## Men vs. Women

Most people contend that men focus more on the physical traits of a woman. Most would also believe that women use a broader range of evaluative criteria when selecting a mate than men. And that contention is supported by this research (Table 6.2).

When asked "What one category of traits most attracted you to the other person," 51.7 percent of males and 41.2 percent of females said physical traits. This difference is statistically significant and indicates that the physical appearance of a woman is more important to men than the inverse. Interestingly, studies of singles advertisements show that women stress their physical attractiveness more than men. Apparently, women have been conditioned correctly to understand that appearance is important to men. However, the emphasis on physical traits by men is not as strong as one might expect.

There were 46.4 percent of men and 53.1 percent of women who said that personality traits most attracted them. Thus, the personality traits of men are much more important to women. For men, the difference between physical traits and personality traits (51.7 percent versus 46.4 percent) is much less than for women (41.2 percent versus 53.1 percent). Hence, men are attracted almost equally by the physical and personality traits of a woman. Women show a clear preference for the personality of a man.

The most striking finding for the career/achievement traits is their minor role in love at first sight. Perhaps, these issues are more unknown in the first sixty minutes of a relationship. It is likely that this category would be more important in a relationship that developed more gradually. Only 1.9 percent of men and 5.7 percent of women mentioned that career/achievement traits were what most attracted them.

While definitely in the minority, women were over twice as likely as men to identify career success as the most important traits. This seems to imply some support for the concept that women want a "good provider" to care for them and any subsequent children.

This question allowed a respondent to pick only one category. It may be that the career/achievements of men would be a more consistent secondary trait used by women. A woman might be attracted to a man's personality, but then evaluate his career achievements or potential as a secondary issue once he passed the initial personality screen.

There is no question that there are differences between men and women regarding which traits that they find most attractive in another. But the differences are not as great as some might expect. While there are differences in traits between men and women, there were no differences across age or education level. It was thought that younger people might focus more on physical traits, but this contention was not supported. It was thought that the better educated would focus more on the personality or career/achievement traits, but this was not supported either. There were significant differences across the times married and across ethnic groups, however.

## Times Married

The more times a person has been married, the more likely they are to be attracted by the physical traits of another (Table 6.3). For a person married only once, the percentage being attracted by physical traits was low at 45.1 percent. But if a person was married twice (48.2 percent), three times (46.7 percent), four times (52.1 percent), or five or more times (53.4 percent), the probability of being most attracted by physical traits increased substantially. This may be a revealing finding.

It may be that those who marry frequently operate on an emotionally shallower level. In other words, they may be attracted most by physical appearance and pay relatively less attention to dimensions of personality. The personality factors could become more important once a relationship is established, and, perhaps, personality differences could also lead to the disintegration of a relationship or marriage. If you will recall, people who married frequently were also more likely to believe in love at first sight and to have experienced it. These people may tend to jump into a relationship very quickly, using more superficial criteria.

## Ethnic Group

There are substantial differences across the ethnic groups in the traits that most attracted people. These results are presented in Table 6.4. Because Caucasians accounted for about 70 percent of the total sample, their views are close to the overall averages. This equates to about 390 respondents who were Caucasian. The remaining ethnic groups varied in size from twenty to fifty respondents. Because of the smaller sample sizes, we must be more cautious in interpreting the results. However, the differences are substantial enough to suggest some very clear trends.

Among the ethnic groups, Native Americans (22.2 percent) and the "other" category placed the least emphasis on physical traits. Hispanics (43.2 percent) and Caucasians (45.6 percent) were roughly equal in being attracted by physical traits. African-Americans (60 percent) tend to be strongly attracted by physical traits.

Native Americans placed the greatest emphasis on personality (77.8 percent). The "other" category (54.5 percent), Hispanics (54.1 percent), and Caucasians (51.0 percent) were very close to one another in being attracted by personality. African-Americans (30 percent) and Asian/Pacific Islanders (29.4 percent) placed the least emphasis on personality.

For career/achievement traits, Asian/Pacific Islanders (11.8 percent) and African-Americans (10 percent) had a substantially higher probability of being attracted by these traits. It is likely that there is some cultural effect working here. The remaining ethnic groups were infrequently attracted by such traits.

## Age of Other Person

The age of the other person when love at first sight occurred apparently does have something to do with the traits that most attracted someone. The younger the other person, the more likely that physical traits most attracted the person. Both of the age brackets under age twenty had large percentages for physical traits (Table 6.5). After age twenty-one, personality became the dominant category of traits. The four brackets over age twenty-one had at least 50 percent of individuals attracted because of personality.

For people attracted to someone over age forty, personality was the dominant trait that attracted others. Between 71 to 75 percent of these people said that personality was key. It appears that age may be the great equalizer of physical appearance for most people.

As humans become older, we are supposed to become more mature and wiser. Apparently that does happen somewhat. Specifically, the personality of another becomes relatively more important in being attracted to someone. With age, we can look deeper into another person and somewhat beyond just the physical attractiveness.

## Summary

The results presented in this chapter show that men are more likely to be attracted by the physical traits of women, and women are more attracted by the personality traits of men. While this question was worded to force respondents to make a choice, it is also quite likely that several categories of traits are used simultaneously by men and women. Men are most apt to use physical and personality traits almost equally when evaluating a potential mate. Women are somewhat more likely to focus on a man's personality and supplement that emphasis with both physical and career/achievement traits. While the use of the various traits as evaluative criteria are unrelated to age and education level, the likelihood to emphasize physical traits is definitely related to the number of times a respondent has been married. The emphasis on physical traits is also more common for several ethnic groups, suggesting a socio-cultural influence.

Table 6.1

## Traits That Attract Others

Physical Appearance

Attractiveness

Personality

Social Skills

Knowledge

Education

Career Success/Status

Wealth

Social Status

Table 6.2

## What Traits Attract Men and Women

|  | Males | Females | Aggregate |
|---|---|---|---|
| Physical | 51.7% | 41.2% | 45.4% |
| Personality | 46.4% | 53.1% | 50.5% |
| Career/Achievement | 1.9% | 5.7% | 4.2% |

Table 6.3

## Traits and Times Married

| Times Married | 1 | 2 | 3 | 4 | 5 or more |
|---|---|---|---|---|---|
| Physical | 45.1% | 48.2% | 46.7% | 52.1% | 53.4% |
| Personality | 50.5% | 49.4% | 53.3% | 47.9% | 46.6% |
| Career/Achievement | 4.4% | 2.4% | 0.0% | 0.0% | 0.0% |

Table 6.4

## Traits and Ethnic Group

|  | Physical | Personality | Achievement |
|---|---|---|---|
| Hispanic | 43.2% | 54.1% | 2.7% |
| African American | 60.0% | 30.0% | 10.0% |
| Caucasian | 45.6% | 51.0% | 3.4% |
| Asian/Pacific Islander | 58.8% | 29.4% | 11.8% |
| Native Amer/ Eskimo | 22.2% | 77.8% | 0.0% |
| Other | 40.9% | 54.5% | 4.5% |

Table 6.5

## Age of Other Person

|  | Physical | Personality | Achievement |
|---|---|---|---|
| 15 & Under | 60.0% | 40.0% | 0.0% |
| 16-20 | 47.7% | 47.2% | 5.1% |
| 21-25 | 41.5% | 55.6% | 3.0% |
| 26-30 | 45.3% | 50.0% | 4.7% |
| 31-40 | 42.9% | 53.1% | 4.1% |
| 41-50 | 20.8% | 75.0% | 4.2% |
| 51 & Over | 28.6% | 71.4% | 0.0% |

# I Was a Skeptic

⬦

$\mathcal{I}$ was a total skeptic. I simply did not believe in love at first sight. That was just stuff for romance novels. I was sure that it didn't happen in real life. I was absolutely certain that you really had to know somebody for quite a while before love developed. I thought love was more like a disease that gradually took over rather than a bolt of lightning. It especially wouldn't happen to me, a divorced mother of four children. But it did.

The precise events of that day will be crystal clear until the day that I die. It was Friday, September 7, 1990, in Portland, Maine. My grandmother had passed away a few days earlier, and she was buried that day. She was a jewel of a lady, spunky and full of life. She felt that age was mostly a state of mind. Her spirit, her heart, her mind were all young. She had a freshness of life each day that was vigorous, adventurous, full of vitality. The only thing that hindered her was that she was trapped in a body that was experiencing life's decline. Her eyes, that window to her soul, remained clear and bright to the very end.

One of her wishes was that she didn't want people sitting around being sad and crying about her death. Instead of a big, fancy funeral, she said keep it simple. She wanted everyone to go out and have a party and celebrate what a great life she had. She wanted people to smile and laugh when they thought of her. So all the family complied with her wishes.

*There were too many of us to go to a house so we went to a local pub. It wasn't the kind of place that I would normally go to, as I wasn't much of a drinker. Consistent with responsible drinking in the 1990s, I was the designated driver for everyone else. Lightning struck at the pub that afternoon.*

*As I said, I was divorced then. My divorce had been final in May of 1990. I hadn't been dating anyone and didn't really expect anyone to be interested in me. I was attractive enough, but, at thirty-eight with four children, two of them teenagers, I wasn't a hot commodity to most men my age. That actually didn't bother me much, as I loved my children a lot and was very comfortable with who I was as a person. I didn't need a man to fulfill me, but having one around had its advantages, too.*

*After I walked in and sat down, we saw each other at the same time. He was sitting at the next table facing me. When our eyes met, we seemed to get lost in each other. His name was Charles. He was about 5 feet, 6 inches and very stocky. He wasn't fat, just very well built. He had black hair and brown eyes.*

*He said, "You look like you could be a Jill." I just laughed and said, "I'm a nurse, so I should be named Karen." It seemed like there were an awful lot of nurses named Karen. He offered to buy me a drink, and I ordered a Coke. He teased me about drinking such strong stuff.*

*He was just a character, he was so funny and engaging. He had a beautiful smile and a great personality. Charles had also just gone through a divorce that was final in August. He had two beautiful daughters.*

*Charles was in the Navy and had just been promoted to Chief Petty Officer. He was thirty-six and had been in the Navy for almost twenty years. He had to go back out to sea about a week after we met.*

*We had a few drinks and talked at the pub. Then everyone wanted to go have dinner. We went to a restaurant called The Home Plate in Portland. I invited Charles to go with us. Neither of us were really hungry so we both had coffee and a muffin. We just talked and talked. Later he told me that he was attracted to me because I was so easy to talk to. We felt like two old friends right from the start.*

*I couldn't understand why I was so attracted to him. I wasn't even looking for a relationship. But I knew that I was in love with him before we even left the pub. Everything was just so comfortable with him. It was definitely love at first sight, with no hesitation or uncertainty at all.*

*We went out several times that week before he went out to sea. He was gone for three months, and we wrote each other constantly. During the process of writing those letters, I told him that I had fallen in love with him that first night. I actually asked him to marry me. He was out to sea from the middle of September until the middle of December. When he got back from his tour of duty, we got married on Christmas Eve, 1990.*

*We had actually only gone out together a few times before we got married. I never would have believed that I could marry someone so quickly. But that was over eight years ago, and we have been so happy.*

*Unfortunately, right after we got married, the Gulf War started. Charles had to ship out for eighteen months to the Persian Gulf. When Charles returned from the Gulf, I immediately got pregnant. I guess that we both had a lot of pent up passion for each other. At my age then, forty, I wasn't planning on having any more children. But having a child with him has been a real treasure. Maybe when you get older you appreciate more what creating a new life is all about.*

*Any man that can marry a woman with four kids, and make it work happily, must completely love you. My teenagers are good kids, but teenagers are still teenagers. He has been so respectful and patient with my children and myself. Having two teenage girls must have helped him to learn patience. I'm not sure that I knew what a wonderful man he was when we married.*

*Charles has taken me to places that I've never been emotionally. I've heard it said that those who completely give and receive love feel more happiness in life. They draw the love and happiness in and multiply it and give it back again. Each person gets back far more than they give. I didn't truly understand that until Charles and I shared our love with each other. And I'm sure that all of our children see and feel the love in our home, too.*

*As a bit of irony, his oldest daughter's birthday is the day we met, September 7. And, he'll never forget getting married on Christmas Eve. Those are two dates neither of us will ever forget.*

*I admit that I was a total skeptic of love at first sight. I'd even discussed it with some friends before. Anybody who doesn't believe in love at first sight is wrong. They just haven't looked in the right places yet, or found the right person.*

# The Hurricane Brought Us Together

*It happened August 21, 1995, at about 9:00 P.M. I own a bar at Pawleys Island, South Carolina, about seventy miles up the coast from Charleston. It was on a Monday and the place was crowded for Monday Night Football.*

*There was bad weather that year, several big hurricanes. There was another big hurricane due to hit the coast in several days. It added to the excitement, I guess. It seems a lot of places have hurricane parties. I was in New Orleans once, right before a hurricane was supposed to hit, and Bourbon Street was absolutely wild that night.*

*Because we were so busy, I was serving food. He was from Michigan and was diving for some offshore gold expedition. His company shut down the dive until the coming storm blew over. He was tall and thin and worked out a lot. He had brown curly hair and brown eyes. He looked at me so adorably when I served him, I thought, "What a little doll."*

*I had just divorced and wasn't looking to get involved at the time. He kept talking to me every chance he got that night. He was very friendly and outgoing. I told him that I had to shut the place down for a while and board up all the windows. That night was going to be the last day that the bar would be open until the hurricane passed. He said that he wanted to help me. It seemed so romantic that he would want to help a stranger.*

*The next day he came over and we bought plywood and the other things we needed. He worked a good part of the day helping me. Then we had to get packed since we had to leave the area.*

*That evening, we went inland to Columbia. My son, who was nine, and I got a room at a hotel. He and a friend of his also got a room there. My son just fell in love with him right away. We had several days to kill and we spent all of our time together. In the day, we all went out and did things together. At night, he and I would go out together.*

*At first, I thought that he might be too young—I was forty-one and he was thirty-two. But it was just so overwhelming and the feelings were so strong. He was very sweet, genuine, honest, and just so adorable. He has a smile that lights up a room and eyes that glow and sparkle. I have red curly hair and his hair is real curly so I really liked that.*

*We have so much in common. We both come from big families and both have brothers that died. We are just able to talk and talk and talk. Being so comfortable with him makes it so easy to talk and share our hearts. We can talk about anything, our hopes and dreams, our fears, our past, our future. Our communication has brought us closer.*

*After about a year and a half of dating, we got married. At the wedding, his father was the best man. He said "He came to South Carolina searching for gold, and a hurricane came in and he found his treasure." That hurricane was a real blessing for us. It really brought us together.*

*Looking back now, I can't pinpoint one thing that attracted me to him. It is really a million things. I never would have believed in love at first sight until it happened to me.*

## Chapter Seven

# The Physical Traits That Attract Men and Women

$\mathcal{A}$s we saw in the previous chapter, the physical traits of men and women are important in attracting potential mates. This chapter will examine this subject in more detail. The first part of the chapter will address the traits of men that attract women, according to the 337 female respondents. The second part of the chapter will address the physical traits of women that attract men, according to the 221 male respondents. First, it might be helpful to identify why the physical traits presented in Table 7.1 were addressed.

A rather extensive review of the literature on interpersonal attraction was conducted. This literature identified a variety of physical traits of both men and women. Rather than have one questionnaire for men and another questionnaire for women, we chose a "unisex" approach. We wanted to have a questionnaire that could be used equally well for male and female respondents. This meant that each trait had to be generic enough to fit both genders. For example, a woman might refer to a man as having a "good build." A man is more likely to refer to a woman as having a "great body." The woman is probably referring to a man being lean and muscular. The man is probably referring to a woman's breasts, waist, hips, and legs. But rather than use specific terms, we choose to use the term "build/body."

The generic terms were used for other reasons as well. The use of more explicit terms might have offended some respondents. We wanted to avoid this as much as possible. And, from a very pragmatic research standpoint, more detailed questions would result in a longer questionnaire. The length of the questionnaire is always a concern in survey research.

## The Physical Traits

Each of the physical traits was included because there was some evidence that the trait was appealing to potential mates. However, some traits were expected to be more commonly used by men, and others were expected to be more commonly used by women.

## Good Looking/Attractive

There is broad support that "good looking" or "attractive" is important to potential mates, whether male or female. However, a person does not have to be drop dead gorgeous to be attractive. Rather, a person must fall into a potential mate's "zone of acceptability." If you recall from chapter six, most couples are of roughly similar attractiveness. The implication is that each person has a perception of who is attractive. Not all women would rate a man equally. Some women might find a particular man very attractive, while other women might find the same man very average. As the old saying goes, "Beauty is in the eye of the beholder."

When love at first sight occurs, the other person may not be even close to our "ideal" mate. One lady felt she always wanted to marry the "Greek god" type of man. She thought he would have blond hair, be over six feet tall, and be lean with well-defined muscles. When she fell in love at first sight, the man who caught her attention had short dark hair, was barely five feet, nine inches, and was of a stocky build. The best laid plans of men and women often go awry when lightening strikes.

## Build/Body

In most countries around the world, men and women prefer the same general body shapes. Men prefer women who are shapely and curvaceous, with proportionate measurements. Long legs are also generally appealing, and men like women who are in reasonably good condition. In short, men like women who look healthy and who have the appearance of being a good mother.

Women prefer men who are V-shaped from the waist up. This implies broad shoulders and a narrower waist. Women like men who are lean and have good muscle definition. And most women like a man who has a good rear end. In general, women want a man who will be a good provider, and physical strength is the traditional surrogate cue that women use.

A woman does not have to have an hour glass figure with large breasts. A man does not have to be chiseled out of stone. The body of both men and women must convey a general statement of health and vitality.

## Height

Everyone has probably heard the saying that a woman is looking for a "tall, dark, and handsome man." Some women do prefer men who are taller than average. And some men do prefer women who are also taller than average. But, again, height is a relative concept. Women prefer men who are taller than they are. Most men prefer women who are shorter than they are. So one woman may view a man as tall while another may not.

While not related to height, the second word in the phrase (dark) also has some research support. Women tend to prefer men who are darker skinned. This could simply be a result of being tanned by the sun. And men, traditionally, prefer women who are fairer skinned. So the hue of a person's skin can influence another's perception of them.

*Hair*

With a billion dollar hair care market in the United States, a lot of people think that a person's hair matters. A woman's flowing tresses have been mentioned in the romantic literature for thousands of years. Certainly someone thinks that hair can attract other people. This is an area that seems to favor women. A woman's hair can be appealing to men. A man's hair is much less likely to be an attractant for women.

The role of hair may be due to socio-cultural influences. Hairstyles and length have varied over time. In general, men wear their hair much shorter than twenty years ago. Women's hairstyles also have varied, with more variety.

This respondent from Vermont clearly indicates how hair was combined with other traits. "He had nice brown hair and he had a couple of little locks that hung down over his forehead. He had those eyes that looked like Hershey kisses, that wonderful brown color. He had a little bit of a tan because he had been down to Georgia. He had picked up sort of a little Southern accent I guess. He was a few years older than I was so I just thought he was old, sexy, wicked, and wonderful."

## Eyes

It has been said that the eyes are the window to a person's soul. Starting with the mother-infant interaction, eye contact became a primary form of nonverbal communication. In a previous chapter, the concept of nonverbal signaling was discussed. Most of the signals, or invitations, involved some aspect of eye contact. Hence, a person's eyes should be an important physical trait in attracting another.

This is illustrated in the following example from a woman in New York. "My girlfriends and I were going to the bar and our eyes kind of locked as we walked up to the entranceway. He had brown hair, blue eyes, was very handsome and very muscular."

Although eyes may be important, the color of eyes is apparently not a major factor. A person's eyes could be blue, green, or brown. The important aspect of eyes is the nonverbal message being conveyed by a lingering, sometimes smoldering, glance.

As with most traits, more than one is usually mentioned. In the following example, eyes are described three ways. "His hair was blond brown. He was very neatly dressed, and had blue-green eyes that were kind of almond shaped. He was very clean cut. His eyes were extremely attractive. He had an after-shave on. He had a scent to him, which I was very attracted to."

Most have heard the term "bedroom eyes." If a person thinks of intimate, passionate thoughts while looking at another, the eyes actually change. The eyelids lower. The pupils get larger and more alluring. Large pupils are consistently viewed, and interpreted, as being very sexy. Typically, the facial expression also can change into a sultry, come-hither look. But this all starts with the eyes.

The eyes also convey nonverbal messages depending upon how long they look at someone. Extended, direct eye contact with another conveys the clearest message of interest and affection. The more the eye contact, the stronger the affection. Couples who are openly in love have much more direct eye contact than couples who are good friends.

Eyes do not have to directly connect with another's to convey a message. Picture this situation. A man and woman are at a party. They have never met, but feel an attraction to one another. Across the room, they make eye contact, neither one looking away. Without blinking, the man slowly shifts his gaze downward across the woman's body and then back up to her eyes once again. What message was conveyed? The slow downward inspection of another's body normally has strong sexual connotations. The woman, by not turning away when this occurred, conveyed a return message of interest or approval.

The implication is that eyes can be a powerful physical trait in attracting another. Where the eyes look, how long they look, and how they look all work together to convey messages. Therefore, the eyes are generally viewed as a key physical trait.

## Sex Appeal

Most of the relationship experts are skeptical that love at first sight occurs. Instead, most feel that "lust" at first sight is much more likely. But lust is more of an emotional response resulting from some type of stimuli. In a general sense, there must be some level of sex appeal for lust to occur. If "lust" at first sight is a frequent occurrence, then sex appeal should be a frequently mentioned physical trait that attracted another.

The following example from a woman in Montana illustrates the ambiguous, but strong power, of innate sex appeal. "When I met him the first time, I couldn't even look at him. I don't know, there was just some kind of thing that made me sick to my stomach, and I simply could not look at him in the eye. It was too much of a physical thing. He had dark hair, and looked rugged. He's not a real big guy, but he had great looking hands. He is Italian. He was married when I met him, was, and still is. Basically, I was just overwhelmed. I just thought he was sexy and I liked everything about him."

## Athletic

Our society places a huge emphasis on sport. Professional and college sports are major media events. Amateur and youth sports involve many millions of people. In addition, the fitness industry is also huge. Exercise equipment, health clubs, exercise and aerobics classes, bicycling, running, and swimming are all prominent activities. Advertisements feature lithe, tanned women and lean, muscular men subtly conveying the message that we should all look that way. Collectively, all of this would suggest that being "athletic" would be very appealing to others.

## Older

It already has been noted that, in most cultures around the world, women like men who are older, to some degree. The older man may be more mature and experienced. They may be better educated and generally be more sophisticated. A man who is older may have an established career, and, therefore, have more resources. But the term older is another relative term. An eighteen-year-old woman might view a twenty-year-old man as "older." A forty-year-old woman may not view a forty-five-year-old man as older, even though the age gap is wider. It appears that the age gap between a woman and man is more significant to the young. But as people age, age gaps become less relevant. Being older should be a trait of men that women find appealing.

While some men prefer older women, the inverse is also true. Men do prefer younger women. This is thought to reflect the greater reproductive capability of younger women. Therefore, men should find being younger an attractive trait of women.

A word of caution is necessary here. Being younger does not mean fifteen or twenty years younger. In most cases, the woman is only a few years younger than the man. When a woman is much younger than the man, images of the "trophy bride" are conjured up, carrying a somewhat negative image in society.

## Smell/Odor

As discussed previously, odor plays an important role in body chemistry and sexual reproduction. The sense of smell is the most acute and sensitive for most humans. Therefore, odor could play a role in interpersonal attraction.

The role of odor could be artificial or natural. An artificial odor might be a perfume, after-shave, or soap. Some of us might find a particular perfume very alluring, while others might find it almost repulsive. A natural odor is the unique odor signature that each human possesses.

For example, a couple liked to cross-country ski in the winter. The man said he found the woman exceptionally sexually arousing after they had been skiing. He was aroused by her perspiration and natural odor, far more than by any perfume. He felt her odor was almost like an aphrodisiac for him.

## Attire

The clothes that a person is wearing at the time of love at first sight may convey a certain image to another. A woman in an evening gown could convey an image of elegance and class. A man in uniform could convey strength and leadership. Expensive, stylish clothes could convey wealth and status. The clothes that a person wears convey an image of some type.

If another finds the projected image very appealing, that person may be attracted. Some relationship experts advise singles to always dress for success. In other words, dress with the expectation that you'll meet Mr./Ms. Wonderful on the next trip to the grocery store. As they say, there is only one chance to make that important first impression.

The following example certainly does not provide support for the dress for success idea. But Dominick remembers Lori's attire clearly. "It was a rainy, misty, and cloudy afternoon at Machu Picchu in Peru. I was visiting the ancient city on my own. She was with a large tour group. She glanced at me as I was staring at her. I noticed she had a scar on her knee. And she was wearing a poncho with a pair of shorts and hiking boots. Amongst the mystical energy contained in the ceremonial grounds of that ancient village, she stood there with this peaceful look about her."

## Smile

If direct eye contact is accompanied by a smile, the invitation is unmistakable. A smile conveys excitement, fun, pleasure, and warmth, all desirable traits. A smile also conveys acceptance, implying there is no need to worry about rejection, at least initially. Therefore, when love at first sight occurs, there are probably mutual smiles exchanged between one another, very frequently. As one lady stated in an interview, "I just couldn't stop smiling when I met him."

## The Research Results

The act of asking questions can influence a respondent's answers. Therefore, this research used two separate approaches when evaluating the physical, personality, and career/achievement traits. In one approach, the interview read the list of traits and the respondent answered "yes" if that trait attracted them to the other person. If the trait had no influence, the respondent said "no." The respondent also was allowed to provide an "other" response if the listed traits were not sufficient. Because a list of traits was read, this was referred to as an "aided" approach.

The other approach was to simply ask the respondent, "What physical traits of the other person attracted you?" The interviewer would check off the trait if it was on the list. If it was not on the list, the trait was captured (written down) by the interviewer. Because the list of traits was not read, this is referred to as an "unaided" approach.

Since the sample sizes were different for the aided and unaided approaches, comparing only the number of times mentioned would be a bit misleading. Therefore, a percentage also was calculated. The percentage indicates the proportion of respondents in each category that mentioned a particular trait. This percentage is very useful in making direct comparisons.

As you might expect, the aided approach led to a much higher number of mentions by the respondents. Both men and women averaged 7.42 physical traits using the aided approach. Using the unaided approach, women averaged 1.59 traits of men, and men averaged 1.73 traits of women. While the magnitude of comments varies from one approach to the other, the message is generally the same.

## The Physical Traits of Men That Attract Women

When prompted with questions, respondents gave a much wider array of responses. Because of these dramatic differences between the aided and unaided approaches (Table 7.2), each will be discussed separately. Then the implications of an integrated data set will be discussed.

## Aided

The aided approach prompted respondents to recall traits that they did not recall on their own. Since the love at first sight experience may have occurred many years previous, this is not necessarily bad. However, the split sample research design certainly illustrates the impact that a research design has on data results.

There are three physical traits of men that were identified by 85 to 89 percent of all women. These were good looking/ attractive (89.4 percent), smile (88.8 percent), and eyes (84.6 percent). Making eye contact and smiling are two very productive ways to attract another person. The good looking/attractive trait may be self-fulfilling. When we love someone, we think they are more attractive. It is a sort of halo effect where positive emotions influence our perceptions. If we love someone, we see them in a more positive light, sort of looking through those rose colored glasses, if you will.

After the first three traits, two others stand out from the rest. Sex appeal (77.1 percent) and body/build (76.6 percent) were mentioned by nearly equal numbers of women. The sex appeal trait seems to be an extension of being attractive. If we love someone, we probably find them sexier in some way. Since over 70 percent of these love at first sight experiences resulted in either marriage or a long-term relationship, sexual intimacy followed for most people. This may result in retrospectively saying the person had sex appeal.

The body/build trait indicates that women do pay attention to all aspects of a man's physique. Other research suggests a woman's preferences can be varied and flexible, suggesting that no one body shape is dominant. However, women do prefer men who are healthy looking, and that usually translates into leaner, more muscular builds that convey strength and power.

There was another cluster of three traits mentioned by 55 to 62 percent of women. These were hair (62.2 percent), attire (56.4 percent), and height (54.8 percent). The importance of hair, relative to some other traits, was surprising. Given the trend to shorter hairstyles for men, I expected hair to be somewhat less important. Obviously, most women do pay attention to a man's hair. Both the color and hairstyle are probably factors that would influence a woman's perception.

The importance of attire was also a bit surprising, being ahead of other traits. Since the exact aspects of attire were not asked, we can't say exactly which types of attire were most appealing to women. Perhaps, the old saying that "clothes make the man" does indeed have merit.

Height was the eighth most frequently mentioned trait. It was thought that height would be more important since other evidence suggested that women prefer taller men. However, height does not appear to be as big of a factor as some might contend.

Being athletic was mentioned by about half (50.5 percent) of the women. This trait is probably related somewhat to body/build, but also implies some degree of physical conditioning. The connotation of being healthy and fit would probably also contribute to this trait.

Smell/odor was mentioned by less than half (43.6 percent) of the women. It is likely that this trait includes both natural and artificial odors. Since pheromones appear to operate on a more subconscious level, this result is not too surprising.

Only 34 percent of women indicated that a man being older was appealing. Since most of the men were older than the women by a few years, this was a bit surprising. Perhaps the role of age is more significant initially, but, over time, this issue of age gaps becomes less relevant. There were only 11.2 percent of women who indicated that the man being younger was appealing. This generally fits with the research that suggests women prefer older, not younger, men.

There were 12.8 percent of the women who provided an "other" response. The most common other traits, and times mentioned, were rear end (4), hands (2), and mannerisms (2). All of the remaining traits were each mentioned once. Therefore, there was no conclusion that could be drawn from the "other" responses.

The aided approach paints a much more detailed picture of the physical traits of men that attract women than an unaided approach. The fact that the 195 women collectively indicated 1,395 traits, an average of 7.42 per respondent, was surprising. These results are even more interesting when compared to the unaided results.

## Unaided

The 142 women surveyed with the unaided approach identified 226 physical traits of men that attracted them. This means, on average, each woman recalled one or two traits. While there were similarities with the aided approach, there also were differences.

The most frequently mentioned trait was eyes, mentioned by 39.4 percent of the women. This result was generally expected. Eyes were in the top three traits using the aided approach.

The second trait, good looking/attractive, was mentioned by 31 percent of women. This, again, was one of the top three traits using the aided approach. Given the intuitive importance of eyes and good looking/attractive, it was a bit surprising that only 30 to 40 percent of women mentioned these traits.

After the first two traits which were clearly most prevalent, four traits were mentioned by 12 to 17 percent of women. These were hair (16.9 percent), smile (16.2 percent), body/build (14.1 percent), and height (12 percent). The most surprising finding here was that smile was indicated by only 16.2 percent of women using an unaided approach compared to 88.8 percent using the aided approach. Since a smile is one of the strongest nonverbal signals, it was expected to be close to eyes in importance, even using the unaided approach.

As would be expected, a larger portion of women (21.1 percent) provided an "other" physical trait. The most common among these, and the times mentioned, were stature/poise (4), cleanliness (4), beard/mustache (3), hands (3), butt (3), muscles (2), and chest (2). There were ten other traits mentioned once each. The only surprise here was the cleanliness trait. Given most American's emphasis on personal hygiene (compared to other countries), cleanliness would seem to be almost a given.

Traits such as sex appeal, attire, and athleticism were mentioned by less than six women. Apparently, these simply are not top of mind issues when falling in love at first sight. Age and smell/odor were not mentioned by anyone.

## The Implications

If the general themes running through both research approaches are integrated, we can develop a set of "how-to" guidelines for men. The most influential traits are eyes and smile. The more of both, the better. If a man is interested in a woman, he should emphasize direct eye contact and reinforce it with a smile. As we will see when the personality traits are discussed in the next chapter, eye contact and smile can be supplemental with other issues as well.

The good looking/attractive, build/body, and hair traits are a bit more problematic. Each of us is cast a combination that we can only partially control. The best advice is to do the best with what you've got, and pay attention to how you look. Being disheveled and slovenly is not going to be appealing to very many women.

## The Physical Traits of Women That Attract Men

The same pattern of frequency of responses emerged with men as it did for women. With the aided approach, men had an identical mean number of physical traits of women identified (7.42). However, men had slightly more unaided traits than women (1.73 versus 1.59). This was somewhat surprising. It is a generally held view that women are more socially and perceptually sensitive than men. This would seem to imply that women would identify more traits, whether physical, personality, or career/achievement, than men. But that did not happen. The implication is that men can recall the love at first sight experience with the same acuity as women.

## Aided

There were two traits that stood out from the rest (Table 7.3). Good looking/attractive was mentioned by 93.9 percent of the men, and smile was mentioned by 86.8 percent of the men. These are the same top two traits identified by women using the aided approach.

After these two traits, there were three physical traits of women that were of roughly equal importance to men. Between 77 to 80 percent of all men identified these traits. These were build/body (79.8 percent), sex appeal (79.8 percent), and eyes (77.2 percent). Considering the way a man views a woman, her body and sex appeal are probably very closely related to one another. If you believe those who say a man thinks about sex almost continuously, it would be hard for a man to look at a woman without noticing her sex appeal. While this may be the case, the incidence that sex appeal was mentioned was roughly equal for men and women. Sex appeal must be equally important to both sexes.

It was a bit surprising that "eyes" was the fifth trait, based on frequency of comments. It may be that women have a wider array of attractive physical characteristics to attract a man's attention. Therefore, some attention may be diverted away from the woman's eyes.

The next most frequently mentioned physical trait was the woman's hair. This was the sixth-ranked trait, the same as for women. But 70.2 percent of men mentioned hair, compared to 62.2 percent for women. The implication is that a woman's hair can definitely attract men.

Sixty-four percent of the men indicated that the woman's attire attracted them. However, since more detailed information was not gathered, it is difficult to identify exactly what aspects of attire were found to be attractive.

The height of a woman was mentioned by slightly over half (53.5 percent) of the men. While height of men is usually inter-preted to mean a woman's preference for taller men, the pattern is not as clear for men. In some cases, height included "tiny" and "petite." In other cases, the woman was "tall and slender." While the height of a woman was noticeable to men, the direction of influence was ambiguous.

The eighth-ranked physical trait of women was smell/odor, mentioned by 43.9 percent of men. This was nearly identical to the 43.6 percent identified by women. Since women tend to use much more perfume than men use cologne, the odor of a woman was expected to be more of an attractant for men. Perhaps in the overall love at first sight experience, smell/odor pales in comparison to other more dominant traits.

A woman being athletic was relatively unimportant to men. Only 36 percent of men identified this trait as attracting them. It may be that build/body and sex appeal subsume the concept of athleticism, thus eroding its influence. However, it appears that most men simply are not concerned with a woman being athletic.

Age of the woman is somewhat of a factor for men. There were 32.5 percent who mentioned that the woman being younger attracted them, compared to only 12.4 percent who found the woman being older appealing. This supports the contention that men prefer younger women, and women prefer older men.

There were 12.4 percent of men who identified an "other" physical trait of women. The most common of these were legs (2), lips (2), and large breasts (2). The other traits each had only one mention. It is interesting that despite all of the silicone breast implants and resulting controversy, large breasts were mentioned by only two men. Apparently, they are not a big deal in reality.

### Unaided

The men identified the same top five physical traits as women when using an unaided approach. And these traits were generally in the same order. There were 34 percent of men who mentioned the woman's eyes, and 29.1 percent who mentioned that the woman was good looking/attractive. These two traits were in the same order as women had identified for men.

Following the first two traits was a cluster of three traits identified by 18 to 21 percent of men. Smile (20.4 percent), hair (19.4 percent), and build/body (18.4 percent) were roughly equal to one another. After these three physical traits of women, no other trait was mentioned by 6 percent of men. The implication is that the preceding five physical traits of women are clearly the most important when attracting a man.

However, the "other" trait category had a clear pattern. There were seventeen men who identified a woman's face as attracting them. This was followed by legs (9), lips (5), skin (4), and teeth (3). The "face" trait is probably closely related to the good looking/attractive category since that is what most refer to when evaluating attractiveness. It is interesting to note that, once again, "breasts" were not mentioned by any man. It is likely that breasts were subsumed into the good body trait. Could it be that breast size has more to do with a woman's self-image than with attracting men?

## Male-Female Contrast

The most striking finding of the research on physical traits is how similar the perceptions of men and women are when comparing the traits that attracted them. To facilitate this comparison, Table 7.4 has been developed.

When examining the aided approach, men are somewhat more likely to be attracted to a woman who is good looking/attractive, by her hair, who is younger, and by her attire. Women are somewhat more likely to be attracted by a man's eyes, by his athleticism, and by him being older. For all other traits, the differences between men and women are statistically insignificant. Being good looking/attractive and smiling are the consistent physical traits that attract men and women.

When using an unaided approach to identify the physical traits that attract men and women, all traits but five fall out. The eyes and being good looking/attractive dominate for both men and women. Smile, hair, and build/body are clearly attractants, but of somewhat lesser influence.

## Summary

The most significant finding of this chapter is how consistent men and women are in their views. Not only do they identify the same number of traits on average, the top five traits are the same and are ranked similarily. This similarity in traits is probably due to genetically imprinted preferences, reenforced by socio-cultural values.

Table 7.1

## The Physical Traits

Good Looking/Attractive

Build/Body

Height

Hair

Eyes

Sex Appeal

Athletic

Older

Smell/Odor

Attire

Smile

Other Physical Traits

Table 7.2

# The Physical Traits of Men That Attract Women

| | Aided (N=195) | Unaided (N=142) |
|---|---|---|
| Trait | % of Response | % of Response |
| Attractive | 89.4% | 31.0% |
| Build/Body | 76.6% | 14.1% |
| Height | 54.8% | 12.0% |
| Hair | 62.2% | 16.9% |
| Eyes | 84.6% | 39.4% |
| Sex Appeal | 77.1% | 1.4% |
| Athletic | 50.5% | 4.2% |
| Older | 34.0% | 0.0% |
| Younger | 11.2% | 0.0% |
| Smell/Odor | 43.6% | 0.0% |
| Attire | 56.4% | 2.8% |
| Smile | 88.8% | 16.2% |
| Other | 12.8% | 21.1% |

Table 7.3

## The Physical Traits of Women That Attract Men

| | Aided (N=120) | Unaided (N=101) |
|---|---|---|
| Trait | % of Response | % of Response |
| Attractive | 93.9% | 29.1% |
| Build/Body | 79.8% | 18.4% |
| Height | 53.5% | 5.8% |
| Hair | 70.2% | 19.4% |
| Eyes | 77.2% | 34.0% |
| Sex Appeal | 79.8% | 2.9% |
| Athletic | 36.0% | 5.8% |
| Older | 12.4% | 1.0% |
| Younger | 32.5% | 0.0% |
| Smell/Odor | 43.9% | 1.0% |
| Attire | 64.0% | 1.9% |
| Smile | 86.8% | 20.4% |
| Other | 12.4% | 33.0% |

Table 7.4

## A Direct Comparison of the Physical Traits That Attract Men and Women

| | Aided (N=315) | | Unaided (N=243) | |
|---|---|---|---|---|
| Trait | % of Response | | % of Response | |
| | male | female | male | female |
| Attractive | 93.9% | 89.4% | 29.1% | 31.0% |
| Build/Body | 79.8% | 76.6% | 18.4% | 14.1% |
| Height | 53.5% | 54.8% | 5.8% | 12.0% |
| Hair | 70.2% | 62.2% | 19.4% | 16.9% |
| Eyes | 77.2% | 84.6% | 34.0% | 39.4% |
| Sex Appeal | 79.8% | 77.1% | 2.9% | 1.4% |
| Athletic | 36.0% | 50.5% | 5.8% | 4.2% |
| Older | 12.4% | 34.0% | 1.0% | 0.0% |
| Younger | 32.5% | 11.2% | 0.0% | 0.0% |
| Smell/Odor | 43.9% | 43.6% | 1.0% | 0.0% |
| Attire | 64.0% | 56.4% | 1.9% | 2.8% |
| Smile | 86.8% | 88.8% | 20.4% | 16.2% |
| Other | 12.4% | 12.8% | 33.0% | 21.1% |

# The Pastor's Daughter

*I* was a sixteen-year-old high school student and had just finished my junior year. My dad was a pastor at a church in New York. Naturally, I was very involved in the youth group at our church. Each year there was a big leadership convention for youth groups in Colorado that drew thousands of young people from all over the U.S. and Canada. In 1971, it was being held at Colorado State University in Ft. Collins. But the story actually begins before that, much earlier than I realized then.

In March that year, I was visiting a friend of mine, Louise. Her dad was also a pastor, so our families had done a lot of things together. This boy, John, had been dating Louise, but Louise wasn't really interested in him. Louise's mother knew both John and myself. Her mother told me that if we ever met, John and I would probably really hit it off. I saw a picture of him at the house and thought he was really handsome. But since he was nineteen and away at college, nothing more was ever said.

I was the only person from the youth group at my church that attended the conference that summer, so I was pretty much out there by myself. At the first meeting, the conference organizers were introducing the counselors. They had introduced quite a few counselors. Then they introduced this guy. As soon as I saw him, I thought, "Whoa, who is that?" I didn't realize until later that it was the John that Louise had dated.

*Oddly enough, later that evening I was walking with a boy that I knew from another youth group. His name was Wes. It was a warm evening so we walked over to the basement of the boy's dorm to get a Coke from the machine there. Just as we got there, John walked in. He and Wes went to college together so they knew each other. Wes said, "John, do you know Julie?"*

*John turned and gave me this long, head to toe look. It was the kind of look where a boy undresses a girl with his eyes. I was just dying inside because I wanted to meet him and now was my chance to get to know more about him. Because he was older and so handsome, I thought that he was completely out of my league. I was excited and was enjoying just having him look at me, but I didn't think I had a chance with him. It seemed like an eternity before he answered. He kept looking at me through those beautiful greenish brown eyes.*

*Then he said, "Yes, actually I do. We lived in the same town when she was five and I was eight. But you've changed a little bit." I was completely shocked. My family and his had lived in the same town in Indiana where my father had been a pastor. Apparently, we had met through some church activities way back then. Because I was so young, however, I didn't remember. I was surprised that he would remember, since he was only eight. The long examination that he gave me was reconciling that I could be the same girl.*

*I was only five feet tall and very petite, with long dark hair. Bell-bottom pants and tie dyed T-shirts were popular back then, which is what I was wearing. I was barefooted, naturally. Somebody had spilled some pop on the floor, and I stepped in it about that time. I was hopping around trying to get out of it because my feet were all sticky. My bell-bottoms were so long and big that my feet didn't even show.*

John looked down and said, "My gosh, do you have any feet?"
I pulled up my bell-bottoms and said, "Yes, I have feet." He said
they were the smallest feet that he had ever seen. I walked over
and stood next to him so my foot was next to his.

He said, "I bet you have small hands, too." I said, "Yes I do."
I stuck out my hand so he could hold his up against it. He said,
"You are the first girl that I ever met that has smaller hands than
me. I think that I'll keep you."

He tucked my hand in his and looked at Wes and said, "We'll
see you later." He led me away with him holding my hand. I was
thinking, "Holy cow! Where is this going?" I was having a good
time so I just went along with it. I was in shock and star struck
that he was showing interest in me. He was so outrageously handsome that I was nervous and had butterflies in my stomach.

We walked and talked for about twenty minutes. I was pretty
sassy and feisty with him, and he was enjoying it. We continued
walking until we got back to my room. Then he leaned over and
gave me a quick goodnight kiss. I was stunned and overwhelmed.
After a short walk, he had the nerve to kiss me good night! He just
turned and walked away like Joe Cool without saying a word. He
didn't say anything about seeing me again or getting together or
anything. Just a "Good night," a quick little kiss, and, poof, he was
walking away. I was irritated and thought, "I'm not going to let
him have the last word."

I said "Hey, wait a minute!" and ran over to him. I threw my
arms around his neck and gave him a real kiss, long, wet, and passionate. Then I turned and walked into my room without saying
a word. He just stood there in shock with his mouth open.

The next day he saw me walking across campus and ran over
and stopped me. We made arrangements to see each other that
evening. After that, we were pretty much inseparable.

*John was the classic, tall, dark and handsome man. He was six feet tall, had a Fu Manchu type mustache like Joe Namath, and the long hair that was popular then. Of course we both had small hands and feet. John had delicate features for a man—small nose, chin, and mouth. There were the typical early, 70s interests as well. We both liked to play the guitar and write poetry and songs. We were into causes and human rights issues. We were both pretty serious teenagers. We weren't hippies or flower children, but we would have blended right in at Woodstock.*

*After one of our dates that week, he was leaning against a building holding me. I said, "I really hate to admit this, but I'm starting to like you an awful lot." He said, "That's okay, just don't fall in love with me." At that moment I knew that I loved him.*

*At the end of that week in August 1971, I returned home and told my mother that I was going to marry John. He hadn't actually asked at that point, however. But I knew in my heart that we were going to be together. We got married the next July after I graduated from high school. We are now going on twenty-seven years of being happily married.*

*It is strange how a person instantly knows who the right one is. I was only sixteen when I first saw him in Colorado. I knew he was the one for me, from that first night. When you lose yourself in someone else, you gain more in life than you give. When both people feel the same way, the sum is far greater than the two parts. That's the way our marriage has been, both of us help each other to grow and be a better person. There is a synergy, a growth and fulfillment that is hard to explain if you've never experienced it. In order to find real love, you first must be able to give love completely.*

# We Met At First Base

❧

*I*t was August 1978. It was one of those exquisitely beautiful, hot sunny days in Puget Sound. It rains a lot there, but days like that make you forget about all the rain. My company had picked a perfect day for the company picnic and baseball game.

The picnic and game were at Marymore Park in Redmond, Washington, just east of Seattle. It was a beautiful day and a beautiful park.

My company is pretty good sized, so there were a lot of people there. After lunch, there was a softball game scheduled. I was at bat and got a hit and ran to first. The first baseman on the other team said, "Nice hit!" That was when I first saw him. My first thought was, "Wow, what a great looking guy!" He had blond, curly hair, green eyes, and a great body. He was a very strong looking man. At first, it was a very powerful physical attraction, I think. Anyway, I kept watching him during the game, and I just liked the way he moved and looked.

After the game, I found that I knew his roommate, and he introduced us. His name was Jerry. It turned out that we were both the same age, thirty. My girlfriend and I invited them to join us for a picnic right after the game, but he already had plans to have dinner with another lady. I was disappointed at not being able to spend more time with him, and, truthfully, I was a little jealous. I didn't see him again for about a month.

*I was a single parent at the time. My daughter was three and really missed her daddy. I was dating a few men, but nothing was very serious. On the way home one Friday night, I saw his roommate's truck at a bar that we used to frequent, so I stopped. When I went in, Jerry was with his roommate.*

*I sat down to talk to them, and we had a few drinks. Once again, they had dates with other women that night. I could feel that rush of jealousy creeping through my body again. I wanted him to spend time with me, not somebody else. While we were talking, Jerry put his hand on my knee and kept it there. In a way, I thought it was kind of forward of him, but there was something about his touch that I liked. I was wearing shorts so it was a skin on skin thing. Finally, Jerry sent his roommate to pick up their dates because Jerry couldn't let go of my knee. I asked Jerry if he had super glue on his hand. He just laughed but kept rubbing my leg. After his roommate left, Jerry told me where they were going for dinner and dancing. Finally, Jerry left to meet his date.*

*After he left, I gathered up several of my girlfriends, and we just "happened" to end up at the same restaurant where Jerry and his roommate were (with their dates). This gave me a chance to evaluate the other woman. Jerry and I danced once, a slow dance, at my request. It felt good to have his body next to me. While we were dancing, he said that he would call me the next day. My friends and I left fairly soon, but I'm sure the other women were not too happy with us. Slow dancing with their dates probably made them mad. Anyway, I was hoping that they were mad.*

*The next day he called me, and I'm sure that he came over to my house as fast as he could get there. It was like he suddenly noticed me the night before, the way I noticed him at the baseball game. There were several friends from out of town at my house that weekend, and we had a camping trip planned. I invited Jerry.*

*We went camping at a lake up in the Cascades. We had a really great time. We all sat around the campfire for hours that evening, drinking wine and telling jokes. We slept in tents that night since there were some mosquitoes.*

*Jerry didn't have a tent so he threw his sleeping bag in my tent. It was pretty late when we decided to turn in. After we got into our sleeping bags, Jerry and I talked for a long time. Then he leaned over and gave me what was supposed to be a goodnight kiss.*

*That kiss ignited some fireworks. We didn't get to sleep for several hours. A tent isn't exactly the most private place to make love, especially the first time. In the morning we got heckled and teased about all the noises that were coming from our tent. From that point, things went pretty quickly for Jerry and I.*

*He was head over heels in love with me. At first, I thought it was going to be just a summer fling. But he was crazy about me and my daughter. My daughter hated him at first. She didn't want her mom involved with anyone else because all of my attention had been devoted to her. But she gradually accepted him.*

*About two weeks after our camping trip, I had to move from the house that I was living in. He invited me to move in with him, which I did. I was unsure about doing that since our relationship was only two weeks old. But we meshed together perfectly. We were married the next summer. Ironically, his roommate married my sister the following summer. We are all still married.*

*We have been married twenty years now. It seems incredible. In addition to my daughter, we had another daughter, so we raised two girls. Now we have three grandchildren. He has been a wonderful husband and father. I love him much more now than I ever thought I could have when we first met. When I hold him, I can still feel his love flow through me, strengthening my soul.*

## Chapter Eight

# The Personality Traits That Attract Men and Women

*A*n individual's personality plays a powerful role in love at first sight. Since love at first sight was defined as falling in love within sixty minutes of meeting someone, the assessment of another's personality must occur very quickly. But this is something that humans do continually and are very good at.

Have you ever met someone and immediately had a strong dislike or liking for the person? What's at work when this occurs is a comparative perceptual assessment. I say "comparative" because we are comparing another's values and personality to our own. If there is a good match, we tend to like the person. If there are many and significant differences, we tend to dislike the person.

We each have our own personality blueprint that we have developed over the years. At the conscious level, most of us probably are unaware of all of the subtle nuances, preferences, and biases we have. Although the psychologists say that the bulk of our personality is developed by age twelve, we continue to make subtle changes as we go down life's highway. Each pothole, or negative experience, teaches us something. Each positive experience teaches us something. Some of the learning is at the conscious, rational level. Some of the learning is at the subconscious level, and this influences our personality in ways that we, individually, don't realize.

In some way, we have both a conscious and subconscious self-image of who we are. Although we may not understand it very well, it is this self-image that forms the template against which we evaluate other people. When we assess another person, we compare what we see in the other person to ourselves.

This evaluation of another person involves perception and projection. We don't pick up on every cue that another person gives off. We pick up only on those that we know something about, that have meaning to us. This involves "perceptual sensitivity." The more perceptually sensitive a person is, the more they notice the verbal and nonverbal cues given off by another. A highly sensitive person is more aware of the personalities of other people. Women are supposed to be better at this than men, in general. Perceptual sensitivity also can be accompanied by perceptual selectivity.

Perceptual selectivity means we notice things that are important to us. If another person has a common interest in our favorite activity, we focus on that, and ignore other cues. You may know someone who claims to be attracted to certain people based on a specific part of their anatomy. This simply means that this person is perceptually sensitive to a chosen body part, and he or she probably pays relatively little attention to other parts of the anatomy. These examples are all at the conscious level of perception. But exactly the same thing happens subconsciously. We may

*Love at First Sight*

notice how another person interacts with other people and pick up numerous cues.

When we see a person giving off cues, we must interpret what the cue means. This is where our own personality template comes in. Our brain notices the cue and interprets the meaning based on our own experience and learning. This is where many misunderstandings occur in an international context. We may be very aware of social cues in the United States, but know very little of the social cues in China, Japan, Germany, or Australia. Either we don't even notice the cue because we haven't been conditioned to it, or we misinterpret it because we don't understand the other socio-cultural context.

Once we interpret the verbal and nonverbal cues of someone else, we make projections of what the other person's personality is like. For example, one of the women in the love stories said, "I noticed him when he first entered the room. I liked the way he moved, he had an air of confidence about him. I hate it when men walk like they are apologizing for being there." This woman noticed the way the man walked and how he held himself. Based on his body language, she projected self-confidence back to the man. She consciously and subconsciously picked up on an array of cues, interpreted them, and made a conclusion about the man's personality.

Another woman was at a party and noticed a man leaning against the wall, watching other people. She said, "He had cat-like eyes, silently standing there, taking in everything." She went on to say that he was the strong, silent type. This lady saw the cues of the man watching people, apparently studying them, and keeping to himself. From this she concluded that he was the strong, silent type who never missed a thing. Again, this is perception and projection at work.

In both of these examples, the whole process of perception, interpretation, and projection took no more than ten seconds. In both of these situations, the perception and projection were very accurate. And in both of these situations, the woman fell in love with and married the man. While falling in love usually takes a little more time, it also can happen very quickly.

Attempting to identify all of the possible cues is beyond the scope of this book. Most are situation specific and would vary with small changes in the situation. While we can't identify all the possible cues, we can identify the personality traits.

## The Personality Traits

As with the physical traits, the literature on interpersonal attraction was reviewed to identify the personality traits that attract others. While it was less of a problem than for physical traits, a similar unisex approach was used. The personality traits were phrased in such a way to be equally appropriate for men and women. The personality traits included in the questionnaire are presented in Table 8.1. Each of these thirteen traits have been found to be, at some point, influential in mate selection in some way.

## Self-Confidence

Self-confidence implies that a person is confident of their abilities. Typically, this means the person is not afraid of risk, of taking a chance. This usually is reflected by a willingness to try new activities, often daring, exciting endeavors. The self-confident person assumes that their innate ability will see them through, and make them successful. A self-confident person is often the Type A, achievement-oriented personality who consistently sets high goals and works hard to achieve them.

In mate selection, self-confidence probably is linked to survival. A self-confident mate is more likely to survive over the long-term, even in perilous situations. On a more modern note, self-confident people are more apt to assume leadership roles and be successful in their careers.

It may be that self-confidence in a man is more appealing to a woman than self-confidence in a woman is appealing to men. This would be consistent with the assumed role that the man is the head of the household. While many might argue that there is no good reason to assume that the man is the head of the household in modern society, there are several people, both men and women, who still accept the traditional family roles.

Regardless of *why* self-confidence is appealing to others, there is consistent research support for self-confidence being an appealing trait. One of the women in the love stories described her man as "so self-assured, he just knew what he wanted in life and how to get there." But like many personality traits, self-confidence is closely related to some of the other traits on our list.

Marie felt her man's self-confidence was sexy: "I just thought he was a very sexy guy. He had such a presence about him. He is one of those stand up and take a look at me type of people when they walk in the door. He is very polite and very well spoken."

Doreen also watched her man's walk and interpreted the walk as self-confident, self-assured: "He had leather heels on his shoes, and his heels clicked as he walked. He had the strongest, sturdiest walk I have ever seen. It was a real deliberate walk, and ooh, I liked that. Here was a guy that really has the stuff. He was very sure of himself. He had a nice smile. He was very friendly and very open. He wasn't pushy, just a real friendly guy. He just had a really nice, warm personality."

## Fun

People like to replicate positive, enjoyable experiences and avoid negative experiences in life. Therefore, being "fun" is an intuitively logical trait that would fit men and women equally well. The logic is that if someone else appears to be fun, some of that fun will rub off. If a person has experienced a difficult time in life, they may be more in need of having fun.

One of the women in the research had gone through a difficult divorce. After the divorce, she sealed herself off for a year. She went to work and went home to her apartment. Other than for work, she seldom left her apartment for any reason. Her big outing was to stop by the grocery store a few days a week. One of her friends was seriously worried about her and talked her into going to a church barbecue. There, after a year of social deprivation, she experienced love at first sight.

She described the man as "Fun, fun, fun. Life was just a big party to him. You never knew what to expect...we went sailing, scuba diving, skiing in Europe." When she described him throughout the interview, fun was the central theme.

## Shared Values/Common Background

As we saw from some of the results presented earlier, most people want someone who is similar in many ways. This similarity reenforces and validates our own self-image. We often feel a kinship with those who have common values and experiences. This similarity is the foundation upon which we can add interesting differences that may complement us in some way.

For example, Julie and John had many similar interests. They came from very religious families in the same state. They both played the guitar and wrote poetry. They were into causes and human rights issues. They were both pretty serious teenagers. It was on this base of a common background and shared values that they built a twenty-nine year (and still going) marriage.

## Dominant/Assertive

Traditionally this is more of a male-oriented trait and one that may be appealing to some women. This trait implies that a person can make a decision and is not wishy-washy. In a relationship, it is the person who makes a decision and takes charge. For example, a man might tell a woman, I've made early dinner reservations at a nice restaurant so we can attend the theater afterwards. As one woman stated, "I hate it when a man always asks what I want to do, forcing me to make the decision. I want a man who is strong enough to anticipate what I'd like, and then surprises me with it."

This trait does not suggest that because a man is dominant that he dominates the woman or vice versa. It simply means that a person is willing to make decisions proactively without waiting for another's seal of approval. This would probably lead to a little more spontaneity in a relationship. Each partner would be willing to surprise the other.

## Aggressive

Being aggressive is related somewhat to the dominant/assertive trait and implies a bias for action. Aggressive does not imply physical aggression. An aggressive person would want to get started soon, and would likely be the pursuer in a relationship.

Some women like to be pursued by a man, knowing that they are desired, wanted. Therefore, being aggressive is more of a male trait that would be appealing to women. While an aggressive woman might be appealing to some men, the level of aggressiveness displayed would probably be lower.

## Outgoing

As a personality trait, outgoing is a bit more ambiguous than the others. Outgoing conjures up images of active, fun, spontaneous, and, perhaps, carefree. Due to mood transference, being around an outgoing person would be enjoyable because they would make us happy.

An outgoing person would probably be the life of the party. Or, the outgoing person might suggest doing something active instead of sitting around watching television. The more daring, active personality would pull others along, getting everyone involved.

For example, Linda felt immersed in a sea of outgoing people. "Working in the Magic Kingdom, with the work environment there, there were some really close friendships that developed. I was always an outgoing person, yet when I got to Disney World, I was all of a sudden thrown into a big group of people who were also outgoing. You have to be a certain kind of person to do that job. So, I automatically knew that he would be an open, fun type of person. The fact that he was really beautiful just added to it. When I found out that he was in college and that he had a good future in front of him, that just showed it all to me, that he was the one for me."

This respondent shows how an outgoing person affects other people. "One of the reasons I was instantly attracted to him was his dancing. I just fell in love with the way he danced. I was in love, that was it. He is very friendly. He is a people person and that attracted me to him too because at that time I was very shy, very, very shy. Just his presence invited you to be a part of whatever he was doing. I couldn't talk to anybody freely and he did. That attracted me to him because he was a total opposite of me at that time."

## Intelligence

At its simplest, intelligence is defined as the ability to learn. People like to be around intelligent people who can discuss a wide range of issues. Intelligent people are often described as interesting or worldly because of their awareness of many subjects.

It may be that intelligence is an admirable trait based on genetic selection. Intelligent people probably had a greater chance of survival historically. They would be able to reason their way through challenges more successfully than less intelligent people. In modern society, intelligence usually implies a greater likelihood of career success. This suggests that intelligent people will have greater wealth and resources, resulting in a more comfortable life.

But intelligence in a potential mate is a relative term. We each assess the intelligence of another based on our own self-image. If we think another person knows more than we do, we might view them as intelligent. Although knowledge and education are somewhat different than intelligence, these are often used as surrogate indicators. High levels of education, for example, would typically imply high intelligence. Since we don't go around administering intelligence tests to others, intelligence is very much of a perceptional trait.

## Generosity

Generosity is the willingness to share with others. This normally implies sharing wealth, but could imply sharing time or affection with another. It may be that generosity is related to being a good provider who shares resources with a mate and children.

Generosity is probably a trait that women would find appealing in a man rather than the inverse. This is due to traditional male-female roles in most societies in the world. For example, during courtship a man often picks up the tab. Or a man will buy his date flowers. These are indicators of generosity.

Regarding love at first sight, generosity may be more difficult to evaluate. Generosity is displayed as a behavior, the sharing of resources. This behavior may not be apparent in the first sixty minutes of meeting someone. Therefore, generosity may not be observable initially and may be relatively more important when a person falls in love more gradually.

## Kindness

Kindness is a type of behavioral interaction with other people. Kindness would be reflected in a caring, empathetic attitude, a genuine concern for others. A kind person would probably be relatively more socially sensitive, pick up on cues given off by others, and then engage in behavior that would elevate the mood of others. In short, kindness means someone is a nice person.

Kindness is probably an appealing trait because most people want to be treated that way. If we see someone treating others with kindness, we assume that we would be treated the same way. The implication is that we generalize this trait broadly based upon relatively few cues.

This respondent from South Carolina shows how kindness is viewed by others. "We had both been widowed when we met. Our mutual friends kept telling me, 'He was good to his wife. He was so good to his wife.' That was a big appeal to me. He was very calm and friendly, and an easy conversationalist. I trusted him because my friends spoke so highly of him, and they knew me from so many years. I knew that they would not introduce me to anybody who was not very special. In conversation, we realized that we had a lot in common. That was a big attraction."

The following lady equated kindness and being nice. "It was just something about him. He was just such a nice person. He was very nice, very soft-spoken, and very pleasant. Something about him caught my eye."

This respondent had a similar view, but expressed it a little differently. "His politeness is what attracted me to him. He was kind. He didn't make any cruel remarks. He was just a gentleman. He hadn't been like any other person or any other man I had known. He was gentle. He is very kind and to this day, he still opens the car door."

## Good with Kids

Good with kids is a trait that women find appealing in a man. This generally is relevant regardless of whether the woman wants children or not. And it is usually relevant regardless of age. According to our respondents, displaying good parenting skills most likely suggests that a man would be a good father. And women have a genetic preference to select a mate who would be a good father.

Good with kids may be a trait of women that is appealing to a man. If we are planning a family, good parenting skills would be a consideration in mate selection for both fathers and mothers. But it is likely that this trait would be more important to a woman since having a child is a bigger physical and emotional investment for her.

Like generosity, this trait may be less relevant for love at first sight. If there are no children present when love at first sight occurs, this trait could not be displayed. Therefore, it would be difficult to evaluate it. However, a liking of children could be verbally expressed.

## Good Communication/Conversation

Open communication is at the heart of a good relationship. There must be a willingness to discuss decisions, values, and dreams. Without good communication, a long-term relationship would be difficult or impossible. At some level, everyone knows this. But this trait is supposed to be more important to women, according to the literature. This may go back to early childhood development where boys are taught to be independent, and girls are taught to be more considerate. Girls are quickly taught to communicate more openly with their friends.

One of the comments made by an astronaut after he returned from a space mission was revealing. A reporter asked him if he was looking forward to seeing his family. He indicated that, of course, he missed his family. But there was one thing that worried him. He had read that the average woman speaks ten thousand words in a day. He had been gone for ten days, so he figured that his wife had one hundred thousand words saved up for him.

Research on interpersonal communication indicates that communication flows, both volume and depth of discussion, are at their highest during courtship. About a year after marriage, the volume of communication begins to decline. The decline in communication continues for ten to fifteen years and then stabilizes at a much lower level.

Initially, in a love at first sight experience, being easy to talk to is probably a good indicator of communication. Many of the love stories say "we talked and talked and talked." Or some said, "It was like we'd known each other for years, he/she was so easy to talk to." One lady said that, "After making love at night, we would talk until dawn. We talked about everything."

Another woman from Seattle provided an array of physical and personality traits, and included communication. "He has blond hair and hazel eyes. He is just funny and really enjoys life. He has a good time, and is just very fun to be around. He has a great personality, and is very attractive in that way. He is very easy to talk to. He just makes you feel very comfortable."

## Humorous

People like to laugh and have a good time. Therefore, having a good sense of humor is appealing to both men and women. Being humorous is also probably closely aligned with the fun trait. There were many of the stories that said, "he made me laugh," or, "she was so funny."

In a social context, being humorous would be an easy trait to observe. But being humorous does not necessarily mean telling jokes. Being humorous could be just a quick wit, a play on words, or a facial expression. Regardless of how humor is displayed, people like to be around others who make them feel good.

## Warmth

Like outgoing, warmth is a somewhat ambiguous trait. Personal warmth implies that a person is easy to approach. Those with warmth would appear to be socially sensitive and express genuine concern for others. They would have some degree of charisma, that innate ability to relate to others very quickly.

While warmth may be hard to tightly define, it is well understood by most people. In the love stories, the term was used frequently. Typically, the term was used in combinations like, "she was so warm and friendly," or, "he was warm and engaging."

## The Research Results

As with the physical traits discussed in the previous chapter, the personality traits were studied using a split research design. Some of the respondents were presented with the traits in Table 8.1, individually. They were asked to identify which personality traits attracted them to the other person by indicating "yes" or "no." The other respondents were asked to list the personality traits that attracted them to the other person using an unaided approach with no prompting.

As you might expect, the aided approach resulted in five to six times as many traits being identified as the unaided approach. And, somewhat unexpectedly, the differences in the number of traits identified by men and women were small. Since women are supposed to be more socially sensitive, I thought they would pick up, and use, a larger number of social cues. Also, since women place a greater emphasis on personality than men, this category was thought to be more critical to them. Neither belief was supported.

## The Traits of Men That Attract Women

There was a substantial contrast between the aided and unaided approaches. When provided a list, the women identified an average of 9.77 personality traits of men. When simply asked to identify the personality traits, women identified an average of 1.53 traits. The top two traits were the same for both approaches, humorous and kindness. After those two traits, there were major differences using the two approaches.

### Aided

When read the list of personality traits, three were identified by over 90 percent of all respondents (Table 8.2). Humorous and kindness were mentioned by 91.2 percent of all respondents. Intelligence was mentioned by 90.8 percent of respondents. Fun was not far behind at 88.8 percent. It appears that humorous, kindness, and fun cluster close together conceptually. After these top four personality traits, there was a bit of a drop off to a second cluster of traits that were mentioned by 80 to 84 percent of respondents.

Warmth (83.7 percent), generosity (82.4 percent), self-confidence (82.3 percent), good communication/conversation (80.7 percent), and outgoing (79.8 percent) were mentioned with about the same frequency. Four of these traits, warmth, self-confidence, good communication, and outgoing, bundle well with the humorous and fun traits. This creates a total package of a fun, upbeat person who "plays well with others."

There was a substantial drop off to shared values/common background (64.5 percent) and good with kids (63.8 percent). It is entirely possible that neither of these are observable in another when love at first sight strikes. Dominance/assertive (40.7 percent) and aggressive (28.3 percent) were mentioned by a minority of women. The lesser importance of these last two traits may reflect the changing values of women in American society.

The women identified relatively few other personality traits when using the aided approach. Of the twenty-three other mentions, only honesty (2) and charisma (2) were identified more than once. There were nineteen personality traits identified just once such as adventurous, mischievous, he loved me, and laugh.

## Unaided

When simply asked what personality traits attracted the women to the men, the volume of traits fell off substantially. The women identified an average of 1.53 per respondent. Interestingly, this was nearly identical to the men's average of 1.54.

Of the traits mentioned, there were two that stood out from the rest. Humorous (33.1 percent) and kindness (25.4 percent) were the two most frequently identified traits. These were the top two traits using the aided approach as well. The implication is that having a good sense of humor and being kind are two aspects of a man's personality that consistently and instantly appeal to women.

After the top two traits, there was a substantial drop off to a cluster of four traits. These were outgoing (12 percent), fun (9.9 percent), generosity (9.2 percent), and intelligence (9.2 percent). Humorous, kindness, and fun were three of the top four traits in both approaches.

The biggest difference in the top traits was for intelligence. When prompted, more than 90 percent of women said that the intelligence of the man attracted them. When the unaided approach was used, less than 10 percent of the women said the man's intelligence attracted them. Perhaps the respondents felt that intelligence *should* be important in a mate, it seems intuitively logical. Therefore, when reminded of the trait, the women would think, "well of course he is smart," and then respond "yes."

This halo effect may also explain the large difference in traits identified using the two approaches. Both men and women may be initially attracted by only a few traits. After they realize that they are falling in love with the other person, they start seeing positive aspects in everything the other person does. This halo effect extends a halo for the key initial traits to all traits.

Women identified forty-four other personality traits of men that attracted them. The most frequently mentioned traits were gentle (5), happy (3), caring (3), witty (2), sweet (2), fun loving (2), romantic (2), personable (2), and attentive (2). These accounted for about half of all the "other" traits. The remaining twenty-one traits were mentioned by only one woman each.

# The Traits of Women That Attract Men
## Aided

When using the aided approach, men identified an average of 9.01 personality traits of women that attracted them. This is almost one trait per respondent less than the women's average of 9.77. While this is statistically significant, the difference is not extremely large. And the average number of traits identified were nearly identical using the unaided approach. While there were no big differences in the volume of traits identified, there were differences in the importance of various traits.

The top personality trait of women that attracted men was fun, identified by 89.3 percent of men (Table 8.3). The next traits were outgoing (84.1 percent), good communication/conversation (83.2 percent), intelligence (81.3 percent), and humorous (80.5 percent). Apparently, men want a woman who is active, fun to be around, and who they can easily talk with.

After these first five traits, there were four that were mentioned. These were kindness (77.0 percent), warmth (75.2 percent), self-confidence (71.7 percent), and generosity (71.4 percent). Following this cluster of four were good with kids (63.9 percent) and shared values/common background (57.5 percent). According to the survey, men don't find the traits of dominance/assertive (35.4 percent) or aggressive (25.4 percent) appealing.

Men identified only eleven "other" personality traits of women that attracted them. Only two of these traits were identified by more than one man. These were honest (3) and loving (2). The remaining traits were identified by only one man each.

## Unaided

When men simply identified the personality traits of women that attracted them, a cluster of four traits stood out. These were outgoing (23.5 percent), kindness (21.4 percent), humorous (21.4 percent), and fun (18.6 percent). No other trait was identified by more than 10 percent of men. These four traits cluster well together conceptually. Men want to be around women who are happy and active.

As expected, the "other" category had a larger number of traits than when using the aided approach. Men identified thirty-two other personality traits. The dominant traits were shy (10), honest (6), loving (4), sincere (2), bubbly (2), and lighthearted (2). The remaining seven traits were each mentioned by only one man.

The most notable finding from the other category was being shy. Men find this appealing in women, but it was not mentioned by women. Being shy and coy is a behavior that some women purposefully engage in when they are attracted to a man. Other women may become nervous and withdrawn when they are around a man that they are strongly attracted to. But regardless of why they are shy, some men find this behavior appealing.

## Men vs. Women

There are some rather significant differences between men and women in the personality traits that attracted them to the other person. Their differences were most apparent using the aided approach (Table 8.4).

Women identified seven personality traits of men much more frequently than men. These all had differences of seven to thirteen percentage points. Kindness, generosity, humor, intelligence, warmth, self-confidence, and shared values/common background were male personality traits that were more appealing to women.

There were only two personality traits of women that men indicated more frequently than women. These were outgoing and good communication/conversation. And the differences here were much smaller than for women, only three to five percentage points. Women do appear to evaluate somewhat more personality traits of men when an aided approach is used.

The top three personality traits of women that men are attracted to are fun, outgoing, and good communication/conversation. The top three traits of men that women are attracted to are humorous, kindness, and intelligence. However, these differences are not as evident when using an unaided approach.

When using an unaided approach, the top three personality traits of women that men are attracted to are outgoing, kindness, and humorous. The top three traits of men that women are attracted to are humorous, kindness, and outgoing. The top three are the same for both men and women. However, women place much greater emphasis on a man being humorous and somewhat more on kindness, while men place greater emphasis on the woman being outgoing.

## Summary

Regardless of which approach is used, the personality traits of humorous, kindness, outgoing, and fun, are generally appealing to both men and women. Being around happy people is a positive, pleasurable experience. A striking finding is that intelligence is quite important when the respondents were reminded of it. But intelligence was mentioned infrequently when not prompted. Perhaps intelligence is something that is evaluated later in a relationship.

Table 8.1

# The Personality Traits

Self-confidence

Fun

Shared Values/Common Background

Dominance/Assertive

Aggressive

Outgoing

Intelligence

Generosity

Kindness

Good With Kids

Good Communication/Conversation

Humorous

Warmth

Other Personality Traits

Table 8.2

## The Personality Traits of Men That Attract Women

|  | Aided (N=195) | Unaided (N=142) |
|---|---|---|
| Trait | % of Response | % of Response |
| Self-confidence | 82.3% | 7.0% |
| Fun | 88.8% | 9.9% |
| Shared Values | 64.5% | 2.8% |
| Assertive | 40.7% | 2.1% |
| Aggressive | 28.3% | 0.7% |
| Outgoing | 79.8% | 12.0% |
| Intelligence | 90.8% | 9.2% |
| Generosity | 82.4% | 9.2% |
| Kindness | 91.2% | 25.4% |
| Good with Kids | 63.8% | 0.0% |
| Communication | 80.7% | 5.6% |
| Humorous | 91.2% | 33.1% |
| Warmth | 83.7% | 4.9% |
| Other | 14.6% | 33.6% |

Table 8.3

# The Personality Traits of Women That Attract Men

|  | Aided (N=120) | Unaided (N=101) |
|---|---|---|
| Trait | % of Response | % of Response |
| Self-confidence | 71.7% | 1.9% |
| Fun | 89.3% | 18.6% |
| Shared Values | 57.5% | 3.0% |
| Assertive | 35.4% | 0.9% |
| Aggressive | 25.4% | 1.9% |
| Outgoing | 84.1% | 23.5% |
| Intelligence | 81.3% | 9.8% |
| Generosity | 71.4% | 5.9% |
| Kindness | 77.0% | 21.4% |
| Good with Kids | 63.9% | 0.9% |
| Communication | 83.2% | 3.9% |
| Humorous | 80.5% | 21.4% |
| Warmth | 75.2% | 8.9% |
| Other | 10.0% | 31.5% |

Table 8.4

# A Direct Comparison of Personality Traits That Attract Men and Women

| | Aided (N=195) | | Unaided (N=142) | |
|---|---|---|---|---|
| Trait | % of Response | | % of Response | |
| | male | female | male | female |
| Self-confidence | 71.7% | 82.3% | 1.9% | 7.0% |
| Fun | 89.3% | 88.8% | 18.6% | 9.9% |
| Shared Values | 57.5% | 64.5% | 3.0% | 2.8% |
| Assertive | 35.4% | 40.7% | 0.9% | 2.1% |
| Aggressive | 25.4% | 28.3% | 1.9% | 0.7% |
| Outgoing | 84.1% | 79.8% | 23.5% | 12.0% |
| Intelligence | 81.3% | 90.8% | 9.8% | 9.2% |
| Generosity | 71.4% | 82.4% | 5.9% | 9.2% |
| Kindness | 77.0% | 91.2% | 21.4% | 25.4% |
| Good with Kids | 63.9% | 63.8% | 0.9% | 0.0% |
| Communication | 83.2% | 80.7% | 3.9% | 5.6% |
| Humorous | 80.5% | 91.2% | 21.4% | 33.1% |
| Warmth | 75.2% | 83.7% | 8.9% | 4.9% |
| Other | 10.0% | 14.6% | 31.5% | 33.6% |

# My Great "What If"

*I*t was the summer of 1984, and I was living in Freeport, Texas. I had been a virtual recluse for the past year since my divorce. I'd go to work and go home and that was it. My big social outing was stopping by the grocery store a few times a week. In the evening and on the weekends, I'd read and watch television. My divorce just seemed to drain all of the emotional energy out of me. Looking back now, it was a pretty pitiful existence. I was probably in a dark depression for the whole year.

There was a lady who lived near me in my apartment complex, and she was genuinely worried about me. She told me that I had to get out and do something. Her church had a big singles group, and she got me to go to that a few times. I went to the meetings mostly to appease my friend. I wasn't really trying to meet someone. It was just a way to kill some time, a bit of a diversion from the walls of my apartment.

Each summer, the singles group would have a "pig roast" on the beach. It was actually more of a big Texas barbecue than an actual pig roast. But singles groups from the surrounding towns would come, so it was a pretty big deal. They would have volleyball, baseball, horseshoes, lots of food, and music. About two hundred people would normally show up.

The pig roast was at a beach house that was owned by a member of our singles group. I wasn't sure that I even wanted to go to the pig roast. After a year of isolation, I was unsure of myself and still pretty socially withdrawn. So I went out to the beach house the night before the barbecue with some other people to help set things up for the next day and check things out. I was partly nervous, partly scared, just a whirl of mixed emotions.

I didn't really know the man who owned the beach house very well, but we had met once. His name was Steve. Steve was very warm and friendly, a real nice person. Knowing him a little meant that there would be at least one person that I could talk to.

Ultimately, I decided to go to the pig roast, but wasn't planning on getting involved in the activities. I was just going to stay off to the side and be a spectator. The back deck of the beach house was actually over the water, so I thought I'd hang out there. Steve, myself, and one other person were sitting on the deck having a glass of wine and talking. Most of the people were down on the beach.

A friend of Steve's, his name was James, walked over to where we were sitting. He was with a very attractive young lady. I felt this immediate physical attraction to James. It was like, "Wow! What is happening?" But since he was with someone else, I kept it to myself. James started teasing me about being so white. I literally had not been out in the sun for a year, and I have a pretty light complexion anyway. He said he had never seen anyone so white. So we bantered back and forth at each other for a while.

It was fun joking around with James, but I wasn't sure I wanted to start anything. Since he was with a pretty young thing, that made the situation complicated. James and his friend left, but I kept thinking about him. Truthfully, I kept glancing over to the beach to see if I could see him. Having such a strong physical attraction to someone was a little scary. I didn't completely trust myself or my feelings.

In about fifteen minutes, James came back alone. I asked him where his girlfriend was, and he just said he got rid of her. Although I was definitely attracted to him, I wasn't going to get involved in a three-way triangle. I wasn't even sure what I wanted. It was a bit confusing. My hesitation and caution apparently came across as very coy and hard-to-get. James told me later this really attracted him.

We talked for a while, throwing jabs back and forth. He was just very quick-witted, a lot of fun. Then he asked me to play volleyball on the beach, which we did. By the time we finished playing volleyball, it was almost dusk. James asked me if I wanted to go sailing. I told him I didn't think so because it was getting dark. He said that sailing in the evening was the best time.

James had a condominium near Steve's beach house. He had a fourteen-foot catamaran sailboat at his place. I was pretty nervous about going sailing with a stranger at night. James said he often sailed at night, and he seemed to know what he was doing. So I threw caution to the wind and went. My plans to be a spectator that day were slipping away pretty quickly. The evening was beautiful, one of those warm Gulf coast nights. There was a light wind, and even the humidity wasn't too bad.

We sailed and talked and talked. We watched the sun go down and cast this rosy haze over the water. The sky and the water seemed to merge together. I looked into his blue eyes, and, oh boy, I just fell in love big time. I just knew it in my heart, but I wasn't about to let it show. I certainly never planned on this happening so fast. I had planned on just going to the pig roast and watching people, and here I was on a sailboat in the Gulf, falling in love.

The sky grew darker and the moon came out. The moon was reflecting off the water and off the sail. It was just so romantic. You could see the lights twinkling along the coastline miles away.

*We were talking, or I should say I was talking, and he reached over, put his arms around me and kissed me. I never finished that sentence. I was so excited that my heart just went pitter-patter, like a little girl having a crush on a boy. He held me and his body felt so good next to me. We had this tremendous connection between us. It was like we'd known each other for so long. Everything felt so comfortable, although I'd only known him for a few hours. After that night, we were inseparable for two and a half years. It was like an endless dream.*

*James' condo was right on the beach. He had a hot tub on the roof. We used to sit in the hot tub and drink wine and listen to the waves crashing on the beach. He was always so romantic.*

*He was fun, fun, fun. Life was just a big party for him. You never knew what to expect. We did so many fun things. He bought a bigger sailboat, and we went sailing every weekend. We would sail out to a drilling rig in the Gulf and tie up to it. Then we'd go scuba diving off the boat and spear fish. He had a barbe-cue grill on the boat, and we'd drink wine and grill our fresh fish. Sometimes we would spend the night out on the boat.*

*We'd always be doing something. We went scuba diving in the Bahamas, and we went snow skiing in Europe. But it got to the point where I wanted to settle down and start a family. And that just wasn't him.*

*He was so much fun to be with, but I couldn't see him settling down. It got to where I was putting pressure on him to change somewhat. He was resisting, so I felt I had to break things off and get on with life. I truly loved him deeply, but I had to walk away to have the family I wanted. I didn't want to waste a lot of years, living for something that wasn't truly me.*

*I really missed his laughter and smile and touch. I felt cold inside, but not at all like after my divorce. Being with James had helped draw me out of my shell and get my life going again, and for that I was thankful. He had helped me realize that having a family was central to my life.*

*He kept trying to come back for a while. We even started seeing each other again. Trying to get together again just reinforced that I made the right decision earlier. James was a fantastic man, but being a father wasn't on his agenda. And that was a high priority on mine. That one issue, and it was a big one, was the only thing that kept us apart.*

*I'm really happy with my life now, but it is completely different than being with James. I have a good husband and family. I have a very stable life. But James was excitement personified.*

*A strange thing happened about five years ago. My husband and I were moving from Freeport, and the movers were packing my house. They mentioned that they had just packed up a house on the beach the previous day. Naturally that peaked my interest so I asked them who it was. It was James' house. He was moving to Tennessee.*

*It was just such a coincidence that I had to phone him and wish him good luck. He was still single. I guess that was our final goodbye as it's been five years since I've seen him or talked to him. It's strange how you never know when the last time that you see someone or talk to them will be. But he was just so much fun that I can't help but think of him from time to time. James will always be my great "what if."*

## ∞ **Chapter Nine** ∞

# *The Career/Achievement Traits That Attract*
# *Men and Women*

*W*hen asked to identify the category of traits that most attracted a person to someone else, the personality and physical traits clearly dominated. Therefore, it is quite likely that the career/achievement traits tend to be implicitly used as supplementary evaluative criteria, more like icing on the cake or maybe even decorations on the icing. For example, a woman might find a man to be very charming, engaging, and humorous. Then she might consider him to be handsome and physically fit. These might be completely adequate to stimulate her interest in him. But when she finds out he also is professionally successful, she may consider him to be "marriage material."

If a woman were to develop a list of criteria that she ideally wanted in a man, and rank ordered the list, career/achievement issues would probably be on the list. But most would be in the bottom half of the criteria. If a man did the same thing, the career/achievement traits would be even lower on the list. And many men, if not most, wouldn't even have career achievement traits on the list at all.

As we will see, women consistently identified career/achievement traits much more frequently than men. In other words, women do find career/achievement traits of men to be appealing. However, men identify these traits of women much less frequently as an attractant.

## The Career/Achievement Traits

As with other categories, a list of traits was developed by reviewing the literature on interpersonal attraction (Table 9.1). However, relatively few studies addressed this issue. Therefore, the list of traits was somewhat shorter than for physical and personality traits. However, there is a justification for each trait. As with other traits, the traits were stated in such a way that they were applicable to both men and women.

### Talent

Being talented implies that a person has good skills for their chosen career. Thus, this term would apply to almost any career. A teacher might be well organized and interact with children very well. An artist might be skilled at capturing emotional depth in the subjects painted. A singer might have a particularly clear voice and good voice control. An accountant may know all of the intricate nuances of tax law.

Regardless of the career choice, being talented implies that a person's skill sets are particularly well suited for their career. But being talented is not quite the same as the next trait, professionally successful. A person may be very talented, but fail to use those talents effectively. A talented person may lack motivation and squander their abilities.

There are numerous examples of young men who excelled at basketball. Their skills are equal to or better than professional basketball players. But, perhaps their grades are low and they can't get into college to showcase their talents. Or, many other events or career goals are pulling them away from utilizing their talents. There are many people around the world who have special talents, but fail to utilize them.

## Professionally Successful

To be successful, a person must have some degree of talent, but there must also be something more. There must be motivation, perseverance, opportunity, and good choices along the way. All of these together create success. However, at its best, success is defined internally.

Being successful means to achieve your heart's true desire and dreams. It means to know who you are and be content with the person in the mirror. It means to be proud of what a person has accomplished in their career. For example, a teacher might be very successful because he/she touched the lives of children in a positive way. A national park service employee might be proud of preserving the natural beauty of America and sharing it with other people. These are commendable ways to evaluate professional success. Society often disregards the internal measures of success and focuses on the external, more observable indicators.

Unfortunately, many people equate professional success with income level. Using this standard, neither the teacher nor park service employee would be viewed as successful by most people. To others, the career itself may convey success. Being a doctor or actor might convey success to some. In some countries, being a college professor is very prestigious, in other countries, it is not. To some, being an attorney implies success, to many, it is one of the lowest professions. The implication is that, like beauty, professional success is in the eye of the beholder. What may constitute success for one person may be abject failure for another.

Given that the majority of people are young (under age thirty), when they experience love at first sight, it is also logical that career/achievement traits are relatively less important. In most careers, success requires a significant amount of learning and experience, and this takes time. Typically, real success doesn't come until after age forty or so. Since there were relatively few respondents over age forty when they experienced love at first sight, professional success may not have happened yet for most people.

## Social Status

People with high social status may be appealing to some. Being a prominent, well-known citizen, such as a politician or an actor, may convey higher social status. In some parts of the U.S., having the right family name conveys status. The logic behind the appeal of social status is that a person would marry into the same social strata and be accepted.

As with being professionally successful, having high social status may take many years to achieve. Therefore, the young age at which love at first sight occurs may constrain the social status trait. And some may not perceive or even know of the other person's social status initially.

There was a tall, six feet, eight inches, very athletic, muscular man who met a very attractive lady. There was obviously a mutual attraction between the two people. She asked him what he did for a living. He said he played for the Utah Jazz, but she still didn't know what that meant. He explained that it was a professional basketball team. The social status of the perennial NBA All

Star who was subsequently selected as MVP of the league was totally oblivious to the woman. They ultimately were married, anyway.

## Well Educated

While professional success and high social status usually take many years to achieve, education comes earlier in life. It is also a more readily apparent trait. As with many other concepts, being well educated is a relative issue. To a person with only a high school education, a college graduate may seem well educated. To a person with a master's or doctorate degree, the person with a bachelor's degree may not be well educated. And, to some, formal education or degrees, may not convey true education at all.

The purpose of formal education is twofold. One purpose is to teach people how to learn. The other purpose is to help people acquire knowledge and/or skills. As a former professor, I have seen many students who never really achieved either. They may have graduated with a bachelor's degree, but they never learned much about learning or acquired much true knowledge. I have seen people who never attended college develop a hunger to learn and acquire far more knowledge.

Despite these issues, education is generally held to be positively related to career success. The more education and knowledge that a person has, the more successful they should end up being. Therefore, education may be an early indicator of subsequent wealth.

## Income Potential

Somewhat akin to education, income potential implies that a person will do well in life. It is more a perceptual expectation than an easily evaluated trait. The young often do not have a set career path. They often do not really know where life's road will take them. They may not realize that they will change their careers numerous times. But academic, and, to a lesser degree, athletic achievements are often used as predictors of subsequent success.

There is a joke about what a high school student would call a "nerd" ten years later. The answer is "Boss." The implication is the focus on academics early leads to success later in life. This does not imply that academic and athletic achievement are mutually exclusive.

## Control of Resources

A person who has a lot of financial resources is often viewed as a "good catch." The implication is that a person with resources will share those resources with another. But, like several other career/achievement traits, the youth factor may work against this trait. It takes time to acquire resources, or assets. Since love at first sight is predominantly an event for the young, most have probably not had time to acquire much.

This concept may be relative, however. To an eighteen-year-old girl, a twenty-one-year-old man who has a job, owns a car, and has a few household effects may be perceived to have resources. He may simply have somewhat more than she does, although neither would have very much from a forty- or fifty-year-old's view.

## Good Provider

Being a good provider for a mate is the quintessential career/achievement trait. In many respects, it rolls most of the previous career/achievement traits together. In the literature, this trait is almost always viewed as a trait of men that women find appealing. Historically, throughout the history of mankind, males protected and provided food and shelter for women and children. While there were (and are) many societies where women shouldered the majority of physical work, men were the hunters. In a very general sense, this concept pervades modern society as well.

The legal system in most industrialized countries requires the husband to pay child support when a divorce occurs. This provides a very clear legal example of a man providing for the children. And, in some states, men are required to provide for their ex-wives, as well. The implication is that the role of the male being a good provider is embedded in most societies.

This may be a trait that men also use to evaluate women. While a woman's definition of a man being a good provider focuses primarily on financial considerations accompanied by emotional nurturing, the man's definition is different. To a man, a woman being a good provider means she will be a good mother and a good companion. For some, it also implies the woman will take a large part of the household responsibilities. A man's expectation of a woman's financial contribution is much less of an element of the woman being a good provider.

## Energy/Enthusiasm

This is a trait that could probably have gone equally well either in the personality or career/achievement categories. It was placed in this category to try to capture the idea of a person liking their work, having a passion for it, being motivated, and hardworking. These were rolled up into energy and enthusiasm. People who are enthusiastic about what they do give off a positive energy that others like.

As I was starting my academic career, a sage old professor gave me some advice about teaching. He told me, above all, to be enthusiastic about what I was teaching. That would yield high teaching evaluations. He stated that students are not experienced enough to know if you are right or wrong, up-to-date or behind the times. But they can tell very quickly if you are passionate about what you are doing. In most careers, having a high energy level and being enthusiastic is viewed positively.

## The Research Results

As with the other categories of traits, an aided and unaided approach was used. Some respondents were read the list of career/achievement traits and were asked to respond "yes" or "no" in response to the question, "Which of the traits attracted you?" The remaining respondents were simply asked to identify any career/achievement traits that attracted them.

The results were quite different than for the physical and personality traits. When using the aided approach, men and women identified roughly nine to ten physical traits and nine to ten personality traits that attracted them. Using the aided approach for career/achievement traits, only three to four traits were identified. Using the unaided approach, each respondent identified one to two physical and personality traits. For the career/achievement category, the mean was only about 0.5 traits per respondent. Stated differently, only about half of all respondents could even identify a trait. While there were fewer traits identified, there were some clear patterns in the data.

## The Traits of Men That Attract Women

When using the aided approach, the women identified an average of 3.9 career/achievement traits of men that attracted them. This is obviously much lower than for the physical and personality traits. Using the unaided approach, the women only identified an average of 0.6 traits. The implication is that women simply could not recall these traits as clearly.

## Aided

The career/achievement traits of men that attract women are presented in Table 9.2. The one trait that really stands out from all of the rest was energy/enthusiasm. This trait was identified by 78.5 percent of all women. Women are obviously attracted to a man who has a high energy level and is enthusiastic.

After this trait, there were three that were identified by 50 to 60 percent of the women. These were good provider (58.6 percent), well educated (54.1 percent), and talent (50.3 percent). Although ranked second and third, respectively, it was a bit surprising that only 54 to 58 percent of women identified good provider and well educated. Based on the literature, these were expected to be more frequently mentioned. Perhaps, a youth factor was at work since love at first sight occurred at a younger age.

All of the remaining traits were identified by only 30 to 40 percent of women. These were control of resources (39.8 percent), professional success (37 percent), income potential (32.6 percent), and social status (29.8 percent). Because of the young age at which love at first sight occurred, it was a bit surprising that control of resources was rated ahead of income potential. Most young men, under age twenty-five, have mostly potential ahead in their careers.

The women only identified thirteen additional "other" career/achievement traits of men that attracted them. None of the traits were mentioned by two or more women. The traits identified were issues such as hardworking, well traveled, self-starter potential, etc. Because of the few responses, no firm conclusions could be drawn from these "other" traits.

Perhaps the most significant finding is the low number of career/achievement traits identified. This certainly implies that physical and personality traits of men are far more important to women. The career/achievement traits are most notable due to their scarcity. This is even more evident using the unaided approach.

## Unaided

If the scarcity of comments was notable for the aided approach, it was even more so for the unaided approach. Only about half of the women could identify a career/achievement trait of men that initially attracted them. The result was a mean number of traits identified of 0.6.

Of the list of traits, only two were identified by 10 percent or more of women. The most frequently mentioned trait of men was professional success, identified by 15.6 percent of women. Well educated was the second most frequently identified trait, by 11.3 percent of women. After these two traits, no other trait was mentioned by 6 percent of respondents. Thus, there were too few mentions to draw meaningful results.

The "other" category contained traits identified by 15.6 percent of women. The most frequently mentioned trait was goal-oriented (4), followed by hardworking (2), and respected (2). No other trait was mentioned by more than one respondent. The career choice influences some women since cowboy, doctor, and lawyer were mentioned.

The biggest difference between the aided and unaided results was for energy/enthusiasm. When this was stated, 78.5 percent of women indicated that this is what attracted them to the man. When unaided, only 4.3 percent of women identified this trait. Since energy/enthusiasm had such overwhelming support with the aided approach, women may not perceive this to be a career/achievement trait. It appears that most women perceive this to be more of a personality trait.

## The Career/Achievement Traits of Women That Attract Men

Men are even less concerned with career/achievement traits than are women. Using the aided approach, men identified an average of 3.2 career/achievement traits of women that attracted them (Table 9.3). When using an unaided approach, men identified an average of only 0.5 traits. Hence, career/achievement traits are less important to men.

### Aided

Using the aided approach, energy/enthusiasm was identified by 75 percent of the men. For both men and women, having a high energy level and being enthusiastic are quite important. Being a "couch potato" isn't going to be appealing to either sex. After energy/enthusiasm, there was a substantial drop-off to two traits.

Talent was identified by 49.1 percent of men. Well educated was identified by 46.9 percent of men. Being talented implies some special skills. Hence, these two traits are probably closely related to one another.

After these first three traits, there were three additional traits identified by 31 to 32 percent of the men. These were good provider (32.2 percent), control of resources (32.2 percent), and professional success (31.3 percent). Since less than one-third of all men identified these three traits, they are relatively unimportant. This may be due to the youth factor. Most men experienced love at first sight by the time they were twenty-five. Most women were younger than the men, by roughly two years. Therefore, being a good provider (if financial implications were present), controlling resources, and being professionally successful would not be expected of women under age twenty-three.

The last two career/achievement traits were social status (22.1 percent) and income potential (21.6 percent). Only 21 to 22 percent of men identified these traits. Social status and the woman's potential to generate income are not top of mind issues when a man experiences love at first sight.

There were very few other traits identified. Only 7.4 percent of the men identified another trait, and no two men identified the same trait. Issues such as good with disabled kids, committed to nursing career, musical ability, and cleverness were mentioned.

## Unaided

There were only three career/achievement traits of women that were identified by men in significant numbers, using the unaided approach. Energy/enthusiasm and well educated were identified by 11.9 percent of the men. Having professional success was mentioned by 8.9 percent of men. Men apparently place more emphasis on a woman having a high energy level and being enthusiastic. Being professionally successful and being well educated is appealing to both sexes.

There were 11 percent of men who identified another career/achievement trait. However, no trait was mentioned twice. Traits such as actress, dancer, same career, and enjoyed bowling were identified. With so few responses, no firm conclusions can be drawn about the "other" category.

## Male vs. Female

When comparing the aided results for both sexes, men and women both found a high energy level and enthusiasm to be particularly appealing. Both men (75 percent) and women (78.5 percent) identified this trait with a high frequency (Table 9.4). Men (49.1 percent) and women (50.3 percent) identified talent with about the same frequency. After these two points of similarity, women placed a greater emphasis on all other traits.

Being a good provider was identified by 58.6 percent of the women but only by 32.2 percent of the men. Obviously, this is much more important to women. All the remaining traits were identified by a larger proportion of women than men with a difference of 7 to 10 percent which is statistically significant.

## Summary

Women identified substantially fewer career/achievement traits of men that attracted them than for physical and personality traits. And men identified even fewer. The implication is that these traits, thought to be quite important when gradually falling in love and/or selecting a mate, are relatively unimportant when love at first sight strikes. Apparently, the people are predominantly overwhelmed by the physical traits and personality of the other person.

Only one career/achievement trait stands out. Having a high energy level and enthusiasm is definitely appealing to both men and women. This fits very closely with the fun, outgoing support in the previous chapter.

Table 9.1

## The Career/Achievement Traits

Talent                          Control Of Resources

Professional Success            Good Provider

Social Status                   Energy/Enthusiasm

Well Educated                   Income Potential

Other Career/Achievement Traits


Table 9.2

## The Career/Achievement Traits of Men That Attract Women

|  | Aided (N=195) | Unaided (N=142) |
|---|---|---|
| Trait | % of Response | % of Response |
| Talent | 50.3% | 5.9% |
| Professional Success | 37.0% | 15.6% |
| Social Status | 29.8% | 0.7% |
| Well Educated | 54.1% | 11.3% |
| Income Potential | 32.6% | 1.0% |
| Control of Resources | 39.8% | 3.5% |
| Good Provider | 58.6% | 5.0% |
| Energy/Enthusiasm | 78.5% | 4.3% |
| Other | 7.2% | 15.6% |

Table 9.3

# The Career/Achievement Traits of Women That Attract Men

| | Aided (N=120) | Unaided (N=101) |
|---|---|---|
| Trait | % of Response | % of Response |
| Talent | 49.1% | 4.3% |
| Professional Success | 31.3% | 8.9% |
| Social Status | 22.1% | 2.0% |
| Well Educated | 46.9% | 11.9% |
| Income Potential | 21.6% | 2.1% |
| Control of Resources | 32.2% | 2.0% |
| Good Provider | 32.2% | 0.0% |
| Energy/Enthusiasm | 75.0% | 11.9% |
| Other | 7.4% | 11.0% |

Table 9.4

## A Direct Comparison of Career/Achievement Traits That Attract Men and Women

| Trait | Aided (N=315) | | Unaided (N=243) | |
|---|---|---|---|---|
| | % of Response | | % of Response | |
| | male | female | male | female |
| Talent | 49.1% | 50.3% | 4.3% | 5.9% |
| Professional Success | 31.3% | 37.0% | 8.9% | 15.6% |
| Social Status | 22.1% | 29.8% | 2.0% | 0.7% |
| Well Educated | 46.9% | 54.1% | 11.9% | 11.3% |
| Income Potential | 21.6% | 32.6% | 2.1% | 1.0% |
| Control of Resources | 32.2% | 39.8% | 2.0% | 3.5% |
| Good Provider | 32.2% | 58.6% | 0.0% | 5.0% |
| Energy/Enthusiasm | 75.0% | 78.5% | 11.9% | 4.3% |
| Other | 7.4% | 7.2% | 11.0% | 15.6% |

# Love at the Drive-Thru

*It happened about six years ago in the drive-thru of the What-A-Burger in Round Rock, Texas, just north of Austin. It was the end of summer, almost fall, just after midnight. The nights were finally starting to cool off, and it was a brisk evening, at least for central Texas.*

*I had been out by myself that night and decided to get a breakfast taco before I went home. I was in the drive-thru waiting for my order that never came. All of the people in the other lane kept ordering and getting served. And I waited and waited and waited. Exasperated, I got out of my truck, went to the window, and said, "You forgot me." Finally, I got it taken care of. But I was holding up the whole line of cars that were behind me.*

*There were two guys and a girl in the car behind me. As I got back into my truck, one of the guys yelled, "Stop! I want to talk to you." They had been watching me go through all the hassle of getting my order. So I pulled over and waited for them. The guy got out, and the other couple left. We sat on the tailgate of my truck and had breakfast. We talked and talked.*

*I was twenty-six at the time and Dan was twenty-nine. He had brown hair and blue eyes. He was tall and had a nice build. I was really attracted to his eyes and his body. He was so cute, and he smelled good. There was definitely an immediate attraction or chemistry.*

*I think he was attracted to my hair at first. I'm a hairdresser, and I have waist length curly brown hair that has a lot of body and bounce to it. I have blue eyes and am pretty athletic. I was wearing shorts that night, so he probably noticed my legs, too.*

*Dan was in the Army and was stationed at Fort Hood. He had just returned from a tour of duty in Germany. I was very excited that night, having breakfast with a total stranger. I was very interested, very intrigued with the things that he had done and places he had been. Dan had been married and had children but was divorced. It was a painful subject so we didn't discuss it that much.*

*He asked for my phone number, but I wouldn't give it to him. I was being coy and playing hard-to-get, I guess. So he asked where I lived. I pointed at the water tower and said that I lived right next to it. I said, "If your can find your way to the water tower, you can have a date with me."*

*The very next day he found the water tower. My truck was parked in front of my house so he knocked on the front door. When I opened the door and saw him, I thought, "Oh my God! He found me!" My father gave me an odd look, implying, "Who is this?"*

*At the time, I had just returned from a year in Connecticut. I was living at my Dad's house temporarily. My Dad is very religious and very strict. That was a bit of a constraint on the relationship at first.*

*We went out together that night and really hit it off. That strong attraction that I felt for him the previous night just got stronger. We felt like we were right for each other from the start.*

*We were both adults. It wasn't very long before we were intimate with each other, the attraction was just too powerful. However, my dad did not approve of premarital sex, so we couldn't spend the night with each other until I moved out and was on my own.*

*We dated steadily for five years. The relationship only had one problem, alcohol. He drank way too much and liked to go to the bars for entertainment. I don't drink much and don't like going to the bars. It was horrible because I loved him so much. He just couldn't give up his drinking.*

*He asked me one day, "Is love enough?" I told him, "No." The alcohol would always be a wedge. I wasn't sure who didn't love who enough. I felt that, if he loved me enough, he would curtail or end his drinking. He felt that if I loved him enough, that I would accept him the way he was.*

*The only time that we ever argued was when he was drinking. He wasn't physically abusive, but he didn't like to be criticized at all. He actually didn't feel like he had a serious problem. He didn't think getting drunk was bad, as long as he didn't drive. Dan simply didn't want to curtail his drinking. He said it helped him to have fun.*

*I am sure that I picked up some of my parents' conservative values—my father never drank. But I tried to be tolerant, accepting, and give Dan encouragement. After several years, it became apparent that he wasn't going to change, and I couldn't go on denying reality. I ultimately told him that I couldn't go on this way anymore.*

*Without him, I feel like I'm drifting alone through the night. Loneliness is always springing up inside me. Everything seems so empty. I call his name at night, just to hear it, and squeeze my pillow, wishing it was him.*

*To this day, he still loves me, and I still love him. I am now thirty-two, and he is the first and only love that I have ever had. Maybe I'll have another encounter with someone and fall in love again. I'm still looking for that better day, but meeting another man is probably going to be difficult since I still love him so much. When you give all of yourself to someone and it ends in pain, you give less next time, and more slowly.*

*Just the other day my mom and I stopped at the What-A-Burger at about midnight. I told her that this is where and when it happened. As we drove through, there was this flood of memories. Most of the memories are pretty bittersweet. There is a lot of good in him.*

## Chapter Ten

# The Emotions Men and Women Feel When Experiencing Love at First Sight

ove stirs the deepest of emotions. It is powerful. It is pervasive. Nearly every human wants love, needs love, experiences love, and loses love during their lifetime. Unfulfilled wants and needs for love elicit one set of emotions. Experiencing love elicits another set of emotions, particularly when love at first sight occurs. Losing love, whether through rejection, divorce, or death elicits another set of emotions. All of these emotions are closely related to love. But no two sets are quite the same.

Although everyone recognizes the concept of love, describing love is difficult for most. Because we each have a unique blueprint for loving, we each have our own conceptualization of love. We each perceive and express love in our own unique way, with all of our own idiosyncrasies we have learned along life's highway. If I asked thirty people to write down a two sentence definition of love, there would be thirty different definitions. I guarantee you that no two descriptions would be exactly the same.

The reasons that no two definitions would be the same are twofold. First, as discussed throughout this book, no two people share the same genetic profile and same life experiences. Each human truly is unique. Second, all humans do not have an equal ability to express themselves. Some can describe life, and love, with a richer palette of words than others. Thus, there would be differences in both the conceptualizations of love and in the ability to express that conceptualization.

While no two definitions would be identical, there would be some common themes that would emerge. The same or very similar words may appear in several, or more, descriptions. There may be the same or very similar concepts expressed. There certainly would be some common ground for the definition of love.

And that is exactly the goal of this chapter. This part of the research attempts to identify an emotional common ground of shared emotions. Is there enough commonality so that emotional themes will emerge? Or, are people so different that the emotions generated by love at first sight will be widely diverse?

## The Emotions Generated by Love at First Sight

As with the traits that attract people, a literature review was conducted to identify the emotional responses that a person might feel when experiencing love at first sight. The most striking finding was the scarcity of research on the emotional responses to falling in love. Only a few works addressed the emotions that a person might associate with love. And none addressed the possible emotions associated with love at first sight.

Despite the lack of relevant research, a list of ten emotional responses was developed (Table 10.1). These were used in the design of the questionnaire. Specifically, the ten possible responses were presented to respondents using the aided approach. The following discussions describe the logic behind each emotion included.

## Hope

Some suggest that hope is among the first emotions that a person feels when falling in love. There is hope for a variety of positive outcomes, such as for happiness, for fulfillment, for security. There could be hope for a life together, hope for having children. There could be hope for the dream of living happily ever after, a common expectation of women. These are all conscious thoughts although some might be rather subtle.

Some psychologists, such as Freud, would suggest that there is hope on a deeper, more subconscious level. Freud would suggest that adult intimate relationships are attempts to replicate the earliest intimate relationship, the mother-infant bond. The lifelong search for a similar relationship is at the core of much Freudian psychology. The warmth and closeness of the unconditional love of the mother leaves a mark on the infant, well before an infant has the understanding or capacity to describe the experience. But the comfort and security of the mother's love is felt and remembered. And each person has a subconscious hope that it can, someday, be replicated.

Plato believed that true love created the feeling of wholeness and completeness through the unity of soul mates. He contended that humans subconsciously search for the lost half of our souls. We feel an emptiness, a longing that is not satiated until we love. It is this hope for completeness that drives people.

## Exhiliration

As discussed in an earlier chapter, when around a passionate love, the brain produces a variety of chemicals, such as endorphins, that create a natural euphoria. These chemicals all work together to make a person feel good. Researchers have shown the natural high from these chemicals is much like a drug-induced high. Some people may express this as feeling good or being exhilarated by another's presence.

People may not know exactly why they feel exhilarated. But they know something is happening to them. One respondent from California said she felt "lightheaded" when she experienced love at first sight. A women from Wyoming said she felt "butterflies." These probably are both manifestations of the exhilaration resulting from chemicals being produced in the brain. And all of this results from experiencing love at first sight.

## Comfort

When experiencing love at first sight, many people said that they just felt instantly comfortable with the other person. This could be caused by a common background, shared values and beliefs, or a broad range of similarities. It could be caused by similar life experiences. It could be caused by similar birth order influences. But whatever the cause, an instant comfort was a term frequently used in the stories.

Some might have stated that they were immediately "completely comfortable." Others might have used the term "compatible." Others felt that the person was an "old friend," but they had never met before. Regardless of how the concept was expressed, the idea of comfort was thought to be important.

## Excitement

Along with the chemicals produced in the brain that create a natural high, there is also a release of adrenaline when a person experiences love at first sight. The adrenaline causes the eyes to get larger and the pupils to dilate. The adrenaline causes an increase in the heart rate and body metabolism. The increase in metabolism results in people blushing and feeling flush or warm. The palms of the hands (and feet) begin to perspire. These all result from a charge of adrenaline.

One respondent in Florida said, "my heart went pitter-patter and I felt all goofy inside." A man in Colorado said "he felt an immediate anxiety and fear of what was happening." One woman said she felt "nauseous." All of these are descriptions of the excitement caused by a release of adrenaline in the body. And this is stimulated by love at first sight.

## Chemistry/Fit

People long have used the term "good chemistry" to describe the meshing of kindred souls. I am not sure where the term originated, but it actually describes reality very well. When two people experience love at first sight, they both experience pleasurable chemical reactions in the brain. The result of the chemical reactions would be described by even the most cynical as good, if they ever felt them. Since chemistry is a term commonly used in describing the compatibility of couples, it was included.

The term "fit" was an added descriptor to illustrate the concept more. Several respondents used this concept colorfully. One man said meeting his love was "like we were the last two pieces of the puzzle in each other's lives. We each fit together perfectly and completed each other's puzzle." Another man said when he met his future wife that "she was like that favorite old pair of jeans that you just love. When you pull them on, everything fits perfectly, they are so comfortable. That is the way she was." Being compared to a faded, old pair of jeans doesn't seem particularly romantic, but he made his point well.

## Lasting Attachment

When people meet "the one," a common feeling they experience is one that connotates "forever" or "happily ever after." There is a sudden realization the person that they just met will be with them for life. Or, at least, that is the expectation. Somehow, the perception shifts from a here and now, day to day view to a long-term expectation.

One woman in Oregon, described the feeling well. She said that within a few minutes of meeting him, she "knew that I'd spend the rest of my life with him." A man in South Dakota said, "As soon as I saw her, I knew she was going to be my wife." There is certainly something in the depth of emotional arousal to realize that the event is the beginning of something long-term, not just a passing fancy.

## Wholeness/Completeness

The logic behind this emotion is based on Plato's philosophies. When we truly love another, it completes us in some way, uniting us with the missing part of our soul. Thus, there is a synergy where the two souls united are each better and more than the two souls individually. This results in a feeling of at least one of the people being made whole.

At the surface level, this could be the bubbly extrovert hooking up with the quiet introvert. They are opposites in many ways, but both long to be more like the other. They hope that the other will bring them something that they currently don't have. They hope that the other's desirable traits will rub off on them, change them for the better.

One woman from Washington noted, that when she met her man, "he was just perfect for me." A man in Boston self-described himself as quiet and reserved. When he first kissed his love, he said, "she just felt wild, absolutely wild." Both people said the other made them feel complete.

## Growth

Somewhat like the synergy discussed with the wholeness/completeness emotion, growth implies that the other person made them better in some way. The growth typically would be some form of psychological or spiritual growth. Perhaps the other person helped by providing a deeper understanding of self, an understanding of those desires and fears that we keep hidden from the light of day, or the eyes and ears of those around us.

Perhaps the growth was spiritual, not just in the religious context, but in the broader meaning of life. The growth could help us understand what's truly important in life, how to put our priorities in order, stripping away the superficiality that most chase. Regardless of exactly how the growth is manifested, the concept implies that we are somehow a better, deeper person because of the other's love.

## Fulfillment

In many ways, this is similar to several of the other emotions such as comfort, wholeness/completeness, and growth. But the term conjures up a slightly different concept as well. Fulfillment also implies that we've reached some demanding goal, that we've arrived at some destination in life. We may not have known consciously what the destination was, but we realize it when we see it.

One man in Pennsylvania put it well. He said, "when I saw her, I immediately knew that she was what I had been looking for throughout my life. I always had this hunger, this emptiness inside me, telling me there had to be more in life. From the instant that I saw her, I never had any of those feelings again. It was as if I had just discovered what life was all about."

## Desire to Have Children

A common emotion associated with love is the desire to have children. This is also referred to as "baby fantasies." And this is usually more common for women than men. A man may see a woman and think, "she is going to be the mother of my children." Or a woman might think, "I want to have his kids."

This emotional reaction to love is probably based on some genetic imprint in our brain associated with survival of the species. Both people who plan to have children, and those who plan not to have children, experience baby fantasies. So the desire to have children does not have to be part of a person's goals or life plan. This emotion is usually a spontaneous up-swelling that often surprises the person. For example, a woman in her thirties had never given a thought to having children. When she fell in love with a man who was fifty, she suddenly wanted to have a baby with him. Perhaps the biological clock was ticking in this example, but baby fantasies occur in people of all ages.

## The Research Results

As with other parts of this research, a split design was used. A portion of the respondents were read the list of emotions and asked to respond "yes" or "no" if they felt that emotion when they experienced love at first sight. The rest of the respondents were simply asked to identify the emotions that they felt.

The pattern of responses was much the same as those that occurred previously. The aided approach resulted in a much higher number of emotions being identified. The average number of emotions identified by each respondent using the aided approach was between seven to eight. Using the unaided approach, only slightly over one emotion was identified by each respondent.

Recalling the emotions felt when love at first sight occurred may have been difficult for respondents. Since most love at first sight experiences resulted in a relationship of some type, the respondent would have had both the physical and personality traits reenforced over time. The respondent would have interacted with the other person for months or years. The emotions, on the other hand, would be fleeting.

There is no question that the love at first sight event would be emotionally charged. This high level of emotional arousal would result in more acute images of the situation. But the initial emotions were probably thought and felt, but not formalized into words. Hence, recalling the exact emotions would likely be more difficult for people. Perhaps this is why there is such a disparity in the results to the aided and unaided approaches.

## The Emotions That Women Felt

As you might expect, women averaged identifying slightly more emotions (7.7) than men (7.1). However, this gap is not particularly large. When using the unaided approach, both men and women identified an average of 1.1 emotions. Given that the literature generally holds that women are more socially sensitive than men, this should have resulted in women experiencing more emotions. Perhaps men are not as unaware of their own emotional state as some think.

### Aided

There were two emotions frequently identified by women when using the aided approach (Table 10.2). These were excitement

(91.1 percent) and chemistry/fit (87.4 percent). These are probably related to one another since excitement is a result of adrenaline being released in the body.

After the two dominant emotions, five others clustered together, being identified by 75 to 80 percent of women. These were lasting attachment (80.0 percent), exhilaration (79.8 percent), comfort (77.4 percent), wholeness/completeness (75.7 percent), and fulfillment (75.0 percent). These top seven emotions are probably experienced almost simultaneously by women when love at first sight occurs.

Hope (70.2 percent), growth (68.6 percent), and desire to have children (54.3 percent) were less frequently identified, but were still mentioned by over half of the women. The implication is that even these three are common emotions when love at first sight occurs. Perhaps the most significant finding is that women experience a whole array of emotions. When an emotion was mentioned, the women would recall having experienced it. However, as the unaided results show, without prompting, women had more difficulty identifying their emotions.

### Unaided

Using the unaided approach, two emotions stood out. Excitement was the most frequently identified emotion, but was mentioned by only 18.1 percent of women. Wholeness/completeness was identified by 13.8 percent of women. After these two, lasting attachment was identified by 8.7 percent of women. While excitement was most frequently identified in both approaches, the diversity of responses was notable.

Over half (52 percent) of the women identified an emotion other than those listed. Most common among these were happiness (11), attraction (9), anxiety (5), obsession (4), and jealousy

(4). After these, an array of emotions were mentioned just once. The emotions of obsession and jealousy were closely related and interesting. As one woman stated, "when I saw him, I was just obsessed with him. I was jealous if he even talked to another woman. It was like I wanted to stand up and say, 'stay away from him, he's mine.' But I hadn't even talked to him yet."

## The Emotions That Men Felt

### Aided

The results for men to the aided and unaided approaches are presented in Table 10.3. With the aided approach, three traits were identified by men most frequently. These were excitement (88.7 percent), chemistry/fit (86.1 percent), and exhilaration (80.2 percent). All were identified by 80 to 89 percent of all men.

There is an interesting thread running through all three of these emotions. All are directly related to the chemical reactions that take place in the brain when love at first sight occurs. The chemical reactions, discussed in chapter two, stir very powerful emotions.

After these first three emotions, most of the others fell into a relatively narrow band, being identified by 66 to 71 percent of men. The implication is that these six emotions are relatively common, but to a lesser degree than the first three. The desire to have children was identified by less than half (45.9 percent) of the men. While much less frequent than other emotions, a substantial number of men do have baby fantasies.

The results to the aided approach suggest that men experience a variety of emotions simultaneously. There is no single emotion that stands out from the others. Hence, men are likely to feel a sort of emotional stew brewing inside, stirring many new emotions.

## Unaided

Using the unaided approach, the volume of emotions identified by men dropped off rather substantially, just as it did for women. As mentioned, men identified an average of 1.1 emotions, exactly the same as women.

When using the unaided approach, only one emotion stood out. Excitement was identified by 25.5 percent of the men. After excitement, lasting attachment (11.8 percent), wholeness/completeness (8.8 percent), and fulfillment (7.8 percent) were identified by 8 to 12 percent of men. Perhaps most notable of these results is the diversity in the way men conceptualized their emotions. There simply was not a single emotion identified by a majority of men.

This is also illustrated by the large "other" percentage. There were 40.9 percent of all identified emotions that were different from the list. The leading emotions in the other category were attraction (7), pleasure (5), anxiety (4), overwhelmed (3), and lust (3). These five emotions accounted for about half of all the other responses. The remaining other emotions had only one mention each. It is interesting that lust was identified by relatively few men. The people who are skeptical of love at first sight often state that lust at first sight is entirely possible. However, if lust was a dominant emotion, there should have been a much higher frequency. Lust does not play much of a role in the initial love at first sight experiences.

## Men vs. Women

Using the aided approach, both men and women identified excitement and chemistry/fit as the top two emotions that they felt when experiencing love at first sight (Table 10.4). Using the

*Love at First Sight*

unaided approach, both men and women identified excitement most frequently. There is obviously strong support for these two emotions.

Using the aided approach, men and women identified hope, exhilaration, and growth in roughly the same frequency. On the remaining emotions, all were identified more frequently by women than by men. The implication is that women experience a broader range of emotions than men when love at first sight occurs. However, the differences are not as great as what might be expected.

Using the unaided approach, the top three emotions, based on frequency of mention were excitement, lasting attachment, and wholeness/completeness. The order was different for the latter two for men and women, however. Both men and women identified a diverse array of emotions when not prompted.

## Summary

While women identified slightly more emotional responses to their love at first sight experience, the most striking finding is the similarity shared by men and women. Excitement, exhilaration, and good chemistry are clearly the most common emotions. Women also feel a lasting attachment somewhat more frequently than men. Apparently, emotions felt by men and women are not so different after all.

Table 10.1

## Emotions Felt When Experiencing Love at First Sight

Hope

Exhilaration

Comfort

Excitement

Chemistry/Fit

Lasting Attachment

Wholeness

Growth

Fulfillment

Desire for Children

Other Emotions

Table 10.2

## What Women Felt When Experiencing Love at First Sight

| | Aided (N=195) | Unaided (N=142) |
|---|---|---|
| Trait | % of Response | % of Response |
| Hope | 70.2% | 2.2% |
| Exhilaration | 79.8% | 4.3% |
| Comfort | 77.4% | 5.8% |
| Excitement | 91.1% | 18.1% |
| Chemistry/Fit | 87.4% | 3.5% |
| Lasting Attachment | 80.0% | 8.7% |
| Wholeness | 75.7% | 13.8% |
| Growth | 68.6% | 0.7% |
| Fulfillment | 75.0% | 2.2% |
| Desire for Children | 54.3% | 0.0% |
| Other | 14.8% | 52.0% |

Table 10.3

## What Men Felt When Experiencing Love at First Sight

| | Aided (N=195) | Unaided (N=142) |
|---|---|---|
| Trait | % of Response | % of Response |
| Hope | 70.7% | 2.9% |
| Exhilaration | 80.2% | 2.0% |
| Comfort | 68.7% | 3.9% |
| Excitement | 88.7% | 25.5% |
| Chemistry/Fit | 86.1% | 5.9% |
| Lasting Attachment | 69.3% | 11.8% |
| Wholeness | 68.1% | 8.8% |
| Growth | 66.4% | 1.0% |
| Fulfillment | 69.0% | 7.8% |
| Desire for Children | 45.9% | 1.0% |
| Other | 19.8% | 40.9% |

Table 10.4

# A Direct Comparison of Men and Women

|  | Aided (N=195) | | Unaided (N=142) | |
| --- | --- | --- | --- | --- |
| Trait | % of Response | | % of Response | |
|  | male | female | male | female |
| Hope | 70.7% | 70.2% | 2.9% | 2.2% |
| Exhilaration | 80.2% | 79.8% | 2.0% | 4.3% |
| Comfort | 68.7% | 77.4% | 3.9% | 5.8% |
| Excitement | 88.7% | 91.1% | 25.5% | 18.1% |
| Chemistry/Fit | 86.1% | 87.4% | 5.9% | 3.5% |
| Lasting Attachment | 69.3% | 80.0% | 11.8% | 8.7% |
| Wholeness | 68.1% | 75.7% | 8.8% | 13.8% |
| Growth | 66.4% | 68.6% | 1.0% | 0.7% |
| Fulfillment | 69.0% | 75.0% | 7.8% | 2.2% |
| Desire for Children | 45.9% | 54.3% | 1.0% | 0.0% |
| Other | 19.8% | 14.8% | 40.9% | 52.0% |

# Two Days In Paradise

&#10148;

*I was involved in one of those relationships with a man who was emotionally exhausting. After it is over, you wonder how you got involved in the first place, and you wonder why you stayed so long.*

*Jack was enough years younger than me to be referred to as a "younger man." At first, that had an appeal. He was more fun and carefree than previous men, he seemed to have high energy. He also seemed to care for me. Somewhere along the way, however, "fun and carefree" evolved into "childish and immature." The "caring" evolved into controlling and jealousy. He wanted to keep track of every move I made every minute of every day. He would get mad if I spent time with any man.*

*Almost four years with him had taken a toll. I was in a depression that seemed to spiral downward. The constant criticism and sarcasm eroded my enthusiasm for life and my self-esteem. Like many women, I was in self-denial that I could suffer from depression. It seemed that I was concentrating only on day to day survival.*

*At about that point, Annie, my long lost best friend, came to Boise, Idaho, for an extended visit. Fortunately, she stayed with me for a while. It was like I had my own live-in therapist. We talked for hours and hours about life. She felt that I was far from being the joyful, fun loving person that she used to know. After a* lot of soul searching, I had to agree with her. Those times of laughter and fun seemed like a daydream or a previous life. She helped me to see my relationship with Jack for what is was, a dead end street with a lot of potholes.

Annie had come to Boise in November 1997. It wouldn't be long before we were into the holiday season. I always try to make the holidays a good time for everyone else, lots of parties, baking, and gifts. But Christmas is a particularly hard time for me personally. My first child died three days before Christmas in 1982. Christmas always brought many bittersweet memories, thoughts that I always held inside and kept to myself. So the whole holiday season was a bit of a downer on top of my deteriorating relationship with Jack.

Annie's boyfriend, Boyd, and his friend, Alex, had come to Idaho to go elk hunting that year. They stopped by to pick up Annie on their way to the mountains, but I was at work when they came through. Unfortunately, I didn't have the opportunity to meet either Boyd or Alex. The hunting trip didn't go quite as planned.

When Annie was jumping out of the big four-wheel drive pickup, the shoulder belt hit her in the eye, cutting her cornea. She had to be taken to the emergency room at a small country hospital, sixty miles away. Her eye injury required ointment, painkillers, and a large gauze bandage. It was pretty painful for her, so the guys ended their hunt a few days early.

When they showed up early at my place, I was surprised to see them. I was in the process of putting up Christmas decorations. I was standing on an oak coffee table stringing lights around the living room and using my trusty staple gun. When they came in, I glanced over my shoulder and just said "Hi!" I continued putting up the lights as I had them lying all over the furniture.

As I was stretching to staple the lights in place, I suddenly felt this intense heat in my body. It was a hard feeling to explain. I turned around and Alex was sitting in a chair at the dining room table, staring directly at me. He kept staring at me intensely, sending sensations pulsing throughout my whole body. I don't mind saying that I enjoyed the sensation immensely. It was a wonderful feeling to have Alex look at me so intensely.

Alex was fifty, much older than myself or Jack, and was very attractive. He was over six feet tall and was very tanned and toned. His silver gray hair made him very wise looking. His striking blues eyes seemed to send many thoughts piercing through my body. He had an air of strength and power about him.

Annie saw us staring at each other and thought she should introduce us. Alex leaned back in his chair and gave me a sweet, adorable, crooked smile, the type of smile that puts a person at ease. He seemed to have a self-confident warmth and his voice was smooth, deep, and soothing.

That Friday evening, Boyd, Annie, Alex, Jack, and I all had dinner together. During the evening, I was just captivated by Alex. He was extremely intelligent and knowledgeable and was so self-assured. He seemed to have a magnetic personality.

On Saturday afternoon, I took Annie back to the doctor as her eye was still quite painful for her. The doctor gave her a different prescription and told her that it will just take time to heal. We were to meet up with Boyd and Alex afterward.

Being men, they wanted to watch some big college football game that was on TV that day. We had chosen to meet at the Crescent Bar since they had several big screen televisions. The Crescent Bar's claim to fame locally is that no lawyers are allowed in the place, which isn't all bad. By the time we got there, the men had already had a few drinks. I sat across from Alex so we could talk easily. I had several vodka cranberries, and the time seemed to fly by talking to Alex. When I realized that I had been there several hours, I hurriedly said my good-byes and left. Jack would be upset and throw a fit if I was gone too long.

The next day Boyd and Alex caught their plane back to Ohio. Annie stayed with me for about another month, through Christmas, and then moved to Ohio to be with Boyd. During that month, there were a lot of phone calls and Annie informed me that Alex was quite taken with me. He commented that he couldn't understand what such a wonderful person was doing with a guy like Jack.

To reciprocate for my hospitality while they were in Idaho, Boyd, Annie, and Alex suggested that I come to Springfield, Ohio for a visit. When I flew out in January, they all met me at the airport. Alex sort of adopted me and took care of me right from the start. He carried my bags and opened doors for me, he was such a gentleman.

My flight had arrived in the evening so we decided to stop by, play pool, and have a few drinks before going home. We had a great time—there was a good chemistry between all four of us. Everyone was very humorous and quick-witted.

Boyd and Annie had a one-bedroom apartment on a golf course nearby, so we went over there and played cards for a while. By that time, it was getting late, or should I say early in the morning. The time zone changes were catching up to me, and I was fading fast. Everyone decided to call it a night.

Since the apartment was small, I was going to sleep on the couch that night. Alex had a big house and suggested that I might be more comfortable at his place since he had several extra bedrooms. Much to the surprise of Boyd and Annie, and even myself, I agreed to go with Alex. It was pretty impulsive of me.

*As we drove to his house, Alex and I talked all the way. I had felt an immediate attraction to him when we met back in Boise, and being around him felt very good. He was a fascinating, intelligent man. When we arrived at his house, his little Yorkshire terrier, Chips, greeted us at the door.*

*Alex said that he needed to go to bed, as he had to get up in a few hours and go to work. He said the bedrooms were upstairs and I could take my pick. He told me to make myself at home and said good night as he was going up the stairs.*

*A few minutes later, I got my bags and went upstairs. As I walked down the hallway, I glanced into a bedroom and saw Alex already in bed. I don't really know what came over me at that point. There was something so alluring about him that I just couldn't control myself. It wasn't just lust. I wanted to be near him and feel his body close to me. I wanted to soak up his warmth and smell.*

*I sat my bags down and walked over to the bed to see if he was already asleep. He rolled over and looked at me and those blue eyes told me everything I wanted to know. We seemed to melt together in a warm passionate kiss that seemed to last an eternity. My body was quivering in anticipation as he slowly undressed me. We were awake the whole night, enthralled in the newness of our passions. He called in sick that day, only a few hours later. Since we had been awake all night, we didn't even get out of bed until the middle of the afternoon that Friday.*

*Alex had awakened a passion that I felt when he first stared at me. I never knew that type of deep love that explodes every time I look at him or hear his voice. His touch makes my heart race and my knees get weak.*

*That whole weekend was a magical time, almost like walking around in a daze. We met up with Boyd and Annie and had fun all weekend, riverboat gambling, dinners, dancing, hockey games. I was so wrapped up with Alex that I can't even remember everything we did.*

*The weekend ended on Sunday evening at the airport. We all gave each other hugs and said our good-byes. Alex gave me a gentle, sweet look and whispered "I love you." That really brought out the tears in me. I wanted to cling to him and have him beg me to stay. But I couldn't, I had other issues back in Idaho to deal with.*

*The plane trip home was a lonely one, filled with emotional ups and downs. Leaving Alex and returning to my situation was saddening. At the same time, I was excited about the possibilities with Alex, and the fact that our paths had crossed in such a loving way.*

*After returning home I received a call from Alex. He told me that he never thought he would fall in love again, until he met me. Our feeling for each other haven't changed since that first night and they never will.*

*Perhaps the most valuable thing Alex gave me that weekend was my self-respect and self esteem. My relationship with Jack had pulled me down far more than I had realized. After a weekend with Alex, he reminded me about what life is all about and how it should really be. The long conversations with Annie and Alex's warmth gave me the strength to give Jack the boot, something that I should have done long ago.*

*For the next two years, my relationship with Alex was a long distance one. We talked on the phone several times a day, shared emails, and had monthly rendezvouses. The love we have for each other has a life its own, a spiritual energy that can't be dampened. The thousands of miles that we were apart didn't matter because we lived within each other's heart. We got married last month.*

# It Was Meant to Be

In August 1951, I was living in Portollo Valley, California. Someone in the neighborhood was having a party and invited my husband and me. There were probably about thirty people there, mostly couples who lived close by.

I was helping the lady who was hosting the party to serve coffee. Back in those days, pantyhose had not been invented. You had to wear a garter belt to keep your hosiery up. As I was serving coffee, one of my garters got caught on a table, and I stumbled, spilling coffee on this man. Luckily, the coffee wasn't extremely hot, so I didn't burn him. But he jumped up.

I remember looking at him and thinking that he looked just like Gene Kelly, whom I adored. Spilling coffee on him was completely inadvertent, I was very embarrassed. But he was so handsome; there was an immediate attraction.

As it turned out, he was married and lived just a few houses from where my husband and I lived. He and his wife became good friends with my husband and I. Neither of us had any children, and we started doing a lot of things socially over the next two months.

The more my husband and I went out socially with them, the more the other man and I realized that we had so much in common. We both loved history, professional football, and spending time by the sea. We liked the same kind of art, books, music, and liked to do the same things. The more we got to know each other, the stronger the attraction became.

I was happy and content in my marriage. But the attraction for this other man just kept getting stronger and stronger. Unlike me, he was not happy in his marriage. He knew his marriage wouldn't last much longer.

It became harder and harder to do things as a foursome. When we'd go out, I'd want to be with him, not my husband. About two months after spilling coffee on him, we started seeing each other without our spouses. That is when the passion really exploded between us. When our souls and bodies met openly, it ignited such passion and unabashed love. When I held him in my arms, we made the sweetest music imaginable.

We knew that we had a lot of things in common before, but, once we were intimate, it was unbelievable, almost magical. We connected on every possible level, mentally, emotionally, and physically. We both felt the same spark at that party in August, and the fire just got deeper and deeper and all consuming.

After about two months of being crazily in love with each other, we knew that we had to do something about it. We couldn't go on seeing each other on a part-time basis. We simply had to be together. Living without him wasn't even really living anymore. We reached that conclusion at a Christmas party that year. We thought that we could hold out until after New Year's, but we couldn't.

A few days after Christmas we ran away together. I was being swept along by this powerful river of emotions. I don't think I could have stopped, even if I had wanted to. I knew that I just had to be with this man. He was my soul's desire, my inspiration in life. No one could tell what the future held, but we were willing to roll the dice. We both felt that our past lives were over, part of our history. We wanted to experience real love, no matter what the cost. We went to Las Vegas and got divorced and married.

When we came back from Las Vegas, we moved back into the same old neighborhood. We started doing things socially with the same friends as before. We were so much in love that it never even occurred to us that somebody might find it a bit bizarre. Looking back now, starting our marriage living near our ex-spouses and old friends was a little strange. Our children couldn't believe that their father and I did that. We were known as the Elizabeth Taylor and Richard Burton of Portollo Valley. We didn't try to hide or apologize for anything. The love we shared shielded us from any petty comments or disapproving looks, we were completely blind to those things.

Many people have told me that I'm eccentric, and, when I stop to analyze it, I probably am. I started my work career as a ballet dancer in New York. I was a newspaper person in Maine. I was a gym teacher in California. Along the way, I got a Ph.D. in education. Through all of that, the common thread was my marriage to this incredible man. He showered me with his love day after day. He was a dream lover who rescued me from a monotonous life. He would comfort me and make the lonely nights disappear.

There are probably people in this world that don't believe that dreams come true, that a love this strong could exist. Some loves are so powerful and strong that they last forever, for an eternity. Time was never able to steal the raging fire that we both felt. Even after he died, I couldn't get him out of my mind. His invisible arms would hold me and comfort me and give me strength. His love made my life like heaven.

Life has an underlying rhythm, a flow. Before I met him, my life was like playing chopsticks on the piano. Yes, it was music, but it was very basic, very simple. When I met him, my life became a *symphony. The music of life was totally different, overwhelming, building to incredible crescendos at times. At other times, life was a peaceful melody, soothing and gentle, with the tranquility of a mother holding a newborn baby. But with him all of the pieces of the complex orchestra of life meshed together perfectly, creating such harmony, such ecstasy.*

*Every time he would walk into a room, I would have this little gasp and my pulse would quicken. It was the same for him. That happened the first time our eyes met. His touch, his kiss would take my breath away. He was like a tranquilizer to all the world's problems. We were married for thirty-seven years, and that didn't change it. We had four children, and that didn't change it. We moved to different places and had different jobs, and that didn't change it.*

*He was eleven years older than me. He was raised in California and graduated from the University of California when I was only eleven years old. I was raised on the East Coast. Despite the difference in age and being raised thousands of miles apart, our paths were destined to cross. Being together was meant to be.*

*I was so lucky to find him in my life. His intellect was awesome. He had a great sense of humor. He was always so romantic and caring. We never lost those powerful feelings for each other, even after so many years. I have a picture of him right in front of me now. My god, he was handsome.*

## Chapter Eleven

# The Outcomes of Love at First Sight

T o this point, we have seen that love at first sight is not a rare and elusive experience. Almost two-thirds (64.1 percent) of the people in the study believe that love at first sight happens. Of those believers, more than half (58.2 percent) have experienced it. This works out to be roughly 40 percent of the total sample. Because of the sample size of nearly 1,500, we can be pretty sure that roughly the same proportion of the general U.S. population would say that they have experienced love at first sight.

The implication is that when you are sitting in the church on Sunday, about 40 percent of the congregation have experienced love at first sight. When you are shopping at your local supermarket, 40 percent of the adults walking around have experienced love at first sight. Are those 40 percent who have experienced love at first sight happier than most? Or was love at first sight a flash in the pan? Did the two people become a couple and live happily ever after? Or was their love unrequited?

## The Outcomes of Love at First Sight

There are a variety of outcomes of love at first sight. These are marriage, a long-term relationship, a short-term relationship, and no relationship at all. Since our research provides a snapshot in time, it cannot tell the whole story. Some may describe their relationship as short-term because they may have experienced love at first sight three or four months ago. Many of these relationships will lead to marriage. Some long-term relationships may lead to marriage, others may not. Even those who said that their love at first sight resulted in no relationship eventually may have a different outcome. It is entirely possible that these people may eventually have a relationship of some type with their love. The implication is that the story told by the statistics is inherently unfinished. There will be some further changes. But the results do give us a very good idea of what might happen.

For 55 percent of all respondents who experienced love at first sight, the outcome was marriage. There were 20.7 percent who had a long-term relationship with the other person, and 16.2 percent who had a short-term relationship. Many of these relationships are still ongoing. Only 8 percent of respondents had no relationship develop from the love at first sight experience.

Initially, the love at first sight experience could have been one-way. One person sees another and immediately falls head over heels in love. But since 92 percent of the love at first sight experiences lead to some type of a relationship, there must have been mutual emotions a good part of the time. At the very least, mutual shared love was the result for the 55 percent who got married. And mutual love was likely there for most of those in a long-term relationship.

If you recall, roughly 80 percent of men and women were unattached at the time of the love at first sight event. The remaining 20 percent were in a relationship of some type with someone else. Since 92 percent of all respondents had some type of relationship with the other person, roughly 60 percent of those already in a relationship with someone else ended up having a relationship with their love anyway. The presence of an existing relationship was not a major constraint for most.

In addition to these findings about the outcomes of love at first sight, there are many other factors that influence the outcomes in some way.

## Men vs. Women

The fact that 55 percent of love at first sight experiences lead to marriage does not tell the whole story. Men and women have different outcomes. When a woman experiences love at first sight, she will marry the man 62.1 percent of the time (Table 11.1). When a man experiences love at first sight, he will marry the woman 43.9 percent of the time. This difference between 62.1 percent and 43.9 percent is very substantial.

As we saw earlier, some of the difference may be explained by the fact that men are more likely to fall in love with someone who is already taken than a woman is. Since the other person is already in a relationship of some type, the probability of marriage is severely constrained. This also may be reflected in the fact that 11.7 percent of the time no relationship ever develops for the men. They may be madly in love with a married woman who will not break her marriage vows, for example. These factors together are not enough to explain the difference of almost twenty percentage points, however.

Perhaps, the large difference is an indicator of the belief that men have a harder time making a commitment than a woman. While the man may experience love at first sight, taking the step to marriage may be more difficult. In the love stories, a variety of men said that they felt "fear" and "scared" when experiencing love at first sight. These feelings could be a severe constraint.

Since men are more likely to experience love at first sight than women, perhaps men are not as careful as women in their selection process. The men may jump into a relationship, only to find that reality did not match their illusion. Hence, the men would realize the mismatch and withdraw from the relationship.

While there are several plausible explanations for the big difference between men and women in the probability of marriage, we can't say for sure why it exists. In all likelihood, the difference is probably due to all three of the factors just discussed working together somehow. Regardless of exactly why the difference occurs, the much higher incidence of marriage for women explains why women are more likely to experience love at first sight only once. The woman is taken out of circulation by the marriage. Men are more likely to end up back in the market again, increasing the probability of experiencing love at first sight more than once.

## What Happened to the Marriage?

For a couple who got married in 1970, the odds that the marriage would end in divorce were 50-50. For a couple married in 1990, the estimates are that roughly 65 to 70 percent will end in divorce.[14] There are many reasons for the high divorce rate, but we won't go into those here. But the implication is, for the general population in the U.S., a divorce rate of at least 50 percent would be expected. This serves as the standard of comparison for our study.

Of those who got married as a result of their love at first sight experience, 75.9 percent are still married. Only 15.9 percent of these marriages have ended in divorce. The remaining 8.2 percent of marriages were ended by the death of one of the spouses. Admittedly, some of the existing marriages for this group may end in divorce, so the divorce rate may go up slightly. But the message here is amazing.

When the difference between men and women is examined, the results are even more astonishing. Of the women who married as a result of their love at first sight experience, only 6.9 percent got a divorce. Of the men who married as a result of their love at first sight experiences, 21.1 percent got a divorce. The divorce rate for women is extremely low. The divorce rate for men is far below the national average, but is three times higher than for women. Could it be that women make better choices than men?

When a person gets married as an outcome of their love at first sight experience, the marriage is far more enduring than for the U.S. population as a whole. Experiencing love at first sight must result in a deeper, more committed relationship than gradually falling in love. The powerful experience must have some fundamental impact on the connection between two people.

Perhaps the love at first sight experience leads to higher levels of communication and trust in the resulting marriage, two very important characteristics in a successful marriage. Maybe the concept of united soul mates is not far off the mark. Whatever the reason, a marriage that results from love at first sight is much more enduring.

## The Impact of Religion, Ethnic Group, and Race

Religion and race appear to influence the outcome of love at first sight. Ethnic group does not. People who are of the same religion have a much higher probability of marrying as a result of their love at first sight experience than those of different religion. For those of the same religion, 63.4 percent got married compared to 54.7 percent of those with different religions (Table 11.2). A person's religion probably shapes their values, making differences more difficult to overcome. Also, there may be less parental approval to the relationship or marriage if the other person is of a different religion.

The differences for ethnic background are too small to be statistically significant. However, being of the same race increases the chance of marriage as an outcome of love at first sight. The difference in the probability of getting married was 55.7 percent for people of the same race versus 50 percent for people of a different race. Religion and race have an influence on the outcome of love at first sight, although not a major one.

## Education Level and Outcome

Education level has a moderate influence on the outcome of love at first sight (Table 11.3). Those who have attended graduate school (48.8 percent) and college graduates (51.9 percent) are the least likely to get married as a result of love at first sight. Those with a high school diploma, or less, are the most likely to get married (59.6 percent).

The most highly educated were also the least likely to believe in love at first sight. There is no question that education influences a person's pattern of loving and relationships. It may be that higher levels of education foster more of an air of independence. This would probably make them a bit more reserved, and aloof.

## Geographic Area and Outcomes

The geographic area where a person lives also exerts a moderate influence on the outcomes of love at first sight. People in rural areas have a higher probability of getting married after experiencing love at first sight. There were 63.9 percent of rural respondents who married the other person, followed by those from small towns with 54.8 percent getting married (Table 11.4). Interestingly, the respondents from other sizes of cities all have about the same probability of getting married, 50 to 51 percent.

Rural respondents were the most likely to believe in love at first sight, but among the least likely to experience it. The higher probability of believing in love at first sight could be due to rural values where other people, even strangers, are treated with respect and held in higher regard. This could also lead to the higher incidence of marriage as an outcome. The lower incidence of experiencing love at first sight for people in rural areas is probably simply due to a lower opportunity to meet a stranger. But when they do experience it, they are most likely to get married.

## Ethnic Group

There are differences in the outcomes of love at first sight based on the respondent's ethnic group. Asian/Pacific Islanders and Caucasians had about the same probability of getting married as a result of love at first sight, 54 to 56 percent. This was close to the overall average for the study (Table 11.5).

Native Americans/Eskimos (63.2 percent) and the "other" group (61.9 percent) had relatively high probabilities of getting married as a result of love at first sight. Conversely, African Americans (33.3 percent) and Hispanics (38.9 percent) had very low probabilities of getting married as a result of love at first sight. Because of the dramatic differences across ethnic groups, there are surely some cultural factors at work here. Unfortunately, this research can't identify exactly what those cultural factors might be.

## Opposites-Similars

Earlier we saw that some people were attracted to others who were opposites and some people were attracted to others who were predominantly similar. Our conclusion was that people want to love another who is similar, but who also possesses some differences that are complementary. The concept is that people like someone who completes them in some way, makes them a better person than they would be alone. When the outcomes of love at first sight are considered, the evidence tilts slightly toward opposites.

The respondents were asked if the other person was different in significant ways, similar in significant ways, both, or neither. The number of people indicating "different" was slightly higher than those indicating "similar." The people who were attracted to someone because they were different were more likely to marry the person (Table 11.6).

If the other person was different in significant ways, 61.1 percent of the time the two people got married. If the other person was similar in significant ways, they got married 52 percent of the time. The difference is statistically significant. The implication is that having significant differences must create a stronger attraction. Perhaps the feeling of being completed by another, like united soulmates, touches us on a deeper level emotionally.

## Similar to Parents

There is some support for the concept that people are attracted to a person who has characteristics of the opposite sex parent (Table 11.7). For example, a woman would be attracted to a man who is similar to her father in some way. And a man would be attracted to a woman who is similar to his mother in some way.

Overall, 62.1 percent of the women who experienced love at first sight married the man. If the man was similar to her father, the woman got married 69.9 percent of the time. Being attracted to a man who is similar to her father must stir some strong emotions in a woman, increasing the probability of marriage. A somewhat weaker relationship was found for men.

Overall, 43.9 percent of the men who experienced love at first sight married the woman. If the woman was similar to the man's mother, the man married her 48.5 percent of the time. Therefore, experiencing love at first sight with a woman who is similar to his mother increases the probability of marriage.

For both men and women, there is research support for the concept of being attracted to someone who is similar to the opposite sex parent. But the magnitude of impact is not extremely large. The probability of getting married increased by only 5 to 8 percent.

## Relationship Status of Respondent and Other

About 80 percent of all respondents were unattached when they experienced love at first sight. However, love at first sight was not blocked out by being in some type of relationship. About 20 percent of respondents were in this situation. But the outcomes of love at first sight are clearly constrained by the presence of a relationship.

Let's look first at the relationship status of the respondents themselves (Table 11.8). The group most likely to get married as a result of love at first sight were those who were married but separated from their spouse. Of these people, 61.9 percent married the other person. A person who is separated from their spouse is usually at the end of a deteriorating relationship. These people have previously experienced emotional intimacy and probably miss it. In other words, they are emotionally ready to find someone new and have a fresh start.

The people who are unattached (56.6 percent) and those who are already in a relationship with someone else (54.7 percent) have about the same probability of getting married as a result of love at first sight. Being in a relationship is obviously not much of a constraint. Apparently, a "relationship" has a connotation of low levels of commitment. Hence, a person is usually willing to terminate the relationship when love at first sight is experienced with someone else. This cannot be said for married respondents.

For a person who is already married to someone else, the odds of love at first sight leading to marriage are low. Nearly one-fourth of the time, no relationship is allowed to develop. Unfortunately, the flip side of this is that roughly 75 percent of the time, the married person has some type of relationship with the other person. Realistically, this probably implies they have an affair. And, 33.3 percent of the time the relationship is viewed as long-term. But in only 23.8 percent of the love at first sight experiences does marriage result. The implication is pretty clear. Experiencing love at first sight with a married person usually does not have a happy ending.

The pattern of outcomes is much the same when the relationship status of the other person is considered. A person who is married but separated is most likely to get married as a result of experiencing love at first sight (Table 11.9). The separated group (58.8 percent) has only a slightly higher probability of getting married than an unattached person (58.3 percent), however.

If the other person was already in a relationship with someone else, this presented somewhat of a constraint. Since a relationship developed roughly 92 percent of the time, the constraint wasn't major. But only 43.1 percent of love at first sight experiences with a person already involved with someone else led to marriage. While the respondent may have been emotionally ready to take the relationship further, the other person was probably not quite as ready. In other words, the other person wasn't quite ready to give up on their existing significant other.

If the other person was married, the probability of getting married to that person is again relatively low at 34.6 percent. As with married respondents, the probability of a long-term relationship is high (34.6 percent). When the other person is married, the probability of a long-term relationship or marriage is a combined 70 percent. In only 15 percent of the cases did a "married other" not lead to some type of relationship.

The implications from these analyses are powerful. If both people are unattached or separated from an existing spouse, the probability of getting married as a result of the love at first sight experience is good. If either party is already in an existing relationship, the probability of a new relationship is high (over 90 percent), but the probability of marriage is lower. If either party is already married, the probability of a relationship is high (75 to 85 percent), but the likelihood of marriage is low, 24 to 35 percent. Having a love at first sight experience where at least one of the people is married decreases the liklihood for marriage.

## The Most Appealing Traits

As discussed throughout much of this book, there were three major categories of traits that could attract someone. These were physical, personality, and career/achievement traits. The role of these traits also has a significant impact on the outcomes of the love at first sight experience (Table 11.10).

People attracted primarily by the physical traits of another are the least likely to marry that person. For the people attracted by physical traits, only 51.1 percent ended up marrying that person. For people attracted by personality traits, 56.9 percent married the object of their love at first sight experience. For people who were attracted by career/achievement traits, 61.1 percent married the other person. The results for physical and personality traits are not unexpected. However, the high probability of marriage for those attracted by career/achievement traits was surprising.

Not to sound too crass, but the person attracted predominantly by career/achievement traits may be also focusing on the wealth that usually accompanies career success. Some of these people may be seeing dollar signs instead of cupid. Therefore, some of these people may consciously be marrying for money. Hence, marriage is a more necessary part of their relationship strategy to gain fuller access to the benefits of career success. Regardless of the reason, marriage is a much more likely outcome when career/achievement traits are important.

## Summary

The number of factors that influence the outcomes of love at first sight were a bit surprising. While love may conquer all, it has a much better chance if certain conditions exist. If you are of the same religion as the other person, are separated or unattached, are attracted by differences, and live in a rural area, you are most likely to end up getting married as a result of your love at first sight experience. And, certainly, being female helps your odds of marriage as an outcome.

If a person is involved in a love at first sight experience, a relationship will develop about 90 percent of the time. Even for a married person, 75 to 85 percent of the time a relationship will develop outside of marriage. The pull of a love at first sight experience is apparently hard for anyone to resist.

Table 11.1

## Men vs. Women and the Outcome of Love at First Sight

| Men vs. Women | Marriage | Long-Term Relationship | Short-Term Relationship | No Relationship |
|---|---|---|---|---|
| Men | 43.9% | 23.8% | 20.6% | 11.7% |
| Women | 62.1% | 18.9% | 13.4% | 5.6% |

Table 11.2

## Religion, Ethnic Group, Race, and the Outcome of Love at First Sight

| | Marriage | Long-Term Relationship | Short-Term Relationship | No Relationship |
|---|---|---|---|---|
| Same Religion | | | | |
| Men | 63.4% | 19.0% | 10.8% | 6.8% |
| Women | 54.7% | 26.3% | 16.2% | 2.8% |
| Same Ethnic Group | | | | |
| Men | 54.8% | 21.4% | 17.0% | 6.8% |
| Women | 57.4% | 20.6% | 11.8% | 10.3% |
| Same Race | | | | |
| Men | 55.5% | 20.2% | 16.4% | 7.9% |
| Women | 50.0% | 27.1% | 16.7% | 6.3% |

Table 11.3

## Education Level and the Outcome of Love at First Sight

| Education Level | Marriage | Long-Term Relationship | Short-Term Relationship | No Relationship |
|---|---|---|---|---|
| High School | 59.6% | 18.5% | 17.4% | 4.5% |
| Some College | 54.4% | 23.5% | 13.2% | 8.8% |
| College Grad | 51.9% | 19.8% | 18.3% | 9.9% |
| Graduate School | 48.8% | 22.6% | 16.7% | 11.9% |

Table 11.4

## Geographic Area and the Outcome of Love at First Sight

| Geographic Area | Marriage | Long-Term Relationship | Short-Term Relationship | No Relationship |
|---|---|---|---|---|
| Greater - 500,000 | 50.0% | 24.2% | 19.7% | 6.1% |
| 100,000-500,000 | 50.8% | 33.8% | 7.7% | 7.7% |
| 10,000-100,000 | 50.7% | 23.1% | 14.9% | 11.2% |
| Less Than 10,000 | 54.8% | 19.3% | 18.5% | 7.4% |
| Rural | 63.9% | 12.0% | 17.3% | 6.8% |

Table 11.5

# Ethnis Group and the Outcome of Love at First Sight

| Ethnic Group | Marriage | Long-Term Relationship | Short-Term Relationship | No Relationship |
|---|---|---|---|---|
| Native Am. /Eskimo | 63.2% | 13.2% | 21.1% | 2.6% |
| Asian/ Pacific Isd. | 54.5% | 18.2% | 9.1% | 18.2% |
| Caucasian | 55.8% | 21.7% | 14.7% | 7.8% |
| African American | 33.3% | 22.2% | 33.3% | 11.1% |
| Hispanic | 38.9% | 27.8% | 22.2% | 11.1% |
| Other | 61.9% | 9.5% | 14.3% | 14.3% |

Table 11.6

## Opposites/Similars and the Outcome of Love at First Sight

| Opposites /Similars | Marriage | Long-Term Relationship | Short-Term Relationship | No Relationship |
|---|---|---|---|---|
| Different | 61.1% | 19.2% | 14.5% | 5.2% |
| Similar | 52.0% | 18.9% | 18.9% | 10.3% |
| Both | 52.9% | 25.0% | 14.0% | 8.1% |
| Neither | 47.6% | 33.3% | 19.0% | 0.0% |

Table 11.7

## Similarity to Parents and the Outcome of Love at First Sight

| Similar to Parents | Marriage | Long-Term Relationship | Short-Term Relationship | No Relationship |
|---|---|---|---|---|
| Father | 69.9% | 15.6% | 8.9% | 7.8% |
| Mother | 48.5% | 15.9% | 18.2% | 11.4% |
| Both | 37.8% | 27.0% | 24.3% | 10.8% |
| Neither | 54.9% | 21.7% | 16.8% | 6.6% |

Table 11.8

## Relationship Status of Respondent and the Outcome of Love at First Sight

| Relationship Status of Respondent | Marriage | Long-Term Relationship | Short-Term Relationship | No Relationship |
|---|---|---|---|---|
| Unattached | 56.6% | 19.6% | 16.5% | 7.3% |
| Attached | 54.7% | 23.4% | 14.1% | 7.8% |
| Married | 23.8% | 33.3% | 19.0% | 23.8% |
| Separated | 61.9% | 23.8% | 9.5% | 4.8% |

Table 11.9

## Relationship Status of Other and the Outcome Of Love At First Sight

| Relationship Status of Other | Marriage | Long-Term Relationship | Short-Term Relationship | No Relationship |
|---|---|---|---|---|
| Unattached | 58.3% | 18.7% | 15.4% | 7.6% |
| Attached | 43.1% | 29.2% | 20.0% | 7.7% |
| Married | 34.6% | 34.6% | 15.4% | 15.4% |
| Separated | 58.8% | 23.5% | 17.6% | 0.0% |

Table 11.10

# The Most Appealing Traits and the Outcome of Love At First Sight

| Most Appealing Traits | Marriage | Long-Term Relationship | Short-Term Relationship | No Relationship |
|---|---|---|---|---|
| Physical | 51.1% | 20.6% | 19.3% | 8.6% |
| Personality | 56.9% | 22.7% | 13.8% | 6.5% |
| Career/ Achievemt | 61.1% | 16.7% | 11.1% | 11.1% |

# I Saw Him By the Cows

*I* was visiting my cousin, who also happens to be my best friend, at my uncle's dairy farm near Winterport, Maine. My cousin had a crush on a guy who lived just up the road from them. This guy, Darrell, would come over and help my uncle occasionally with different jobs while he was in high school and college. Actually, my cousin thought that she was in love with him, but they had never even dated. She had what is probably best described as a wishful relationship with him. She wished she had a relationship with Darrell, but it never seemed to quite materialize. But for several years I had heard what a great guy he was. Although I only lived a few miles away, I had never met him until that day.

This happened in the summer of 1987. Winterport is at the mouth of the Penobscot River, about twenty miles south of Bangor. Being so close to the ocean, the summers are beautiful, everything is lush and green. The winters can be pretty harsh, though. It happened on a beautiful, sunny day.

I was sixteen that summer, and my cousin was twenty-one. Although she was five years older than me, our families had always been really close and tight-knit. My cousin and I had done things together since we were small, and we evolved into best friends over the years. Our close relationship was important to both of us.

I was always on the shy side, a little quiet. I was five feet, six inches tall, and slender with brown hair and brown eyes. I was very straight-laced, probably due to those conservative New England values. I was the role model for the girl next door, a jeans and flannel shirt type of person.

That first time I saw Darrell, he and my uncle were working with the dairy cows. They were sorting the cows into different groups for feeding. I emphasize the word "saw" because we never actually talked that day. My cousin and I just happened to wander down by the barn so she could show him to me. As soon as I saw him, my heart fluttered and my eyes got big. Just seeing him caused me to get excited. I had never experienced that kind of reaction when I met a boy before. I can still remember every detail of that moment, it is etched in my memory forever.

Darrell was twenty-one at the time. He was tall, blond, very good looking, and always had a big smile on his face. He seemed to have an innocence about him. He also seemed to have a dangerous appeal. The dangerous appeal was hard to explain. Since he was five years older than me, he just seemed more worldly and mature. Perhaps some of the danger was because he was probably more experienced sexually.

At sixteen, I was starting to think about that stuff more, and there was definitely an allure about an older man. Whatever the cause, when I saw him, it was love at first sight. There is no other way to explain it.

When I went back home that day, I told my younger brother, "Wouldn't it be neat if Darrell and I got married." He said that my cousin probably wouldn't like it. My brother was probably right, it seemed that my cousin had first rights to Darrell. She had been telling me all about him for years. I didn't want to steal Darrell from her, even if they didn't have an actual relationship.

Nothing happened between Darrell and me for the next two years. Out of respect for my cousin, I didn't try to contact him. I *thought that I might be too young for such a fantastic guy. In my heart, I also knew he was the one for me, but I pined away for him until the summer of 1989. Poor Darrell had at least two women in love with him, and he didn't even know it.*

*I had just finished my freshman year in college and was working at a general store that summer. Darrell came into the store one day, and we started talking. He had graduated from college the previous year, with a degree in forest management and surveying, so he was working full-time. He was dating someone else rather steadily at the time and so was I. After we talked for a while, he asked if I'd like to go out with him. I immediately said yes.*

*Saying yes was so unlike me. I had a relationship with someone else, and I had never run around on anyone before. I didn't really want to get involved with someone who had a relationship with another woman. Plus, my cousin still had a crush on him after all those years, and I really valued her friendship. It was a real love triangle that I was stepping into. But this was Darrell, the guy who I knew was the one years ago. I couldn't resist, it was like my fantasy was coming true.*

*When I first saw Darrell, it was purely a physical attraction. As we started going out, I found he had this magnetic personality. He was so much fun and very outgoing. He had so much energy. As I sensed two years earlier, he had this dangerous appeal. We'd do things like whitewater rafting and riding four wheelers that were wild and reckless, things I'd never done alone. He seemed to push my boundaries and get me to do a lot of exciting things. I was really attracted by his zest for life. He was so fascinating.*

*After our first date, the sparks really flew for both of us. He was as crazy about me as I was for him. Within a week of our first date, we both ended our other relationships. The issue of my cousin still remained, though. I felt bad sharing my excitement for him with my* cousin, but she was pretty cool about it. She said that when things are meant to be, you can't stop them. She was certainly right about that.

We got engaged just four months after we had that first date, and got married the next year. I finished college, got my degree in education, and am now a schoolteacher. We have two children who are just like their dad.

Even after being married for eight years, my heart just flutters when he walks into a room, just like it did that first day that I saw him by the cows. Isn't that a romantic spot to meet the love of your life…in a barnyard? As long as we're both alive, we know that we'll be together. This is our own little success story, which, unfortunately, is getting more and more rare. Oh yes, my cousin and I are still best friends.

## Chapter Twelve

# A Few Concluding Comments

∞

$\mathcal{T}$he need to give and receive love is terribly powerful in humans. Our genetic code imprints us with a drive that is ultimately shaped by our parents, our family, society, and our own unique collection of experiences. The result of all of this is that we each have developed a unique pattern of loving.

Undoubtedly, falling in love with another person has much to do with the meshing of two very compatible patterns of loving. This can occur very gradually over a period of time. Or it can happen very quickly, within minutes of meeting someone. The relationship experts suggest that virtually all falling in love experiences are gradual, passing through a series of stages. Our research indicates otherwise.

This research was prompted by a single question, "Does love at first sight really happen?" There were many aspects of the results that were quite surprising. The first surprise was the relatively high proportion of people who believe that love at first sight can happen. We expected many people to believe in love at first sight, but we were surprised to have nearly two-thirds of the people say they believed in it. Frankly, I would have guessed a figure around 30 percent.

A second surprise was that more than half of all believers actually have experienced love at first sight. Apparently, simply believing that love at first sight can happen makes a person more likely to let it happen. Experiencing love at first sight is not the rare, elusive experience that some suggest. A good portion of the U.S. population has experienced it.

Love at first sight can happen to people of all ages, but it is most likely to happen to men and women under age twenty-five. It may be that young people are a bit more idealistic and have yet to have their souls hardened by life's travails. Perhaps the young are simply more willing to jump into the consuming fire of love on very short notice. Perhaps they are in a very active search mode for a mate, early in their life cycles.

Experiencing love at first sight is most likely to be a once-in-a-lifetime experience, particularly for women. The reason for this must have something to do with the profound, emotional impact of love at first sight. But, certainly, the outcomes of love at first sight also exert influence. More than 60 percent of women marry the object of their affection. And only 7 percent of these women get divorced. Thus, a woman who experiences love at first sight is likely to be taken off the market.

If this research produced a single shocker, it was the extremely low divorce rate. In our increasingly fast-paced, transitory society, divorce rates continue to rise, falling in the 50 to 70 percent range. Only 7 percent of women and 22 percent of men divorced after marrying the person with whom they fell in love with at first sight. The love at first sight experience must create an incredibly strong husband-wife bond, typified by extremely high levels of commitment. Understanding why this divorce rate is so low could be valuable to all couples.

This research has some pretty obvious implications for people who would like to experience love at first sight. First, it helps to be unattached or in a light relationship. Beyond that, the lyrics to the song, "Don't Worry, Be Happy" come to mind. People are attracted to other people who are happy and are having fun. If you want to attract a mate, smile, laugh, be active, and enjoy life. Your behavior will be noticed. And most men and women will find such behaviors very appealing.

As you read the love stories, you'll see that love at first sight can happen anywhere, anytime. It could happen at noon in a gas station or at midnight in the drive-thru of a fast food restaurant. It could happen at school or at the beach. It could happen in Seattle or in Stowe, Vermont. But, be ready, the lightening bolt of love at first sight could strike you at any time.

# Appendix A: Aided Survey

Hello, this is _____ with Naumann & Associates, a research firm. We are conducting a study of love at first sight. The interview should take less than ten minutes.

Are you at least twenty-one years old? (if no, thank and terminate interview)

Yes
No
Don't Know/Refused

For this study, "love at first sight" is defined as falling in love with someone within sixty minutes of first seeing or meeting the person.

1.Do you believe in love at first sight?

2 Yes—continue
1 No—go to demographics
0 Don't Know/Refused

2. Have you ever experienced love at first sight?

2 Yes—continue
1 No—go to demographics
0 Don't Know/Refused

3. How many times have you experienced love at first sight?

_____

4. What was your age the first time that you experienced love at first sight? _____

5. What was the age of the other person at the time? _____

6. Was the other person of the same or different religion?

    2 Same
    1 Different
    0 Don't Know/Refused

7. Was the other person of the same or different ethnic group?

    2 Same
    1 Different
    0 Don't Know/Refused

8. Was the other person of the same or different race?

    2 Same
    1 Different
    0 Don't Know/Refused

9. Was the other person of the same or different sex?

    2 Same
    1 Different
    0 Don't Know/Refused

10. Which one of the following categories of traits of the other person most attracted you?

3 Physical
2 Personality
1 Career/Achievements
0 Don't Know/Refused

Which of the following physical traits of the other person attracted you? Yes=2, No=1, D/K=0

|  | Yes | No | DK |
| --- | --- | --- | --- |
| 11. Good-looking/attractive | 2 | 1 | 0 |
| 12. Build, body | 2 | 1 | 0 |
| 13. Height | 2 | 1 | 0 |
| 14. Hair | 2 | 1 | 0 |
| 15. Eyes | 2 | 1 | 0 |
| 16. Sex appeal | 2 | 1 | 0 |
| 17. Athletic | 2 | 1 | 0 |
| 18. Older | 2 | 1 | 0 |
| 19. Younger | 2 | 1 | 0 |
| 20. Smell, odor | 2 | 1 | 0 |
| 21. Attire | 2 | 1 | 0 |
| 22. Smile | 2 | 1 | 0 |
| 23. Other_____(capture) |  |  |  |

Which of the following personality traits of the other person attracted you? Yes=2, No=1, D/K=0

|  | Yes | No | DK |
|---|---|---|---|
| 24. Self-confidence | 2 | 1 | 0 |
| 25. Fun | 2 | 1 | 0 |
| 26. Shared values/common background | 2 | 1 | 0 |
| 27. Dominance/assertive | 2 | 1 | 0 |
| 28. Aggressive | 2 | 1 | 0 |
| 29. Outgoing | 2 | 1 | 0 |
| 30. Intelligence | 2 | 1 | 0 |
| 31. Generosity | 2 | 1 | 0 |
| 32. Kindness | 2 | 1 | 0 |
| 33. Good with kids | 2 | 1 | 0 |
| 34. Good communication/ conversation | 2 | 1 | 0 |
| 35. Humorous | 2 | 1 | 0 |
| 36. Warmth | 2 | 1 | 0 |
| 37. Other_____(capture) | | | |

Which of the following career/achievement traits attracted you? Yes=2, No=1, D/K=0

|  | Yes | No | DK |
|---|---|---|---|
| 38. Talent | 2 | 1 | 0 |
| 39. Professional success | 2 | 1 | 0 |
| 40. Social status | 2 | 1 | 0 |

| | | | |
|---|---|---|---|
| 41. Well educated | 2 | 1 | 0 |
| 42. Income potential | 2 | 1 | 0 |
| 43. Control of resources | 2 | 1 | 0 |
| 44. Good provider | 2 | 1 | 0 |
| 45. Energy/enthusiasm | 2 | 1 | 0 |
| 46. Other_____(capture) | | | |

What emotional feelings did you experience with love at first sight? Yes=2, No=1, D/K=0

| | Yes | No | DK |
|---|---|---|---|
| 47. Hope | 2 | 1 | 0 |
| 48. Exhilaration | 2 | 1 | 0 |
| 49. Comfort | 2 | 1 | 0 |
| 50. Excitement | 2 | 1 | 0 |
| 51. Chemistry/fit | 2 | 1 | 0 |
| 52. Lasting attachment | 2 | 1 | 0 |
| 53. Wholeness, completeness | 2 | 1 | 0 |
| 54. Growth | 2 | 1 | 0 |
| 55. Fulfillment | 2 | 1 | 0 |
| 56. Desire to have children | 2 | 1 | 0 |
| 57. Other_____(capture) | | | |

58. Some people say "opposites attract" and some say, "similarity attracts." Would you say that the other person was:

    4 Different from you in significant ways
    3 Similar to you in significant ways
    2 Both
    1 Neither
    0 Don't Know/Refused

59. Would you say the other person was similar to your parents in significant ways?

4 Similar to father
3 Similar to mother
2 Both
1 Neither
0 Don't Know/Refused

60. At the time that you most recently experienced love at first sight, were you:

4 Unattached (not in a relationship with anyone)
3 In a relationship with someone else
2 Married to someone else
1 Married to but separated from someone else
0 Don't Know/Refused

61. At the time that you most recently experienced love at first sight, was the other person.

4 Unattached (not in a relationship with anyone)
3 In a relationship with someone else
2 Married to someone else
1 Married to but separated from someone else
0 Don't Know/Refused

62. Was the outcome of your first love at first sight?

4 No relationship
3 Short-term relationship
2 Long-term relationship
1 Marriage
0 Don't Know/Refused

63. How long did it last? (For 3, 2, or 1 on #62)

## Demographics

Now, I'd like to ask a few questions about yourself.

64. What is your sex? (don't ask just mark)

2 Male
1 Female
0 Don't Know/Refused

65. Are you:

3 Single (never married)—skip question 66
2 Married
1 Divorced
0 Don't Know/Refused

66. How many times have you been married?

    5 five or more
    4 four
    3 three
    2 two
    1 one
    0 Don't Know/Refused

67. What is your education level?

    4 High school diploma or less
    3 Some college
    2 College graduate
    1 Graduate school
    0 Don't Know/Refused

68. Do you live in:

    5 An urban area with a population over 500,000
    4 An urban area with a population of 100,000-500,000
    3 A city with a population of 10,000 –100,000
    2 A town of less than 10,000
    1 A rural area
    0 Don't Know/Refused

69. What is your current age? _____

70. Although this is a sensitive question, the answer is for demographic use only. It is not intended to offend. How would you classify yourself?

6 Native American/Eskimo
5 Asian/Pacific Islander
4 Caucasian
3 African American
2 Hispanic
1 Other
0 Refused

71. Which one of the following best describes the family structure you were raised?

6 Single male head of household
5 Single female head of household
4 Raised by both biological parents
3 Raised with a step-parent
2 Raised by relatives
1 Other
0 Don't Know/Refused

72. Which one of the following best describes the situation?

5 Parents still married (or married until death of one)
4 Parents divorced after you left home
3 Parents divorced while you lived at home
2 Parents never married
1 Other
0 Don't Know/Refused

Where did love at first sight occur?

73. Church or church event
74. At work, office
75. Restaurant
76. Bar, nightclub, pub casino
77. Party, social event
78. At school, college, university
79. Sports event
80. Supermarket, grocery store
81. Shopping center, mall
82. Concert, play, theatre
83. Friends, friend's place
84. Airplane, bus, subway
85. Other

# Appendix B: Unaided Survey

Hello, this is _____ with Naumann & Associates, a research firm. We are conducting a study of love at first sight. The interview should take less than ten minutes.

Are you at least twenty-one years old? (if no thank and terminate interview)

Yes
No
Don't Know/Refused

For this study, love at first sight is defined as falling in love with someone within sixty minutes of first seeing or meeting the person.

1. Do you believe in love at first sight?

    2 Yes—continue
    1 No—go to demographics
    0 Don't Know/Refused

2. Have you ever experienced love at first sight?

    2 Yes—continue
    1 No—go to demographics
    0 Don't Know/Refused

3. How many times have you experienced love at first sight?

_____

4. What was your age the first time that you experienced love at first sight? _____

5. What was the age of the other person at the time? _____

6. Was the other person of the same or different religion?

   2 Same
   1 Different
   0 Don't Know/Refused

7. Was the other person of the same or different ethnic group?

   2 Same
   1 Different
   0 Don't Know/Refused

8. Was the other person of the same or different race?

   2 Same
   1 Different
   0 Don't Know/Refused

9. Was the other person of the same or different sex?

   2 Same
   1 Different
   0 Don't Know/Refused

10. Which one of the following categories of traits of the other person most attracted you?

3 Physical
2 Personality
1 Career/Achievements
0 Don't Know/Refused

11. What physical traits of the other person attracted you? (Capture)

Good-looking, attractive
Build, body
Height
Hair
Eyes
Sex appeal
Athletic
Older
Younger
Smell, odor
Attire
Smile
Other

12. What personality traits of the other person attracted you? (Capture)

Self-confidence
Fun
Shared values/common background
Dominance/assertive
Aggressive
Outgoing
Intelligence
Generosity
Kindness
Good with kids
Good communication/conversation
Humorous
Warmth
Other

13. What career/achievement traits attracted you? (Capture)

Talent
Professional success
Social status
Well educated
Income potential
Control of resources
Good provider
Energy/enthusiasm
Other

14. What emotional feelings did you experience with love at first sight? (Capture)

Hope
Exhilaration
Comfort
Excitement
Chemistry/fit
Lasting attachment
Wholeness, completeness
Growth
Fulfillment
Desire to have children
Other

15. Some people say "opposites attract" and some say, "similarity attracts." Would you say that the other person was:

4 Different from you in significant ways
3 Similar to you in significant ways
2 Both
1 Neither
0 Don't Know/Refused

16. Would you say the other person was similar to your parents in significant ways?

4 Similar to father
3 Similar to mother
2 Both
1 Neither
0 Don't Know/Refused

17. At the time that you most recently experienced love at first sight, were you:

    4 Unattached (not in a relationship with anyone)
    3 In a relationship with someone else
    2 Married to someone else
    1 Married to but separated from someone else
    0 Don't Know/Refused

18. At the time that you most recently experienced love at first sight, was the other person:

    4 Unattached (not in a relationship with anyone)
    3 In a relationship with someone else
    2 Married to someone else
    1 Married to but separated from someone else
    0 Don't Know/Refused

19. Was the outcome of your first love at first sight?

    4 No relationship
    3 Short-term relationship
    2 Long-term relationship
    1 Marriage
    0 Don't Know/Refused

20. How long did it last? (For 3, 2, or 1 on #19)

# Demographics

Now, I'd like to ask a few questions about yourself.

21. What is your sex? (don't ask just mark)

2 Male
1 Female
0 Don't Know/Refused

22. Are you:

3 Single (never married)—skip to question 66
2 Married
1 Divorced
0 Don't Know/Refused

23. How many times have you been married?

5 five or more
4 four
3 three
2 two
1 one
0 Don't Know/Refused

24. What is your education level?

4 High school diploma or less
3 Some College
2 College graduate
1 Graduate school
0 Don't Know/Refused

25. Do you live in:

5 An urban area with a population over 500,000
4 An urban area with a population of 100,000-500,000
3 A city with a population of 10,000 –100,000
2 A town of less than 10,000
1 A rural area
0 Don't Know/Refused

26. What is your current age?(capture)

27. Although this is a sensitive question, the answer is for demographic use only. It is not intended to offend. How would you classify yourself?

6 Native American/Eskimo
5 Asian/Pacific Islander
4 Caucasian
3 African American
2 Hispanic
1 Other
0 Refused

28. Which one of the following best describes the family structure you were raised?

6 Single male head of household
5 Single female head of household
4 Raised by both biological parents
3 Raised with a step-parent
2 Raised by relatives
1 Other
0 Don't Know/Refused

29. Which one of the following best describes the situation?

5 Parents still married (or married until death of one)
4 Parents divorced after you left home
3 Parents divorced while you lived at home
2 Parents never married
1 Other
0 Don't Know/Refused

30. Where did love at first sight occur? (Capture)

Church or church event
At work, office
Restaurant
Bar, nightclub, pub casino
Party, social event
At school, college, university
Sports event
Supermarket, grocery store
Shopping center, mall
Concert, play, theatre
Friends, friends place
Airplane, bus, subway
Other

# Endnotes

**Preface**

1. John Gray, *Men are From Mars, Women are From Venus* (New York: Harper Collins, 1992).

2. Cathy Troupp, *Why Do We Fall in Love?: The Psychology of Choosing a Partner* (New York: St. Martin's Press, 1994).

3. Leil Lowndes, *How to Make Anyone Fall in Love with You* (Chicago: Contemporary Books, 1996).

4. Anthony Walsh, *The Science of Love: Understanding Love and Its Effects on Mind & Body* (New York: Prometheus Books, 1991).

**Chapter 1**

5. Heather Trexler Remoff, *Sexual Choice: A Woman's Decision—Why and How Women Choose The Men They Do As Sexual Partners* (New York: Dutton/Lewis Publishing, 1984).

6. Maggie Scarf, *Intimate Partners: Patterns in Love and Marriage* (New York: Random House, 1987).

**Chapter 2**

7. Anthony Walsh, *The Science of Love: Understanding Love and Its Effects on Mind & Body* (New York: Prometheus Books, 1991).

8. Ruth Winter, *The Smell Book* (New York: JB Lippincott Company, 1976).

9. William C. Agosta, *Chemical Communication: The Language of Pheromones* (New York: Scientific American Library, 1992).

## Chapter 3

10. Anthony Walsh, *The Science of Love: Understanding Love and Its Effects on Mind & Body* (New York: Prometheus Books, 1991).

11. G. Peterson and L. Mehl, "Some Determinants of Maternal Attachment," *American Journal of Psychiatry* 135 (1978): 1168-73.

12. M. Hofer, "Early Social Relationships: A Psychologists View," *Child Development* 58 (1987): 633-47.

13. Anthony Walsh, *The Science of Love: Understanding Love and Its Effects on Mind & Body*. (New York: Prometheus Books, 1991).

## Chapter 4

14. Leslie R. Brody and Judith A. Hall, "Gender and Emotion," *Handbook of Emotions*, ed. Michael Lewis and Jeannette Havland (New York: Guilford Press, 1993).

15. ibid.

16. Daniel Goleman, *Emotional Intelligence* (New York: Bantam Books, 1997).

17. ibid.

18. Heather Trexler Remoff, *Sexual Choice: A Woman's Decision—Why and How Women Choose The Men They Do As Sexual Partners*. (New York: Dulfon/Lewis Publishing, 1984).

19. Monica Moore, "Nonverbal Courtship Patterns in Women: Context and Consequences," *Ethnology and Sociobiology* 6 (1985): 237-47.

20. Timothy Perper, *Sex Signals: The Biology of Love* (Philadelphia: ISI Press, 1986).

## Chapter 6

21. I. Silverman, "Physical Attractiveness and Courtship," *Sexual Behavior* (Sept., 1971): 22-25.

22. Leil Lowndes, *How To Make Anyone Fall In Love With You* (Chicago: Contemporary Books, 1996).

## Chapter 11

23. Daniel Goleman, *Emotional Intelligence* (New York: Bantam Books, 1997).

# Bibliography

Agosta, William C. *Chemical Communication: The Language of Pheromones*. New York: Scientific American Library, 1992.

Brody, Leslie R., and Judith A. Hall. "Gender and Emotion." *Handbook of Emotions*, edited by Michael Lewis and Jeannette Havland. New York: Guilford Press, 1993.

Forer, Lucille and Henry Still. *The Birth Order Factor: How Your Personality Is Influenced By Your Place In the Family*. New York: David McKay Company, Inc., 1976.

Goleman, Daniel. *Emotional Intelligence*. New York: Bantam Books, 1997.

Gray, John. *Men are From Mars, Women are From Venus*. New York: Harper Collins, 1992.

Hofer, M. "Early Social Relationships: A Psychologists View." *Child Development* 58 (1987): 633-47.

Leman, Kevin. *Were You Born For Each Other?: Finding, Catching, and Keeping the Love Of Your Life*. New York: Delacorte Press, 1991.

Lowndes, Leil. *How To Make Anyone Fall In Love With You*. Chicago: Contemporary Books, 1996.

Moore, Monica. "Nonverbal Courtship Patterns in Women: Context and Consequences." *Ethnology and Sociobiology* 6 (1985): 237-47.

Perper, Timothy. *Sex Signals: The Biology of Love*. Philidelphia: ISI Press, 1986.

Peterson, G. and L. Mehl. "Some Determinants of Maternal Attachment." *American Journal of Psychiatry* 135 (1978): 1168-73.

Scarf, Maggie. *Intimate Partners: Patterns in Love and Marriage.* New York: Random House, 1987.

Silverman, I. "Physical Attractiveness and Courtship." *Sexual Behavior* (Sept., 1971): 22-25.

Sulloway, Frank J. *Born To Rebel: Birth Order, Family Dynamics, and Creative Lives.* New York: Vintage Books, 1996.

Trexler Remoff, Heather. Sexual Choice: *A Woman's Decision— Why and How Women Choose The Men They Do As Sexual Partners.* New York: Dutton/Lewis Publishing, 1984.

Troupp, Cathy. *Why Do We Fall in Love?: The Psychology of Choosing a Partner.* New York: St. Martin's Press, 1994.

Walsh, Anthony. *The Science of Love: Understanding Love and Its Effects on Mind & Body.* New York: Prometheus Books, 1991.

Winter, Ruth. *The Smell Book.* New York: JB Lippincott Company, 1976.

# Index

## A

alexithymia, 28

amygdala, 27, 28, 30, 34, 35, 40

androgen bath, 32

aphrodisiac, 162

apocrine glands, 39

## B

baby fantasies, 240

birth order, 10, 68, 62-69, 71, 92, 122, 236

brain stem, 25

## C

career/achievement traits, 139, 140, 143, 213-27, 271, 272; ethnicity relating to, 142

chemistry, 7, 23, 35, 162, 237, 242, 243, 244

cystine, 60

## D

dopamine, 35

## E

eccrine glands, 39

education, 217

eldest child, 64-66

emotional synchrony. *See* social attunement

endorphins, 235

epinephrine, 34

equity theory, the, 12, 137

extero-gestation, 24

## F

father-child bond, 61, 66, 121

Freud, 235

## G

genetic imprinting, 6-8

genetics, 234

## H

hypothalamus, 35

## L

lastborns, the, 68-69

limbic structure, 25, 26, 30, 31, 35

love at first sight, 13, 23, 24, 28, 29, 30, 35, 42, 61, 71, 106, 107, 108, 109, 110, 111, 112, 113, 114, 115, 116, 122, 139, 140, 142, 157, 162, 165, 168, 185, 190, 194, 195, 196, 216, 221, 224, 225, 233, 234, 236, 237, 240, 241, 242, 243, 244, 245, 261, 262, 263, 264, 265, 266, 267, 269, 270, 271, 272, 285, 286, 287; education, 266, 274; ethnic group, 265-66, 267, 273, 276; family structure, 113-15, 125; geographic location, 107-9, 123, 266-67, 275; importance of attractiveness, 137-38; level of education,

111-12, 124; marital status, 109-11, 123; outcome of, 262-65; parents' marital status, 112-13, 125

love, 3-5, 233, 234, 235, 285

## ℳ

middle child, 66-68

Moore, Monica, 87

mother-child bond, 3, 9, 24, 26-27, 40, 58-61, 64, 69, 121, 159, 235; emotional synchrony, 60

## 𝒩

neocortex, 25, 27, 30, 31-33, 34, 35, 36, 40

nonverbal, 116, 159, 186, 187

norepinephrine, 34

## 𝒪

olfactory, 39, 40, 41

only child, 62-64

oxytocin, 60

## 𝒫

perceptual selectivity, 186

perceptual sensitivity, 186

Perper, Timothy, 88

personality traits, 139, 140, 143, 185-207, 241, 225, 271, 272; ethnic group, 142

phenylethylamine, 35

pheromones, 28, 36-41, 166

physical traits, 139-40, 143, 144, 155, 156-73, 174-77, 188, 225, 241, 271, 272; age, 142-43; ethnic group, 142; male-female contrast, 172; times married, 141

Plato, 4-5, 118, 235, 238

prostagladins, 39

psychological growth, 239

## R

Reptilian brain, 25

## S

seratonin, 34, 35

shared traits, 117-21, 128

signaling, 86-87, 159; body language, 88-89; eye contact, 90; nonverbal, 88, 92, 93; synchronization, 89; touch, 89

similarities, 268, 277

social attunement, 91

soul mate, 4

spiritual growth, 239

## T

thalamus, 35

trimethylamine, 38

## U

Utero-gestation, 24

# About the Author

Earl Naumann is an author and business consultant. Through his research and consulting firm, Naumann performed primary research on the little-studied phenomenon of love at first sight. His business books, *Creating Customer Value* and *Customer Satisfaction Measurement and Management*, are among the leading professional books in their respective fields. Naumann holds a Ph.D. in marketing from Arizona State University. He resides in Boise, Idaho.